Marx, Engels, and Marxisms

Series Editors

Marcello Musto, York University, Toronto, ON, Canada

Terrell Carver, University of Bristol, Bristol, UK

The Marx renaissance is underway on a global scale. Wherever the critique of capitalism re-emerges, there is an intellectual and political demand for new, critical engagements with Marxism. The peer-reviewed series Marx, Engels and Marxisms (edited by Marcello Musto & Terrell Carver, with Babak Amini, Francesca Antonini, Paula Rauhala & Kohei Saito as Assistant Editors) publishes monographs, edited volumes, critical editions, reprints of old texts, as well as translations of books already published in other languages. Our volumes come from a wide range of political perspectives, subject matters, academic disciplines and geographical areas, producing an eclectic and informative collection that appeals to a diverse and international audience. Our main areas of focus include: the oeuvre of Marx and Engels, Marxist authors and traditions of the 19th and 20th centuries, labour and social movements, Marxist analyses of contemporary issues, and reception of Marxism in the world.

Alfonso García Vela · Alberto Bonnet
Editors

The Political Thought of John Holloway

Struggle, Critique, Emancipation

palgrave
macmillan

Editors
Alfonso García Vela
Instituto de Ciencias Sociales
y Humanidades
Benemérita Universidad Autonóma
de Puebla (BUAP)
Puebla, México

Alberto Bonnet
Department of Economics
and Administration
National University of Quilmes
Buenos Aires, Argentina

ISSN 2524-7123 ISSN 2524-7131 (electronic)
Marx, Engels, and Marxisms
ISBN 978-3-031-34570-8 ISBN 978-3-031-34571-5 (eBook)
https://doi.org/10.1007/978-3-031-34571-5

Cover illustration: Javier Porras/500px/Getty Images

This Palgrave Macmillan imprint is published by the registered company Springer Nature Switzerland AG
The registered company address is: Gewerbestrasse 11, 6330 Cham, Switzerland

Titles Published

1. Terrell Carver & Daniel Blank, *A Political History of the Editions of Marx and Engels's "German Ideology" Manuscripts*, 2014.
2. Terrell Carver & Daniel Blank, *Marx and Engels's "German Ideology" Manuscripts: Presentation and Analysis of the "Feuerbach chapter,"* 2014.
3. Alfonso Maurizio Iacono, *The History and Theory of Fetishism*, 2015.
4. Paresh Chattopadhyay, *Marx's Associated Mode of Production: A Critique of Marxism*, 2016.
5. Domenico Losurdo, *Class Struggle: A Political and Philosophical History*, 2016.
6. Frederick Harry Pitts, *Critiquing Capitalism Today: New Ways to Read Marx*, 2017.
7. Ranabir Samaddar, *Karl Marx and the Postcolonial Age*, 2017.
8. George Comninel, *Alienation and Emancipation in the Work of Karl Marx*, 2018.
9. Jean-Numa Ducange & Razmig Keucheyan (Eds.), *The End of the Democratic State: Nicos Poulantzas, a Marxism for the 21st Century*, 2018.
10. Robert X. Ware, *Marx on Emancipation and Socialist Goals: Retrieving Marx for the Future*, 2018.
11. Xavier LaFrance & Charles Post (Eds.), *Case Studies in the Origins of Capitalism*, 2018.

12. John Gregson, *Marxism, Ethics, and Politics: The Work of Alasdair MacIntyre*, 2018.
13. Vladimir Puzone & Luis Felipe Miguel (Eds.), *The Brazilian Left in the 21st Century: Conflict and Conciliation in Peripheral Capitalism*, 2019.
14. James Muldoon & Gaard Kets (Eds.), *The German Revolution and Political Theory*, 2019.
15. Michael Brie, *Rediscovering Lenin: Dialectics of Revolution and Metaphysics of Domination*, 2019.
16. August H. Nimtz, *Marxism versus Liberalism: Comparative Real-Time Political Analysis*, 2019.
17. Gustavo Moura de Cavalcanti Mello and Mauricio de Souza Sabadini (Eds.), *Financial Speculation and Fictitious Profits: A Marxist Analysis*, 2019.
18. Shaibal Gupta, Marcello Musto & Babak Amini (Eds.), *Karl Marx's Life, Ideas, and Influences: A Critical Examination on the Bicentenary*, 2019.
19. Igor Shoikhedbrod, *Revisiting Marx's Critique of Liberalism: Rethinking Justice, Legality, and Rights*, 2019.
20. Juan Pablo Rodríguez, *Resisting Neoliberal Capitalism in Chile: The Possibility of Social Critique*, 2019.
21. Kaan Kangal, *Friedrich Engels and the Dialectics of Nature*, 2020.
22. Victor Wallis, *Socialist Practice: Histories and Theories*, 2020.
23. Alfonso Maurizio Iacono, *The Bourgeois and the Savage: A Marxian Critique of the Image of the Isolated Individual in Defoe, Turgot and Smith*, 2020.
24. Terrell Carver, *Engels before Marx*, 2020.
25. Jean-Numa Ducange, *Jules Guesde: The Birth of Socialism and Marxism in France*, 2020.
26. Antonio Oliva, Ivan Novara & Angel Oliva (Eds.), *Marx and Contemporary Critical Theory: The Philosophy of Real Abstraction*, 2020.
27. Francesco Biagi, *Henri Lefebvre's Critical Theory of Space*, 2020.
28. Stefano Petrucciani, *The Ideas of Karl Marx: A Critical Introduction*, 2020.
29. Terrell Carver, *The Life and Thought of Friedrich Engels, 30th Anniversary Edition*, 2020.
30. Giuseppe Vacca, *Alternative Modernities: Antonio Gramsci's Twentieth Century*, 2020.

31. Kevin B. Anderson, Kieran Durkin & Heather Brown (Eds.), *Raya Dunayevskaya's Intersectional Marxism: Race, Gender, and the Dialectics of Liberation*, 2020.
32. Marco Di Maggio, *The Rise and Fall of Communist Parties in France and Italy*, 2020.
33. Farhang Rajaee, *Presence and the Political*, 2021.
34. Ryuji Sasaki, *A New Introduction to Karl Marx: New Materialism, Critique of Political Economy, and the Concept of Metabolism*, 2021.
35. Kohei Saito (Ed.), *Reexamining Engels's Legacy in the 21st Century*, 2021.
36. Paresh Chattopadhyay, *Socialism in Marx's Capital: Towards a Dealienated World*, 2021.
37. Marcello Musto, *Karl Marx's Writings on Alienation*, 2021.
38. Michael Brie & Jörn Schütrumpf, *Rosa Luxemburg: A Revolutionary Marxist at the Limits of Marxism*, 2021.
39. Stefano Petrucciani, *Theodor W. Adorno's Philosophy, Society, and Aesthetics*, 2021.
40. Miguel Vedda, *Siegfried Kracauer, or, The Allegories of Improvisation: Critical Studies*, 2021.
41. Ronaldo Munck, *Rethinking Development: Marxist Perspectives*, 2021.
42. Jean-Numa Ducange & Elisa Marcobelli (Eds.), *Selected Writings of Jean Jaurès: On Socialism, Pacifism and Marxism*, 2021.
43. Elisa Marcobelli, *Internationalism Toward Diplomatic Crisis: The Second International and French, German and Italian Socialists*, 2021.
44. James Steinhoff, *Automation and Autonomy: Labour, Capital and Machines in the Artificial Intelligence Industry*, 2021.
45. Juan Dal Maso, *Hegemony and Class Struggle: Trotsky, Gramsci and Marxism*, 2021.
46. Gianfranco Ragona & Monica Quirico, *Frontier Socialism: Self-organisation and Anti-capitalism*, 2021.
47. Tsuyoshi Yuki, *Socialism, Markets and the Critique of Money: The Theory of "Labour Notes,"* 2021.
48. Gustavo Moura de Cavalcanti Mello & Henrique Pereira Braga (Eds.), *Wealth and Poverty in Contemporary Brazilian Capitalism*, 2021.
49. Paolo Favilli, *Historiography and Marxism: Innovations in Mid-Century Italy*, 2021.

50. Levy del Aguila Marchena, *Communism, Political Power and Personal Freedom in Marx*, 2021.
51. V. Geetha, *Bhimrao Ramji Ambedkar and the Question of Socialism in India*, 2021.
52. Satoshi Matsui, *Normative Theories of Liberalism and Socialism: Marxist Analysis of Values*, 2022.
53. Kei Ehara (Ed.), *Japanese Discourse on the Marxian Theory of Finance*, 2022.
54. Achim Szepanski, *Financial Capital in the 21st Century*, 2022.
55. Stephen Maher, *Corporate Capitalism and the Integral State: General Electric and a Century of American Power*, 2022.
56. Rémy Herrera, *Confronting Mainstream Economics to Overcome Capitalism*, 2022.
57. Peter McMylor, Graeme Kirkpatrick & Simin Fadaee (Eds.), *Marxism, Religion, and Emancipatory Politics*, 2022.
58. Genevieve Ritchie, Sara Carpenter & Shahrzad Mojab (Eds.), *Marxism and Migration*, 2022.
59. Fabio Perocco (Ed.), *Racism in and for the Welfare State*, 2022.
60. Dong-Min Rieu, *A Mathematical Approach to Marxian Value Theory: Time, Money, and Labor Productivity*, 2022.
61. Adriana Petra, *Intellectuals and Communist Culture: Itineraries, Problems and Debates in Post-war Argentina*, 2022.
62. Kolja Lindner, *Marx, Marxism and the Question of Eurocentrism*, 2022.
63. Marcello Mustè, *Marxism and Philosophy of Praxis: An Italian Perspective from Labriola to Gramsci*, 2022.
64. Lelio Demichelis, *Marx, Alienation and Techno-capitalism*, 2022.
65. Terrell Carver, Smail Rapic (Eds.), *Friedrich Engels for the 21st Century: Perspectives and Problems*, 2022.
66. Alexandros Chrysis, *The Marx of Communism: Setting Limits in the Realm of Communism*, 2022.
67. Paul Raekstad, *Karl Marx's Realist Critique of Capitalism: Freedom, Alienation, and Socialism*, 2022.
68. Marcello Musto, *Rethinking Alternatives with Marx*, 2022.
69. José Ricardo Villanueva Lira, *Marxism and the Origins of International Relations*, 2022.
70. Bertel Nygaard, *Marxism, Labor Movements, and Historiography*, 2022.

71. Marcos Del Roio, *Gramsci and the Emancipation of the Subaltern Classes*, 2022.
72. Marcelo Badaró, *The Working Class from Marx to Our Times*, 2022.
73. Jean Vigreux, Roger Martelli, & Serge Wolikow, *One Hundred Years of History of the French Communist Party*, 2022.
74. Vincenzo Mele, *City and Modernity in George Simmel and Walter Benjamin: Fragments of Metropolis*, 2023.

Titles Forthcoming

Vesa Oittinen, *Marx's Russian Moment*

Spencer A. Leonard, *Marx, the India Question, and the Crisis of Cosmopolitanism*

Joe Collins, *Applying Marx's Capital to the 21st century*

Jeong Seongjin, *Korean Capitalism in the 21st Century: Marxist Analysis and Alternatives*

Marcello Mustè, *Marxism and Philosophy of Praxis: An Italian Perspective from Labriola to Gramsci*

Shannon Brincat, *Dialectical Dialogues in Contemporary World Politics: A Meeting of Traditions in Global Comparative Philosophy*

Francesca Antonini, *Reassessing Marx's Eighteenth Brumaire: Dictatorship, State, and Revolution*

Thomas Kemple, *Marx's Wager: Das Kapital and Classical Sociology*

Xavier Vigna, *A Political History of Factories in France: The Workers' Insubordination of 1968*

Attila Melegh, *Anti-Migrant Populism in Eastern Europe and Hungary: A Marxist Analysis*

Marie-Cecile Bouju, *A Political History of the Publishing Houses of the French Communist Party*

Mauro Buccheri, *Radical Humanism for the Left: The Quest for Meaning in Late Capitalism*

Tamás Krausz, Eszter Bartha (Eds.), *Socialist Experiences in Eastern Europe: A Hungarian Perspective*

Martin Cortés, *Marxism, Time and Politics: On the Autonomy of the Political*

João Antonio de Paula, Huga da Gama Cerqueira, Eduardo da Motta e Albuquer & Leonardo de Deus, *Marxian Economics for the 21st Century: Revaluating Marx's Critique of Political Economy*

Lelio Demichelis, *Marx, Alienation and Techno-capitalism*

Salvatore Prinzi, *Representation, Expression, and Institution: The Philosophy of Merleau-Ponty and Castoriadis*

Agon Hamza, *Slavoj Žižek and the Reconstruction of Marxism*

Éric Aunoble, *French Views on the Russian Revolution*

Patrizia Dogliani, *A Political History of the International Union of Socialist Youth*

Alexis Cukier, *Democratic Work: Radical Democracy and the Future of Labour*

Christoph Henning, *Theories of Alienation: From Rousseau to the Present*

Daniel Egan, *Capitalism, War, and Revolution: A Marxist Analysis*

Emanuela Conversano, *Capital from Afar: Anthropology and Critique of Political Economy in the Late Marx*

David Norman Smith, *Self-Emancipation: Marx's Unfinished Theory of the Working Class*

Tomonaga Tairako, *A New Perspective on Marx's Philosophy and Political Economy*

Matthias Bohlender, Anna-Sophie Schönfelder, & Matthias Spekker, *Truth and Revolution in Marx's Critique of Society*

Mauricio Vieira Martins, *Marx, Spinoza and Darwin: Materialism, Subjectivity and Critique of Religion*

Aditya Nigam, *Border-Marxisms and Historical Materialism*

Fred Moseley, *Marx's Theory of Value in Chapter 1 of Capital: A Critique of Heinrich's Value-Form Interpretation*

Armando Boito, *The State, Politics, and Social Classes: Theory and History*

Anjan Chakrabarti & Anup Dhar, *World of the Third and Hegemonic Capital: Between Marx and Freud*

Hira Singh, *Annihilation of Caste in India: Ambedkar, Ghandi, and Marx*

Salvatore Engel-Di Mauro, *An Introduction to Ecosocialism*

Mike Berry, *A Theory of Housing Provision under Capitalism*

Maria Chehonadskih, *Alexander Bogdanov and Soviet Epistemologies: The Transformation of Knowledge After the October Revolution*
Peter Lamb, *Harold Laski, the Reluctant Marxist: Socialist Democracy for a World in Turmoil*
Raju Das, *Marxism and Revisionism Today: Contours of Marxist Theory for the 21st Century*
Gary Teeple, *The Democracy That Never Was: A Critique of Liberal Democracy*
Erick Omena, *Urban Planning as Class Domination: The Games of Land Dispossession*

Acknowledgments

We would like to express our warmest thanks to the Instituto de Ciencias Sociales y Humanidades "Alfonso Vélez Pliego" of the Benemérita Universidad Autónoma de Puebla and the Instituto de Estudios de Economía y Sociedad en la Argentina Contemporánea of the Universidad de Quilmes for supporting the cost of translation of several of the chapters of this book (Chapters 1, 4, 6, 8–10). We also like to thank Anna-Maeve Holloway for her fine work of translation of a number of the chapters of this book (Chapters 1, 6–9).

BENEMÉRITA UNIVERSIDAD AUTÓNOMA DE PUEBLA · 1578 ·
BUAP

IESAC
Instituto de Economía y Sociedad en la Argentina Contemporánea
UNIVERSIDAD NACIONAL DE QUILMES

Contents

Notes on Contributors

Werner Bonefeld (York University, United Kingdom). He is a co-editor of the three *Open Marxism* volumes published by Pluto Press in the 1990s. Recent book publications include *Critical Theory and the Critique of Political Economy* (Bloomsbury, 2014), *The Strong State and the Free Economy* (Rowman & Littlefield, 2017), and *A Critical Theory of Economic Compulsion* (Routledge, 2023). With Chris O'Kane is he co-editor of *Adorno and Marx* (Bloomsbury, 2022) and with Beverley Best and Chris O'Kane he is co-editor of *The Sage Handbook of Frankfurt School Critical Theory* (Sage, 2018).

Alberto Bonnet, Ph.D. in Sociology (Institute of Social Sciences and Humanities, Autonomous University of Puebla, Mexico, 2006); Master's degree in Economic History and Economic Policies (Faculty of Economic Sciences, University of Buenos Aires, Argentina, 2000); Degree in Philosophy (Faculty of Philosophy and Letters, University of Buenos Aires, Argentina, 1992). Professor in undergraduate and postgraduate courses in economic and political theory and the analysis of contemporary Argentine society at the University of Buenos Aires and the National University of Quilmes (and at other national universities, as visiting professor). Director of Accredited Research Projects and Programs of interdisciplinary analysis of contemporary Argentine society from 2001 to date. Author/co-author of Crítica de las políticas públicas. Propuesta teórica y análisis de casos (Critique of public policies. Theoretical proposal and case analysis, 2022); Estado y capital. El debate derivacionista (State and capital.

The Derivation Debate, 2020); La insurrección como restauración. El kirchnerismo 2002–2015 (The insurrection as restoration. Kirchnerism 2002–2015, 2015); La hegemonía menemista. El neoconservadurismo en Argentina, 1989–2001 (The Menemist hegemony. Neoconservatism in Argentina, 1989–2001, 2008); Marxismo abierto. Una visión europea y latinoamericana (Open Marxism. A European and Latin American vision, two volumes, 2007 y 2005); and other volumes. Also, author/co-author of several dozen articles in journals and book chapters published in Argentina and abroad.

Panagiotis Doulos (Universidad Autónoma de Puebla, México) obtained his Master's degree at the Panteion University of Social and Political Sciences (Greece) and his Ph.D. in Sociology at the Institute of Social Sciences and Humanities "Alfonso Vélez Pliego" of the Benemérita Universidad Autónoma de Puebla, Mexico. He is a professor-researcher in the Programa de Investigadoras e Investigadores por México-CONAHCYT at the Instituto de Ciencias Sociales y Humanidades "Alfonso Vélez Pliego"—BUAP (ICSyH-BUAP), Mexico. He is a member of the National System of Researchers (SNI-I). His research interests are violence, social struggles, and critical theory. He is co-editor of *Beyond Crisis: After the Collapse of Institutional Hope in Greece, What?* (with John Holloway and Katerina Nasioka, PM Press, 2020) and has published several articles on violence, fetishism of the concrete, and the crisis of capitalist relations.

Alfonso García Vela studied at Benemérita Universidad Autónoma de Puebla where he received his doctorate in Sociology, is currently Professor and researcher at the Instituto de Ciencias Sociales y Humanidades, at the Benemérita Universidad Autónoma de Puebla, Mexico. He was a postdoctoral fellow at Universidad Nacional Autónoma de México and Visiting Scholar in the Department of History at the University of Chicago. His fields of research and teaching are Frankfurt School critical theory, Western Marxism, contemporary Marxist theory, and classical and contemporary social theory. He is editor of Bajo el Volcán. Revista del Posgrado en Sociología. BUAP. His publication includes *The Concept of Social Class in Contemporary Marxist Theory* (ibidem Press, 2022) with Massimo Modonesi and María Vignau Loria, and *Open Marxism 4. Against a Closing World* (Pluto Press, 2020) with Ana Cecilia Dinerstein, John Holloway, and Edith González Cruz.

Edith González Cruz obtained her Master's and Ph.D. degrees in Sociology at the Institute of Social Sciences and Humanities "Alfonso Vélez Pliego"—BUAP (ICSyH-BUAP), Mexico. The author is a member of the National System of Researchers (SNI-I). Her research interests are the critique of political economy and the Value Dissociation, Latin American critical thought, and issues related to social struggles and resistance. With Ana C. Dinerstein, Alfonso García Vela, and John Holloway, they edited the book *Open Marxism 4. Against a Closing World* (Pluto Press, 2019), and she has published articles on the fetishism of the concrete, the value dissociation, and its relation to the current corona crisis.

Vasilis Grollios has been awarded a Ph.D. in political philosophy from the Aristotle University of Thessaloniki, Greece. He has taught in Greek universities. He has published on critical Marxism and J.S. Mill on journals like *Constellations*, *Capital and Class*, *Critique: A Journal of Socialist Philosophy*, *Critical Sociology* and *Philosophy and Social Criticism.* He is the author of *Negativity and Democracy: Marxism and the Critical Theory Tradition*, Routledge, New York and Oxon, 2017. He has finished his next book which is under review. Its title will be Illusion and Fetishism in the Critical Theory of Nietzsche, Benjamin, Castoriadis, and the Situationists.

Richard Gunn was born in Inverness, Scotland, in 1947. He was educated at Edinburgh University, where he lectured in political theory until he retired in 2011, Since he retired, he has been an independent researcher. Many of his theoretical papers are jointly written with Adrian Wilding. In 2021, Richard and Adrian published a book-length statement of their views: *Revolutionary Recognition* (London: Bloomsbury Academic 2021). A paperback edition has just appeared.

Yiorgos Moraitis studied History of Modern Political and Social Philosophy at the Aristotle University of Thessaloniki. His Ph.D. thesis explores the concept of sovereignty in Thomas Hobbes' and Jean-Jacques Rousseau's social and political thought. He worked for two years as a postdoctoral researcher at the Institute of Intercultural and International Studies (In.I.I.S.) of the University of Bremen, under the supervision of Professor Dr. Martin Nonhoff. He has taught moral philosophy and modern social and political theory at the Department of Philosophy of the University of Patras. He has co-edited with John Holloway a Greek collected volume on Open Marxism that is going to be published in the very next months by Nissos Publications.

Katerina Nasioka completed her doctoral studies in sociology in the Instituto de Ciencias Sociales y Humanidades, Benemérita Universidad Autónoma de Puebla, Mexico. Her research interests address issues related to urban space, critical theory, and social insurrections. She participates in self-organized collectives and projects in Greece and published and presented articles and papers on recent Greek social struggles. She is co-author of *Gender and Journalism in Greece* (2008), author of *Ciudades en Insurrección, Oaxaca 2006/Atenas 2008* (2017), and co-editor of *Beyond Crisis: After the Collapse of the Institutional Hope in Greece, What?* (PM Press, 2018).

Marios Panierakis became politically active in December of 2008, after the assassination of the student Alexandros Grigoropoulos by the police in Athens. He took part in various social struggles. These actions included the movement of the Squares, which he studied in his undergraduate thesis. He is currently a Ph.D. candidate in Sociology at the Instituto de Ciencias Sociales y Humanidades, at the Benemérita Universidad Autónoma de Puebla, Mexico. In the context of which he is researching the new forms of social struggles, focusing on occupied social centers.

Adrián Piva, a sociologist by the University of Buenos Aires and Doctor in Social Sciences by Quilmes University, Argentina. He is currently a professor of sociology for historians at the University of Buenos Aires. He is a researcher at the National Council of Scientific Research of Argentina (CONICET). He has extensively researched the relationship between the mode of capital accumulation, class struggle, and the mode of political domination in contemporary Argentina; and on the theory of classes, the state, and hegemony. He has published Estado y Capital. El debate derivacionista. Madrid: Dado ediciones, 2021 (with Alberto Bonnet), and Economía y política en la Argentina Kirchnerista. Buenos Aires: Batalla de Ideas, 2015.

Marcel Stoetzler is Senior Lecturer in Sociology at Bangor University, UK. He is a sociologist and historian working on social theory, in particular the Critical Theory of the "Frankfurt School", as well as antisemitism, nationalism, race, and gender. His publications include *Beginning Classical Social Theory* (Manchester University Press, 2017), *Antisemitism and the Constitution of Sociology* (University of Nebraska Press, 2014), and *The State, the Nation and the Jews. Liberalism and the Antisemitism Dispute in Bismarck's Germany* (University of Nebraska Press, 2008). He is a member of the editorial board of Patterns of Prejudice, an Associate Research Fellow at the Birkbeck Institute for the study of Antisemitism, London, and an Honorary Research Fellow at the Centre for Jewish Studies, The University of Manchester. Recent articles on critical theory were published in Constelaciones, *Journal of Social Justice*, *Marxism 21*, *The Sage Handbook of Frankfurt School Critical Theory*, the *European Journal of Social Theory*, openDemocracy, and fast capitalism.

Adrian Wilding studied Politics at Edinburgh University, where his teachers were Richard Gunn and John Holloway. His Ph.D. thesis (Warwick University) explored Walter Benjamin's philosophy of history. He currently teaches at the Institut für Soziologie, Friedrich-Schiller Universität Jena and is also Fellow of the Großbritannien-Zentrum, Humboldt Universität zu Berlin. His book co-written with Richard Gunn, Revolutionary Recognition, is published by Bloomsbury.

José A. Zamora is Senior Researcher at the Institute of Philosophy (Spanish Council for Scientific Research—CSIC), Madrid-Spain. Member of the Spanish Society of Critical Theory and Co-Editor of Constelaciones. Revista de Teoría Crítica. Coordinator of the research project "Constellations of authoritarianism: memory and actuality of a threat to democracy in a philosophical and interdisciplinary perspective".

CHAPTER 1

John Holloway and the Meaning of Revolution Today

Alfonso García Vela and Alberto Bonnet

Two decades have gone by since John Holloway embarked on a journey with *Change the World without Taking Power* (Pluto Press, 2010a), one he continued with *Crack Capitalism* (Pluto Press, 2010b) ten years later; now, he adds yet another stretch with his new book, *Hope in Hopeless Times* (Pluto Press, 2022). This is his new attempt to rethink revolution. To understand revolution not in the traditional terms of taking state power and subsequently transforming society from the state, but rather in those of a process of multiplication and convergence of the different cracks that run through capitalist domination every single day.

A. García Vela (✉)
Instituto de Ciencias Sociales y Humanidades, Benemérita Universidad Autónoma de Puebla (BUAP), Puebla, México
e-mail: galileo.vela@correo.buap.mx

A. Bonnet
Department of Economics and Administration, National University of Quilmes, Buenos Aires, Argentina
e-mail: abonnetprivado@gmail.com

A. García Vela and A. Bonnet (eds.), *The Political Thought of John Holloway*, Marx, Engels, and Marxisms,
https://doi.org/10.1007/978-3-031-34571-5_1

This endeavour took on great challenges even before the book was published. A driver who repeatedly steers his car through a paved highway he is familiarized with can do so with certainty. Regardless of whether his car does not work anymore, his highway leads to nowhere, or even of it leads to an abyss; he can drive with certainty, as long as he has given up on the hope of reaching a destination, any destination. On the contrary, he who ventures into an unknown path knows there will be unforeseeable risks; but he also knows that, without venturing into the unknown, no goal can be accomplished. And so, he walks; even if he walks asking, as the Zapatistas do, because he feels uncertain. The aim of this book is to discuss and critically reflect—while walking side by side with John Holloway—on some of the problems facing this adventure of his, the adventure of rewriting the grammar of revolution.

Change the World was published in Spanish in Argentina in mid-2002, before it appeared in its original version in English. That is, it was published a few months after a popular insurrection put an end to an entire decade of neoliberal despotism. And, in that explosive conjuncture, it became one of the most widely read and discussed books amongst the activists involved in the uprising. *Crack Capitalism* was published in English in mid-2010; once again, it found itself at the heart of militant readings and discussions, this time in other geographies, such as the Greek revolts or the Arab Spring of 2010–2012. This, of course, speaks highly of the two books: unlike other intellectual interventions from the Left, those made by Holloway were able to resonate with the people fighting in the streets. And this explains the enormous attention that the books attracted. *Change the World* was reprinted in English in 2005 and 2019 and translated into eleven languages; *Crack Capitalism* was translated into twelve languages. Both books inspired innumerable debates in books and dossiers of prestigious reviews.

Why did Holloway's question on the meaning of revolution resonate with those militants? And why does it continue to do so today? Part of the answer to this question might seem obvious. At the beginning of its expansion, capitalism might have placed humanity before complex dilemmas as a result of the inextricable combination of its both emancipating and oppressive consequences. However, in our days, when it has spread across the globe, all that capitalism admittedly has to offer to humankind is a miserable choice between different forms of annihilation. We are no longer faced with the contradictory consequences of servants becoming wage labourers, but rather with the dilemma of being annihilated by a series of pandemics emerging in the food chain, a new world war involving global powers, or any other similar catastrophe. The development of capitalism is, as Holloway describes in one of his most recent writings, a train that is out of control and is rushing headlong towards the abyss. Our abyss. "The train rushes forward into the night, faster, faster. Where is it going? To the concentration camps? Or to nuclear war? Or to annihilation by global warming and ecological disaster? To extinction?" (2020: 168). To stop this train on time requires nothing less than a radical and generalized transformation of the way in which our social relations are organized. Many words can be used to describe such a transformation; however, they would all be synonymous with "revolution". In this sense, it is obvious that Holloway's question on the meaning of revolution today is not only relevant but also urgently needed.

However, there is another side to the answer to this question, one that might seem less obvious. For the question refers not only to the *timeliness* of revolution in our days, but also to its *meaning*. And, in this sense, it is more defiant. At the moment of its publication, *Change the World* caused quite a commotion because of this. Arguably, it was quite foreseeable that a book that suggested changing the world without taking power would cause such a stir. The matter, however, is not that simple. In fact, when one carefully reviews the debates that took place around *Change the World*, one realizes that in most cases the scandal was not the result of the specific way in which Holloway thought of revolution, but rather of the mere fact that he had dared to rethink it. Indeed, that book, unlike *Crack Capitalism*, was destructive in its essence. That is, it elaborated more on why we should let go of the idea of revolution in terms of the taking and exercising of state power than on what we should think about in its place. Holloway himself openly acknowledged it and even claimed it. "How then do we change the world without taking power? At the end of the book, as at the beginning, we do not know. The Leninists know or used to know. We do not. [...] In part, our not-knowing is the not-knowing of those who are historically lost: the knowing of the revolutionaries of the last century has been defeated. But it is more than that: our not-knowing is also the not-knowing of those who understand that the not-knowing is part of the revolutionary process" (2010a: 215). This "not knowing" that he admitted to was what shocked most of his expert detractors.

The call to the alleged "lessons of history" was the favourite tactic of said detractors. Holloway at times referred to the failure of social democratic and Leninist experiences, as well as to the promises contained in historical alternative experiences of a communitarian or council-related nature and, obviously, to the ongoing Zapatista experience. Although, admittedly, he did not discuss any of these historical experiences in detail. The objections formulated in these terms seemed reasonable. To criticize our revolutionary experiences of the past (a critique that, for the time being, is still in its infancy) is a significant input for rethinking revolution in the present. However, the call of most critics to the "lessons of history" concealed much darker implications. For, to them, history taught that revolution *had already been thought* (by Lenin and his followers, *par excellence*), even if the Leninist conception of the revolution degenerated (in the hands of Stalin and his people). Consequently, Holloway's pretension of ignoring the "lessons of history" amounted, to them, to making *tabula rasa* of the Soviet experience as an outright failure, throwing away the rosy baby of Leninism with the dirty bathwater of Stalinism.

We cannot settle accounts with such an objection in this brief introduction, but we must include a comment to continue advancing. Neither the Soviet experience nor any other historical experience should, naturally, become the victim of such *tabula rasa*. The problem is that we cannot wait for historical research to shed all the light it can on these experiences. Not even if we were to assume that this light would be enough to settle the pivotal polemics surrounding them. We must make do, in the meantime, with formulating hypotheses that will guide us through the terrain of an ongoing class struggle. Holloway has formulated one of these hypotheses: "The apparent impossibility of revolution at the beginning of the twenty-first century reflects in reality the historical failure of a particular concept of revolution, the concept that identified revolution with control of the state" (2010a: 12). And he appropriately responded to these objections with the well-known verse from Blake's *Proverbs of Hell*: "drive your cart and your plough over the bones of the dead". The never-ending discussions on the true "lessons of history", Holloway argued, cannot be used as an excuse to avoid the task of rethinking revolution in our days. We must reject "the common use of history on the Left as a way of avoiding thinking about the meaning of revolution in the present, and particularly the use of the term 'Stalinism'" (Holloway, 2005: 280).

That said, the Leninist conception of revolution that underlies most of the objections played an insignificant role, if any, in the social struggles recorded at the time. There were, naturally, no vanguard parties or strategies to take state power in the struggle launched by the Zapatistas in 1995, neither in the antiglobalization movements that began in Seattle in 1999, nor in the struggles fought in Argentina around 2001 or in Bolivia between 2000 and 2005, nor amongst the Oaxaca rebels of 2006 or the clashes that took place in Greece in 2008 and in 2010–2012, nor in the Arab Spring of 2010–2012 or the French and Spanish *indignados* of 2016, nor in any other significant experience. The objections against Holloway that were inspired by the Leninist conception of revolution became, in this context, a scholastic affair. However, this does not imply that other conceptions that focused on taking state power and transforming society from the state did not influence different experiences that have emerged since then. Such is the case, for example, of the ones akin to the so-called *Socialism of the 21st Century*, inspired rather in the nationalist and populist tradition of the Latin American Left.

Even before the publication of *Change the World*, Holloway had put forward some of his main arguments in his analysis of the 1994 Zapatista uprising. For Holloway, Zapatismo itself had broken with the "state illusion", that is, with "the paradigm that has dominated left thought for over a century" that "perceives revolution as the taking of power state and the transformation of society through the state" and had undertaken "the project of changing the world without taking power" (Holloway, 2001: 174). Those assertions made by Holloway, as well as the positions adopted by the Zapatistas themselves, had been heavily criticized. Meanwhile, a few years after the Zapatista uprising, in 1999, Hugo Chavez rose to power and announced a few years later a new project of transforming society from the state, the so-called *Socialism of the 21st Century*. In this context, the discussion deployed in *Change the World* acquired a much more concrete meaning.

The result in the longer term was that history, tired of being called upon in vain, decided to take vengeance. Many of Holloway's most ardent detractors in those debates became apologists for a new authoritarian regime that was just turning into a grotesque version of the old Stalinism. And this passing from the old defence of Stalinism to a new defence of Chavism did not even require a substantial change in the arguments of the detractors: classes and class struggle were once again replaced by the states and by struggles amongst states, and the old defence of the "labour classes" against the "imperialist states" of the cold war merely muted into the defence of "Socialism of the twenty-first century" against the aggressions of "Yankee imperialism". The one party and the cult of the leader, the electoral frauds and the repression, the corruption of the ruling political-military caste and even the social and economic catastrophe, as well as the massive migration, were accepted as the necessary cost of constructing this new experiment of state socialism. And, in the meantime, the Zapatistas faced enormous limitations and continued, often through failed initiatives, to consolidate their autonomy and expand it to include new communities, determined to change the world without taking power…

In sum: those who had called upon the "lessons of history" in the past to avoid all efforts to rethink revolution were now ignoring these lessons and repeating the worst facets of said history. Holloway's question on the meaning of revolution today was and still is an inescapable affair. The experiences of building authoritarian regimes in the name of socialism, repeated ad nauseam, seemed to have been—and continue to be—linked to the centralized exercise of state power. In this sense, Holloway's hypothesis of changing the world without taking power also was, and continues to be, plausible.

That said, how can we rethink revolution on the basis of this hypothesis? To this end, Holloway leans on three fundamental inputs. Firstly, on the characteristics of the major social struggles of the past decades: the Zapatista uprising, above all, but also more or less insurrectional movements according to the cases registered at the national and international scale, such as the aforementioned. These characteristics include their diverse composition, the assembly forms of organization and the horizontal and democratic decision-making processes, intervention through direct action and the drive towards the creation of new ways of organizing society rather than the taking of state power. Particularly his interpretation of the Zapatista uprising, as we already mentioned, largely inspired the arguments that Holloway would go on to develop in his following books.

Secondly, Holloway could count on the effort he had already dedicated to "opening" up Marxian categories to class struggle and the resulting contingency of social processes. The three volumes of *Open Marxism* had been the programmatical expression of this endeavour. Particularly the "opening" of the concept of the state as an antagonistic mode of existence of social relations, a critical approach to the German state derivation debate, has been at the centre of Holloway's concerns and underlies his approach to the relation between the revolution and the state in the two books (Holloway, 2010a: 91 and ss. and 2010b: 130 and ss.). However, even if the concept of the state is key in Holloway's argumentation, it is not the only one. His distinction between *power-over* and *power-to* and between *hard-fetishism* and *fetishism-as-process* in *Change de World*, as well as his formulation of the antagonism between *doing* and *labour* in *Crack Capitalism*—that is, the theoretical cores of his entire argumentation—can well be considered the ultimate developments of this effort to open up Marxian categories, in this case of abstract and concrete labour, commodity, value, money and capital. In this sense, the two books can be read as the incursion of an *open Marxist* into the thorny terrain of revolutionary theory.

And, thirdly, Holloway can also rely on the input of the tradition of critical theory in a broader sense (Lukacs, Bloch, Horkheimer, Marcuse) and, more specifically, on Adorno's negative dialectics. The influence of critical theory was already present in *Open Marxism* from the onset; however, in the books by Holloway that we are referring to, its influence is more significant than in other cases. According to Holloway, negative dialectics in particular is the dialectics of revolution. "This is the central theme in Adorno's thought: dialectics as the consistent sense of non-identity, of that which does not fit. It is both libertarian and revolutionary" (Holloway, 2009: 13). In other words, negative dialectics becomes in the hands of Holloway the mode of thinking that accordingly allows for the promotion of the effort of opening up categories.

This brief outlining of Holloway's journey to rethinking revolution from *Change the World*, passing through *Crack Capitalism* and reaching our days, with his luggage of class struggles, open Marxism and critical theory, is enough to give the reader an idea of the diversity of reflections and discussions that the journey stimulates throughout this volume.

The first part considers certain key aspects of Holloway's interpretation of Marxist political theory. In the first chapter, Richard Gunn and Adrian Wilding recover Holloway's conception of Marxism, not as a theory of domination anymore but as that of the fragility of this domination, and offer an alternative explanation to this distinction on the basis of the Hegelian notion of recognition. In the second chapter, Werner Bonefeld discusses Holloway's comprehension of one of the Marxian concepts that play a key role in his argumentation; namely, that of abstract labour. In the third chapter, Adrian Piva discusses the identification of the notion of contradiction with that of antagonism explicitly assumed by Holloway in his approach to classes and class struggle. And in the fourth chapter, Yiorgos Moraitis and Vasilis Grollios link Holloway's interstitial conception of revolution to Rousseau's radical democracy.

The second part of this compilation focuses rather on the impact of Holloway's theorizing on negativity, social struggles, and emancipation. In the fifth chapter, Edith González Cruz and Panagiotis Doulos identify an ontological foundation in Holloway's concept of *doing* as presented in the specific books and discuss its political implications. In the sixth chapter, Katerina Nasioka and Marios Panierakis reflect on existing cracks in the context of the biopolitical control enforced during the recent pandemic.

The third and final part of this volume is dedicated to questions linked to the assimilation of critical theory by Holloway. Alfonso Garcia Vela discerns, in the seventh chapter, an anthropological core inspired in Marcuse; that is, a human nature or essence behind Holloway's anti-identitarian concept of the subject. Jose Antonio Zamora recovers in the eighth chapter the critique against authoritarianism—a highly notorious phenomenon in our times—of the Frankfurt School to reflect on "the urgent impossibility of revolution" posited by Holloway. In the ninth chapter, Alberto Bonnet reflects on the way in which Holloway assimilates Adorno's negative dialectics as a dialectic of revolution and its political implications. In the tenth chapter, Marcel Stoetzler revisits one the nodes both of critical theory as well as of Holloway's own theorizing, that of the issue of reification and the relation between subject and object. The volume closes with an afterword by John Holloway, who invites us to keep reflecting on and discussing his question on the meaning of revolution today.

The political landscape changed considerably in the decade following the appearance of *Crack Capitalism*. The ebb of social struggles, the rise of the new Right and of authoritarianism, the growing tensions between international powers, the pandemic and the ongoing war have inaugurated a new world where it seems increasingly difficult to identify the *cracks* in domination. Within this new political landscape, in our opinion, this recovery and discussion of Holloway's political thought make sense. And this also seems to be the opinion of Holloway himself, who has precisely chosen to title his recent book *Hope in hopeless times*...

References

Holloway. (2001). El zapatismo y las ciencias sociales en América Latina. In *Revista del OSAL* (Vol. 4). CLACSO.

Holloway, J. (2005). No. In *Historical Materialism* (Vol. 13, No. 4). Brill.

Holloway, J. (2009). Why adorno?. In J. Holloway, F. Matamoros & S. Tischler (Eds.). *Negativity and revolution. Adorno and political activism*. Pluto Press.

Holloway, J. (2010a). *Change the world without taking power: The meaning of revolution today* (New). Pluto Press.

Holloway, J. (2010b). *Crack capitalism*. Pluto Press.

Holloway, J. (2020). The train. In A. C. Dinerstein, A. García Vela, E. González & J. Holloway (Eds.) *Open marxism 4. Against a closing world*. Pluto Press.

Holloway, J. (2022). *Hope in hopeless times*. Pluto Press.

PART I

Marxism and Political Theory

CHAPTER 2

On Domination and Its Fragility

Richard Gunn and Adrian Wilding

In his 'Variations on Different Themes' of 2012, John Holloway suggests that 'little is served by telling ourselves how bleak the outlook is'. He continues: 'We need a theory not of domination but of the fragility or crisis of that domination, of the possibility of cracking that domination' (Holloway, 2012: 333). The authors of this chapter are immensely indebted to Holloway's writings and conversations, and agree wholeheartedly that the crisis of capitalist domination should be Marxism's focus. Yet our understanding of domination and its fragility is expressed in a somewhat different vocabulary to Holloway's. What we attempt in this article is to explain how and why our approach differs and what the implications of this are. In what follows we sketch issues treated more fully in

R. Gunn · A. Wilding (✉)
Edinburgh University, Retired, Edinburgh, Scotland
e-mail: Adrian.Wilding@uni-jena.de

R. Gunn
e-mail: richardmgunn@googlemail.com

A. Wilding
Friedrich-Schiller-Universität, Jena, Germany

A. García Vela and A. Bonnet (eds.), *The Political Thought of John Holloway*, Marx, Engels, and Marxisms,
https://doi.org/10.1007/978-3-031-34571-5_2

our book *Revolutionary Recognition* (Gunn & Wilding, 2021), for which Holloway has written a powerful Foreword. We argue that the Hegelian notion of *recognition* can supply a unifying and thorough explanation for both domination and its fragility. Indeed only when domination is understood in recognitive terms, we argue, is domination's strength and its fragility fully explicable.

*

Before we can explain our understanding of recognition and its revolutionary implications, however, some clearing of the theoretical field is needed. This is not least because most readers will have a preconception about what 'recognition' means. This in turn is because the field has been shaped by two particularly influential academic interpretations. Since 1992, when Charles Taylor published an article entitled 'The Politics of Recognition' (reprinted in Taylor, 1994), the theme has gained academic respectability within both left-wing and liberal circles. Taylor's aim was to provide liberalism with a term that could gain purchase on multiculturalist questions. In a parallel development, Axel Honneth, former director of the Frankfurt School, sought to ground critical (i.e. left-wing) theory on a recognitive basis (see e.g. Honneth, 2015). Our own view of recognition can only be understood once it is seen as *breaking decisively with both of these approaches*. To put in a nutshell what is problematic in these approaches, the school of thinking launched by Taylor seeks to redress the lack of esteem suffered by marginalized or oppressed cultural groups, whereas the school indebted to Honneth seeks to reform the institutions of civil society and the state by looking to the 'promise of freedom' they contain. Both Taylor and Honneth and the academic industry to which their work has given rise take key elements of our capitalist world for granted: on the one hand, the division into cultural groupings and the assumption that oppression is primarily cultural; on the other, that while the institutions of bourgeois society change over time, they will always be with us. Taylor's and Honneth's approaches share what we call in our book a 'less-than-revolutionary' outlook. Their 'less-than-revolutionary' outlook can be traced, we argue, to a specific—a specifically wrongheaded—understanding of recognition. Briefly put: in Taylor it comes down to assuming that recognition is a 'resource' to be distributed equally; in Honneth it comes down to assuming that human freedom can be adequately recognized by the institutions of civil society and the state. In Honneth's case, the misunderstanding of recognition has a partly textual basis. He draws heavily upon the later Hegel—the Hegel of the *Philosophy of Right* (1821), the Hegel who tried to find a rational justification for the institutions of Restoration Europe. By stark contrast, Gunn and Wilding draw upon the young Hegel—the Hegel of the *Phenomenology of Spirit* (1807)—a work written when the French Revolution and the Revolutionary Wars were still burning issues. Our book *Revolutionary Recognition* opens with a chapter headed 'Hegel's Dangerous Idea'—the dangerous idea being that of 'mutual recognition', which plays a pivotal part in the *Phenomenology of Spirit*'s argument. Already, a reader may surmise something of the difference between Honneth, Taylor and ourselves.

A short paper is not the place to explore, in detail, interpretation of Hegel's writings. Our comments here merely touch on points which our book *Revolutionary Recognition* makes more fully and which are pertinent to Holloway's own concerns.[1] In the *Phenomenology* (especially Chapter 6), much attention is paid to history. Successive phases or epochs of history are seen as shapes or patterns that recognition may take. Different patterns have their own distinctive features, but one is shared by the patterns concerned. It is that, throughout history, recognition exists in a contradictory or 'alienated' fashion. In Hegel's account of history in the *Phenomenology* two such types of 'contradictory recognition' can be distinguished. The one is well known: it is where a relationship of recognition is 'one-sided and unequal'—paradigmatically the relation of Master and Slave (which, as Hegel makes clear, is not confined to the Ancient world). The other is less familiar: we refer to it as 'institutional recognition'. It is to be found wherever institutions and the social roles that go with them channel and limit social interaction. Hegel calls institutions 'social masses' (*geistigen Massen*)—he means by this that they have a weight and an inertia that inevitably produce conformity and obedience. Institutions and the role definitions to which they give rise become a second nature. Yet institutions recognize us in a fundamentally contradictory way: they can only acknowledge us as instances of universals, as

[1] Besides *Revolutionary Recognition*, R. Gunn's Lo que usted siempre quiso saber sobre Hegel y no se atrevió a preguntar (Gunn, 2015) may help to fill the gaps in our discussion here.

types.[2] Institutions constrain the to-and-fro of interaction, channeling it according to norms, regulations and the leaden character of tradition.

Though the two types of contradictory recognition are distinct, it is clear that they may exist contemporaneously. Indeed they can be seen to be internally related. In the slave-owning societies of Ancient Greece and Ancient Rome, recognition that is 'one-sided and unequal' (Hegel, 1977: 116) exists in a paradigmatic way, yet slavery also amounts to an institution that defines the roles of those involved. In the markets of present-day capitalism, individuals 'recognize one another…as proprietors' (Marx, 1973: 243), i.e. in terms of roles, yet these roles presuppose the exploitation—the domination—that characterizes the labor process.[3] Seldom, if ever, does a single form of contradictory recognition exist on its own.

We have said something—all too briefly—about contradictory recognition. Is there then an *uncontradictory* form of recognition? Hegel answers us in the positive: it is what he calls 'mutual recognition'. For the young Hegel this was no mere ideal or utopia but had a historical actuality. The French Revolution is, for the *Phenomenology*, a decisive or critical event since it is then, for the very first time, that uncontradicted and non-alienated recognition makes its appearance. Uncontradicted or, as Hegel has it, 'pure' recognition is recognition of a 'mutual' kind (1977: 112). Where recognition is mutual, the freedom or self-determination of individuals is cast into relief and emancipation obtains. It is no coincidence that the paradigmatic moment of the French Revolution is, for Hegel, the crowd's storming of the Bastille—a despised institution which symbolized the cruelty of the Ancien Régime.[4] In the Revolutionary crowd that rushes to the Bastille, 'each, undivided from the whole,

[2] Institutions recognize us, Hannah Arendt notes, 'as such and such, that is, as something which we fundamentally are not' (2003: 14).

[3] This seems to us the upshot of the famous passage in *Capital* vol. 1 concerning the need to go beyond the 'sphere of circulation' into the 'hidden abode of production' (Marx, 1975: 279).

[4] Susan Buck-Morss (2009) has shown convincingly that Hegel would have had in mind not only the French Revolution but also the Haitian Revolution of 1791–1804, an uprising which overthrew colonial slavery on the island and placed the wider slave system radically in question. For us it is no surprise that Hegel's thoughts on the relation of master and slave encompass those of racial exploitation. His *Phenomenology* targets *all* forms of domination. This is what makes his idea of mutual recognition, so revolutionary, so 'dangerous'.

always does everything, and what appears to be done by the whole is the direct and conscious deed of each' (Hegel, 1977: 357). As Hegel phrases the point elsewhere, an 'I that is We and We that is I' (Hegel, 1977: 110) comes into being. However, mutual recognition arises here only in a fleeting way. The problem faced by the French Revolution, according to the *Phenomenology*, is that attempts to instantiate mutual recognition—through constitution-building or revolutionary war or state terror—undermine freedom and re-instate alienation in this or that way. The difficult task of *instantiating* mutual recognition without *building institutions* is one which is left to subsequent generations to address.

The task fell to Hegel's radical followers—the Young Hegelians or Left Hegelians, among them Karl Marx. In this light it is of interest that, when the *Communist Manifesto* refers to communist society, Marx's phrasing has a mutually recognitive ring. There, Marx describes communism as 'an association, in which the free development of each is the condition for the free development of all' (Marx & Engels, 1976: 506). Communism is the 'I that is We and We that is I' at which Hegelian and French Revolutionary emancipation aims. It is true that Marx is seldom read as a theorist of recognition: economistic interpretations have often prevailed.[5] But read carefully, Marx's work—from youth to old age—tells us that *contradictory recognition* is what stands in emancipation's way. In particular, the analyses of commodity exchange, property and class that fill the *Grundrisse* and the three volumes of *Capital* can each be understood as manifestations of the two forms of contradictory recognition we have set out above.[6]

So far, a reader of the present article may form the impression that Gunn and Wilding's chief interest is in the history of ideas—and that this is where our agreement or disagreement with Holloway lies. In the opening chapters of *Revolutionary Recognition*, we do indeed engage with questions about how Hegel and Marx are to be seen. In the second half of our book, however, we explore practical issues to which a politics of mutual recognition give rise.

If mutual recognition is in existence, it has a dynamic that it is important to note. This dynamic is through and through informal and is of a

[5] In a world where Marx is commonly viewed as a political economist, John Holloway—Gunn and Wilding note in passing—is one of the few commentators who gets Marx's emphasis the right way round (see esp. Holloway, 2015).

[6] This argument is substantiated in Chapter 2 of our *Revolutionary Recognition*.

grassroots rather than a top-down kind. Living examples of mutual recognition, we argue, are to be found in today's social movements, above all in the 'movement of the squares' which has come to replace the vanguard party as the model of revolutionary organization. Here our and Holloway's arguments run in parallel. Today's most radical social movements (indebted in many ways to the Zapatistas) put into practice the egalitarian and participatory social relations that they seek to bring about at a global scale. When Holloway calls such movements 'the breakthrough of another world, perhaps' (2010: 250),[7] or 'fissures' in the edifice of capital that have the capacity to join into fatal 'cracks' (Holloway, 2010: 74) his thought is in unison with our own. For us it is because *a crisis of domination is a crisis of recognition* that one can say, with Holloway, that 'We are the crisis of capitalism' (Holloway, 2010: 250).

Another respect in which Holloway's and our concerns coincide—and this becomes clearer still in his forthcoming book *Hope in Hopeless Times*—is that emancipation must be conceived not just in social but also in ecological terms. In *Crack Capitalism* this is visible in his engagement with theories of the commons, an idea which his latest book renews. For us, commons are to be endorsed precisely because they are a further living example of mutual recognition. They are a form of association in which a mutually recognitive community collectively determines its reproduction. The commons challenges the rule of property and the law of the market whereby individuals view each other only as proprietors. Commoning is a deeply recognitive process. It entails an interaction which renders the egoism of the proprietor irrational (since self-interested exploitation of a commons is contradictory and unsustainable). It encourages concern for the other and a realization of human interdependence, just as it provides a justification for democratic decision-making about the commons itself. Commoning is a mode of production where each individual exists cooperatively *through* others, not *in spite of* others. The vocabulary here is

[7] If this is the case, then it is down to one particular characteristic of these movements: their 'horizontalism', i.e. their egalitarian and participative decision-making. Horizontalism, we suggest, can be pictured as a conversation—a 'good' conversation which, proverbially, follows its subject matter wherever it leads. By contrast, any activist who has experience of membership of a vanguard party will know that if a conversation or interaction is made to follow channels laid down in advance the reciprocal or to-and-fro dynamic is disrupted. The stifling frustration of orthodoxy and traditional authority is the result. What obtains is the quasi-natural inertia that keeps an institution in being. Power is exercised for power's sake and the iron law of oligarchy sets in.

Hegelian and Marxian but one could just as well put it in older terms, those of the English Revolution: a commons is not a state of nature which may become 'any one's property' (see Locke, 1988: Chapter 5) but is 'everyone's birthright' (see Winstanley, 1973: 342). We follow Holloway (along with Silvia Federici upon whom Holloway draws—see esp. Federici, 2019: 110) in placing the notion of commoning at the center of our thinking. What we add to their arguments is this: that when commoning is understood in mutually recognitive terms we have a principle that could bring left-wing and ecological politics together.

We mentioned above that though the two forms of contradictory recognition are distinct, they may exist contemporaneously. How are the two related? We have to acknowledge that, in almost each and every historical instance, *both* forms of contradictory recognition are present. To give an example: the Master–Slave relation is a paradigm example of recognition that is 'one sided and unequal'. But, of course, 'Master' and 'Slave' are themselves social definitions which predominate in the social institutions of the Ancient and slave-owning world. In the modern world, the capitalist and the worker form a relation of one-sided and unequal recognition—although, as *Capital* Volume One emphasizes, 'capitalist' and 'worker' are role definitions ('personifications') for their part. It is, in short, the interweaving of these two forms of unfreedom which make relations of domination seem so difficult to change. So to say, relations of domination are 'double locked'. Many other historical and present instances of this 'double locking' of contradictory recognition could be cited.

If we draw attention to this 'double lock' of domination, do we inevitably downplay domination's 'fragility'? Our answer is: this need not be the case. To explain why, we turn once again to Hegel. At one point in the Preface to the *Phenomenology*, during a seemingly complex discussion of space and time, Hegel remarks critically on the 'mathematical' outlook that would reduce everything to quantity and to identity. He says that the flaw in the mathematical outlook is that it cannot cope with the 'sheer unrest of life and absolute differentiation' (1970: 46; 1977: 27).[8] What does Hegel mean by this cryptic phrase? Our answer is that it he is thinking not only about life in general but about the fundamentally self-determining character of human existence. He is thinking of the

[8] In conversation, Holloway has shown great interest in this line from Hegel.

same thing which Holloway refers to as 'the misfitting-overflowing of our power-to-do' (Holloway, 2010: 250). Let us explain.

For Hegel, human social existence is existence of a *negative* kind. Humans exist by negating what they are at any given moment, by differentiating themselves from what they are. This 'differentiation' is 'absolute' because it is determined not by outside forces but only by ourselves. Our ability to differentiate ourselves from ourselves—to *be what we are not* and to *not be what we are*—is the reason we can determine ourselves and be free. We 'misfit' (Holloway) because we are 'absolute differentiation' (Hegel). Something—some *thing*—that remained the same, self-identical, could never determine itself. Only difference—life's 'unrest'—allows for freedom. Whatever outside social or economic forces then constrain us, these are, so to say, modifications of our essential substance: the ineluctable power of self-determination. Specifically, unfreedom is our self-determination existing 'in the mode of being denied' (Gunn, 1992: 14). It is for this reason that, however dominated or passive or reactive we may seem at any given moment, we remain inescapably 'actual, active' beings [*wirklichen, wirkenden Menschen*], as Marx and Engels put it in a highly Hegelian formulation (Marx & Engels, 1969: 26).[9] Domination cannot have the final word because 'life' never ceases to be 'sheer unrest'.

Hegel's argument about contradictory recognition which we set out above is effectively a restatement of this point about the 'unrest of life'. Domination involves recognition, but recognition of a contradictory sort, a sort that contradicts our essence as self-determining beings. Where domination prevails, our self-determination is not nullified but exists in contradicted form. If this is so, Gunn and Wilding feel, important implications follow. The circumstance that, in virtually every instance of domination, both 'one sided and unequal recognition', and 'institutional recognition' are present—the circumstance that, so to say, relations of domination are 'double locked'—will often make it difficult to see how our self-determination may take place. To use *Crack Capitalism*'s metaphor, the pack-ice of reification (Holloway, 2010: 17) seems formidably deep. For us this shows that domination *is and is not* fragile. One may unmask a recognition that is 'one sided and unequal'—and yet

[9] The Lawrence and Wishart *Complete Works* of Marx and Engels translates this as 'real, active men' thereby missing the passage's Hegelian point.

encounter a role-defined recognition that everyday consciousness takes for granted.[10]

This notion of a double lock of contradictory recognition provides, we suggest, a fuller explanation of domination than, for instance, a notion grounded in 'voluntary servitude' (which Holloway invokes at several points in *Crack Capitalism*). A notion of voluntary servitude, as the etymology indicates, can only view domination and liberation as acts of will. Its appeal lies precisely in its simplicity: that one could straightforwardly 'resolve to serve no more' and 'at once' become free (La Boétie cited in Holloway, 2010: 5; for a fuller discussion see Gunn & Wilding, 2012). Holloway acknowledges a 'difficulty' with such a notion (Holloway, 2010: 6) but the source of the difficulty remains unclear in his book. For us, while La Boétie may evoke (or presage—he was writing two centuries beforehand) Hegel's Master and Slave, he only acknowledges 'one-sided and unequal recognition' and not 'institutional recognition'. For Hegel a relationship of domination is one which can also take on the character of an *institution*: it often has a leaden, intransigent quality that can frustrate even the strongest will to refuse it. For Marx, the situation is more complex still: in capitalism we find not 'immediate relations of domination and servitude' (Marx, 1975: 93, 354), but the highly mediated and 'impersonal'[11] rule of capital as such. Domination is exerted not so much by a particular Lord (as in feudalism or slavery) to whom we could say No, as by the diffuse Lordship of capital itself.[12] The revolutionary finds no *axis mundi* to push against.

[10] The circumstance that individuals often affirm a role definition because it offers at least the means to be *more than nothing*, to at least cling to a rung in the ladder of hierarchy and not fall into the abyss of social non-existence, is one reason why such roles—and the alienation they involve—prove highly tenacious. For the sake of having *something* rather than *nothing* we perpetuate our unfreedom.

[11] To use William Clare Roberts's apt term (2017: 82).

[12] Arguably, Guy Debord's notion of the 'spectacle' is an elaboration of Marx's point. It is regrettable that Debord's *Society of the Spectacle* is often misread as describing a ubiquitous and insuperable alienation when in fact, just like Marx's *Capital*, struggle lies at its heart. We suggest that it is no coincidence that the final chapter of *Society of the Spectacle*, where struggle comes center-stage, opens with an epigraph from Hegel: 'Self-consciousness [or human individuality] exists *in itself* and *for itself* in that, and by the fact that it exists for another self-consciousness; that is to say, it *is* only by being acknowledged or recognized' (Debord, 1987: Chapter 9; Hegel, 1977: 111).

Where does this leave our opening question of how to 'crack domination'? Have we erred on the side of domination rather than on the side of its fragility? This may be for the reader to decide.[13] For our part, we maintain that seeing domination in terms of recognition is—with Holloway—to see its human and malleable root. It is—again with Holloway—to find hope in the 'sheer unrest of life'. Yet at the same time it is to see a complexity in domination which should not be underestimated. To Holloway's 'resolve to serve no more!' we answer with a comradely 'yes, but…'. Yes, but: the will 'to serve no more' exists everywhere in highly mediated and often contradicted form.

Mutual recognition exists today, as we have seen, but it exists in the interstices, in the 'cracks' between a stubborn and near ubiquitous capitalist rule. And where it comes gloriously to life it is often threatened, endangered. The world in a time of pandemic is a case in point. On the eve of the Coronavirus lockdown, the streets were filled with activists for whom capital's destruction of the climate and the state's racist violence were vital issues. These issues brought people together in unprecedented ways and gave new hope to anti-capitalist struggle. But just as these issues were on every activists' lips, the pandemic came crashing down. The streets emptied. Protesters were faced with the dilemma of caring best for their fellow humans by socially distancing from them. Left-wing struggle was silenced precisely by the co-opting of left-wing principles. Mutual recognition was put on hold. Capital's destruction of the climate, and the deadly pandemics thereby set free, seemed to be locking down even the hope of resisting them.

What now? In an ideal world, the ending of lockdown would see the streets filled with protesters once more. The conversations regarding climate change, the state's racist violence and the iniquities of disaster capitalism would be resumed where they were left off. But can a discussion, however unrestricted and free to follow its own dynamic, ever *go back*? In a world where capitalist distraction is uppermost and mainstream news programs are conformist, have we not missed our opportunity?

[13] Of course, whether one errs to one side may be a pragmatic and not just a scientific question. In a revealing moment, Oskar Negt remarks: 'I am true to Antonio Gramsci's line when he says that he is a pessimist in his analysis, because the worst conceivable development cannot be excluded. But one cannot live with that, so one has to be an optimist in political practice. That's why it is the task of intellectuals to look for alternatives. I add, as a father, you can't tell your children that all roads are blocked. For this reason alone, I consider a form of pedagogical optimism to be a necessity' (Negt, 2017).

We do not, and cannot, know. Perhaps lockdown has, against the odds, pent up an anger that will make protest all the more widespread and urgent. Perhaps those tired of the isolation in their households will more readily take up the threads of interaction that were broken off. It is noteworthy that, in *Crack Capitalism*, points from which cracks radiate include moments where thoughtfulness and reflection and critical thinking take place. A book such as this, which reflects on Holloway's vital contribution to revolutionary thought, is perhaps just such a moment—it can itself be a prologue to revolution. We would then return to the unrest of struggle with renewed understanding and renewed hope.

References

Arendt, H. (2003). *Responsibility and Judgment*. Schocken Books.

Buck-Morss, S. (2009). *Hegel, Haiti and Universal History*. University of Pittsburgh Press.

Debord, G. (1987). *Society of the Spectacle* (K. Knabb, Trans.). Rebel Press.

Federici, S. (2019). *Re-enchanting the World*. PM Press.

Gunn, R. (1992). Against Historical Materialism: Marxism as a First-Order Discourse. In W. Bonefeld, R. Gunn & K. Psychopedis (Eds.), *Open Marxism. Volume II: Theory and Practice* (pp. 1–45). Pluto Press.

Gunn, R. (2015), *Lo que usted siempre quiso sobre Hegel y no se atrevió a preguntar*. Herramienta.

Gunn, R., & Wilding, A. (2012). Holloway, La Boetie, Hegel. *Journal of Classical Sociology, 12*(2) (special issue on *Crack Capitalism*), 173–190.

Gunn, R., & Wilding, A. (2021). *Revolutionary Recognition*. Bloomsbury.

Hegel, G. W. F. (1970). *Phänomenologie des Geistes*. Suhrkamp.

Hegel, G. W. F. (1977). *Phenomenology of Spirit* (A. V. Miller, Trans.). Clarendon Press.

Holloway, J. (2010). *Crack Capitalism*. Pluto.

Holloway, J. (2012). Variations on Different Themes: A Response. *Journal of Classical Sociology, 12*(2) (special issue on *Crack Capitalism*), 332–348.

Holloway, J. (2015), Read *Capital*: Or *Capital* starts with wealth, not with the Commodity. *Historical Materialism, 23*(3), 3–26.

Honneth, A. (2015). *Freedom's Right: The Social Foundations of Democratic Life*. Columbia University Press.

Locke, J. (1988). *Two Treatises of Government*. Cambridge University Press.

Marx, K. (1973). *Grundrisse* (M. Nicolaus, Trans.). Penguin Books.

Marx, K. (1975). *Capital* (Vol. 1) (B. Fowkes, Trans.). Penguin Books.

Marx, K., & Engels, F. (1969). *Werke*, Band (Vol. 3). Dietz Verlag.

Marx, K., & Engels, F. (1976). *Collected Works* (Vol. 6). Lawrence and Wishart.

Negt, O. (2017, June 2). Verrohung ist eine falsche Vorstellung von Freiheit. *Süddeutsche Zeitung*.
Roberts, W. C. (2017). *Marx's Inferno: The Political Theory of Capital*. Princeton University Press.
Taylor, C. (1994). The Politics of Recognition. In A. Gutman (Ed.), *Multiculturalism*. Princeton University Press.
Winstanley, G. (1973). *The Law of Freedom and Other Writings*. Penguin.

CHAPTER 3

Suffering and Its Social Validation: On Abstract Labour

Werner Bonefeld

Marx conceives of his historical materialism as critique of the existing social relations. It is to 'develop from the actual, given relations of life the forms in which these have been apotheosized' (Marx, 1990: 494, fn. 4). Instead of tracing the evolution of labour economy throughout history first to establish and legitimize its capitalist anatomy and then, second, to demand its further development towards its socialist actualization, as traditional Marxism has it, Marx's historical materialism is critique of the existing social relations. For Marx the distinctive character of capitalist wealth, its necessities and dynamic, is founded on the double character of capitalist labour, as both concrete labour and abstract labour in one. He holds that its double character is 'peculiar' (Marx, 1990: 165) and that it is fundamental 'to all understanding of the facts' (Marx, 1987a: 407). The chapter examines three 'facts'—the meaning of productive labour, the social form of concrete labour, and the temporality of abstract labour.

W. Bonefeld (✉)
York University, York, UK
e-mail: werner.bonefeld@york.ac.uk

A. García Vela and A. Bonnet (eds.), *The Political Thought of John Holloway*, Marx, Engels, and Marxisms,
https://doi.org/10.1007/978-3-031-34571-5_3

John Holloway (2010a, 2010b) is one of a few scholars who has taken Marx's statement about the peculiar character of capitalist labour seriously and he expounds the dual character of the capitalist labour with critical intent, seeking to locate its cracks. However, I am not at all certain about his view that, in capitalism, 'our activity (doing) is transformed into abstract labour' (2010a: 913). His conception suggests an automaticity, which, if true, would make capitalist social reproduction 'crisis-free'. Is it not also possible that 'concrete labour' might not be transformed into not abstract labour and what would be the consequence of the failure? In addition, he views concrete labour as joyful and abstract labour as a joyless and argues that in capitalism activity as such, doing, has transformed into a joyless expenditure of abstract labour (see ibid.). I am not sure whether it makes any sense to establish the distinction between abstract labour and concrete labour on the grounds that the one is enjoyable and creative, and that the other is oppressive and alienated so that 'enjoyment is no longer part of the [labour] process' (ibid.). What I am certain about, however, is that is not possible to labour in the abstract. Abstract labour is not a form of actual labouring, as he seems to suggest. However, if it really is not, what is it?

I argue that abstract labour is the socially necessary expenditure of concrete labour. Not every expenditure of concrete labour produces use-values. It produces use-values only on the condition that it takes the form of its opposite, that is, abstract labour, which is the social labour that produces value in the form of money. Use-value producing labour that fails to achieve validation in exchange for money counts for nothing. Its expenditure produced a failed commodity, that is, a mere product of a socially unnecessary expenditure of labour. The concrete labour that went into it was not productive of the capitalist form of social wealth. Instead it represents a waste of resource. As a product of a socially unnecessary expenditure of concrete labour, their use-values are socially speaking invalid and they might as well be burnt or left to rot, as indeed they are, regardless of the certain fact that their consumption would have satisfied many, often basic needs. The coincidence of abject poverty and glutted markets of, say, basic food stuff that is thrown away because money is not forthcoming to present social value to them, is not a market contingency. Rather, it expresses the logic of capitalist wealth, according to which the satisfaction of human needs is a mere sideshow. Money is the form of value. What matters is value in exchange.

I argue further that a concrete labour that created only ***products*** threatens its employer with devaluation and liquidation, and its seller with redundancy. On the one hand the employer of living labour will do his utmost to ensure that his investment is not sunk and that, instead, its employment produces a commodity, which is characterized by the simple fact that it has an exchange value. The expenditure of socially necessary labour time creates value in the form of money. Time is money—and there is therefore no time to waste in the expenditure of concrete labour. There is, then, the 'nibbling and cribbling at meal times...petty pilfering of minutes' and 'snatching a few minutes' (Marx, 1990: 352) to ensure, in competition with all other employers of living labour, that the expenditure of concrete labour achieves social validation in exchange for money before the time of socially necessary labour is up. Also, the existence of the sellers of labour power hangs by the value-validity of their labour. If, despite every conceivable effort to make the time of concrete labour count for profit, crippled and wasted by their effort, their concrete labour does not assume the form of its opposite, abstract social labour, its expenditure is socially speaking invalid, which threatens the sellers of labour power with unemployment, with being cut off from the means of subsistence. If the expenditure of their labour turns out to have be unproductive of exchange value, it will put its employer on the edge. Unprofitable exploiters of labour do not hire labour power. They shed labour. That is to say, the macro-economic calculation of the unemployed as economic zeros is not untrue. On the pain of being cut off from the means of subsistence, the living labour of the direct producers either produces value in the form of money or it does not, in which case, and regardless of their effort and the quality of their product, their labour fails to make the cut. The sheer unrest of live, the daily struggle to maintain the strength of the link to the means of subsistence, human suffering, is premised on the social validity of the expended concrete labour in competition with all other expended concrete labour on a global scale. Pace Holloway's point about enjoyment, it is not the boredom of the capitalist labour process, or the lack of enjoyment that is felt by the worker, that is oppressive. What is oppressive is the threat of redundancy. The living labour that produces failed commodities is socially speaking redundant, and so is the labourer unless she finds alternative forms of wage income.

The paper discusses the double character of labour focusing on Marx's characterization of abstract labour as a purely social form. The next section expounds abstract labour as the socially necessary labour. It includes brief summaries of rival interpretations, including Holloway's, to illuminate its meaning. Two Sections follow, one explores the double character of labour and the other expounds the temporality of abstract labour. The concluding Section examines abstract labour as the labour of silent economic compulsion.

On Abstract Labour as Purely Social

In the Marxist tradition, the dominant approach to abstract labour conceives of it as a natural labour. It picks up on Marx's reference to it as a physiological labour (Marx, 1990: 137). In this view, abstract labour is actually expended in the concrete labour processes and embodied in the commodities. It is expenditure of human energy regardless of the concrete purposes to which it is put. Abstract labour refers thus to the physiological fact that 'muscles burn sugar' (Haug, 2005: 34). In this perspective, Marx's concept of abstract labour is said to establish that in every society 'human beings expend their corporeal power' (Starosta, 2008: 31). Indeed, according to Makoto Itoh, Marx recognized the basic condition 'of the metabolism between human beings and nature as general economic norms in the analysis of the labour-and-production process' (1988: 121). Thus, this approach holds that the critique of abstract labour is fundamentally a critique of its capitalist modality, and that it is an argument also for its socialist transformation, that is, the rational planning of the expenditure of human energy by central authority in socialism. Indeed, as argued by Starosta (2008: 36), the 'material specificity of [capitalism]...consists, precisely, in the development of the human productive capacity to organize social labour in a fully conscious fashion' in socialism. It seems as if the—trans-historically conceived, or in any case naturally determined—forces of production rebel against the social relations of production with a history making dynamic and force, transitioning labour economy from mode of production to mode of production. Starosta's (2008: 34, see also 24) point that the forces of production express the 'contradictory unity between materiality and social form' is reminiscent of those same dogmatic notions that Adorno (1990: 355–360) rejected as 'a perversion' of Marx's materialism: it substitutes Marx's critique of society for a trans-historical 'metaphysics' according to which, as Murray (2005: 64, fn. 21) put it, 'the "forces of production" are not social-form-determined but, on the contrary, are the ultimate determinant of the "relations of production"'.

Marx's physiological definition of abstract labour directly contradicts his point about it being a purely social labour. The further development of this conception is recent. It emerged in the late 1960s from a Rubin-inspired critique of the embodied labour theory of value. Michael Heinrich is one of the foremost contemporary exponents of this critique. He argues that although the magnitude of value appears as a reified property of a commodity, it expresses in fact a social relationship between the labour expended on the individual commodity and the labour that is socially necessary for its production. The value magnitude of a commodity represents therefore a relationship between 'the individual labour of the producers and the total social labour' (2004: 52; see also Bonefeld, 2010). Following Marx's insight that in capitalism labour is directly social, everybody works for everybody else, its social character manifests itself in the exchange relations. Exchange for money is the capitalist form of social synthesis and mediation. Money is the socially valid form of capitalist wealth.[1] The value of a commodity manifests therefore a social relationship between the commodities expressed in the form of money. Money establishes the social validity of the privately expended labour in relation to all other commodities and the labour that produced them. Whether the labour expended by the dissociated producers was productive of value, and to what magnitude, appears in its exchangeability for a certain amount of money. Expenditure of concrete labour as such does not create value. For it to have value it has to take the form of abstract labour, which, I argue, is the name of the socially valid expenditure of concrete labour, which manifests itself a posteriori in exchange for money. The value-being (*Wertsein*) of a commodity is thus effected in exchange; it is not created in production as it is argued by the proponents of an embodied labour theory, and also by John Holloway when he argues that 'my doing has become a completely indifferent to its contents; there has been a complete abstraction from its concrete characteristics' (2010a: 193). On the contrary, it is by means of exchange that the concrete expenditure of labour is validated as an expenditure of social necessary labour in the form of a certain quantity of money. Money represents to them their social value. In Heinrich's argument, abstract labour is the necessary social labour. It produces value as the socially necessary expenditure of

[1] On Marx's concept of validity, see Reichelt (2005). On Marx's value theory as a monetary theory of value, see, for example, Heinrich (1999), Arthur (2005), Backhaus (1975), Bonefeld (2020).

concrete labour. Therefore, abstract labour manifests an irresistible force of economic compulsion. Failure to live up to its requirements is exacting to point of ruin. The pressure to increase labour productivity through the use of ever more sophisticated, labour-saving methods of production is relentless.

Marx discusses of the consequences of the impact of the introduction of new methods of production on the character of concrete labour as a tendency towards a general labour. Some commentators conceive of general labour as a standardized, abstract form of labour (see, for example, Finelli, 2007; Holloway, 2010a, 2010b; and also Vincent, 1991). It is an 'activity that is devoid of concrete specificities' (Holloway, 2010a, 2010b: 913). According to this view, in capitalism, concrete labour becomes abstract in character due to its increasing simplification and technologization. It is seen to become deskilled, repetitive, monotonous, and boring. It becomes a joyless labour. Indeed, in *Capital*, Marx speaks eloquently and with prescient foresight about this labour in the chapter about machinery and large-scale industry: 'Thus large-scale industry, by its very nature, necessitates variation of labour, fluidity of functions, and mobility of the worker in all directions' (Marx, 1990: 617). Therefore, the argument that labour expended in production is immediately social in character because it can be employed with ease and effectiveness in any kind of production process, with seemingly boundless fluidity and mobility, and application. In fact, it represents, as seen by Horkheimer and Adorno (1989: 207), the 'universal reduction of all specific energy to the one, same abstract form of labor, from the battlefield to the studio'. According to Finelli (2007), therefore, abstract labour is characterized by its homogeneous and undifferentiated character, and above all by the relations of technological effectiveness and rationalization. He rejects any consideration of concrete labour in relation to the capitalist labour process because it opens, he argues, Marx's critique to a humanist misreading of *Capital*. Holloway rightly rejects the anti-humanist critique of capitalism. In fact, the subjective reason of his account is founded on the humanism of the early Marx, and he rightly sees the mature Marx as a wiser humanist. Nevertheless, he conceives of abstract labour in terms similar to those offered by Finelli. According to Holloway, 'useful labour exists *in the form* of abstract labour' (2020a: 194). Useful, concrete labour, thus vanishes and disappears into its opposite, and what has vanished and disappeared has no independent reality. Its reality is the reality of abstract labour. In his account, therefore, concrete labour exists in the 'mode of being denied' (ibid., quoting Gunn) and he thus considers it as a hidden, secret ontological force—it asserts as 'useful doing ***in-and-against-and-beyond*** abstract labour' (ibid.), cracking its abstract reality. Be that as it may, Finelli's and Holloway's identification of concrete labour with the 'pleasure principle' is unhelpful. Concrete labour is the labour of a specific utility and boring, unpleasant, and repetitive assembly line work remains a labour of a specific utility. Whether it assumes the form of abstract labour by means of its exchangeability for money is a different matter altogether. It has nothing to do with character of the expended concrete labour. Rather, it has to do with its exchangeability as an expenditure of concrete labour that was socially necessary and that was therefore productive of value. Should the expenditure of boring assembly line work have created a mere product, a good that is not exchangeable, the labour that produced it created a failed commodity. As a mere product of a socially unnecessary concrete labour, and regardless of whether its expenditure was pleasurable or unpleasurable in the living experience of the worker, it produced neither a social use value nor exchange value. The expended labour is socially speaking redundant, which devalues its employer and threatens the labourer with redundancy.

I have argued that abstract labour is the social labour. It is effected in exchange. It is the socially necessary expenditure of concrete labour, which 'appears in the form of money' (Clarke, 1988: 13). That is to say, 'money (...) is the form of existence of abstract labour' (Kay, 1979: 58). In explanation, the value of a commodity is its social value. Value is thus a property of exchangeability and money is the independent form of that property. That is, money is not the measure of value. This conception presupposes a pre-monetary existence of value, which is the forte of those approaches that see abstract labour as expenditure of human energy (Starosta, Itoh) or as abstract activity (Holloway). Rather money is the socially valid form of measurability (see Arthur, 2005). In distinction to the labour theory of value, this or that concrete labour, or this or that consumption of human energy, or this or that supposed abstract activity, does not count. What counts is the social validity of this or that labour. Marx conceives of the socially valid expenditure of concrete labour as abstract labour (see Bonefeld, 2010). Exchange, says Marx (1990: 165), establishes the 'labour of the private individuals .... as an element of the total labour of society'. Whether this or that expenditure of concrete labour is a socially valid expenditure of abstract labour, becomes clear only post-festum in exchange for money.

On the Double Character of Labour

In his *Notes on Adolph Wagner* Marx made the point that 'Man' (*Mensch*) in general has no natural tendency, needs, consciousness, etc. Man has needs only as concrete Man and that is, the 'determinate character of this social man is to be brought forward as the starting point, i. e. the determinate character of the existing community in which he lives' (Marx, 1962: 362). What does this hold in relation to the capitalist labour economy? Regarding use-value producing concrete labour, its social constitution is easily understood despite the fact that 'use-values...constitute the substance of all wealth, whatever may be the social form of that wealth' (Marx, 1990: 126) Commodity production entails use-values as produced for others, 'social use-values'. Exchange is the medium of sociability and social synthesis. What therefore makes use-values 'historically-specific [in] character' (Marx, 1962: 370; 1990: 131) is their social form. They are not the use-values, or simply products, of the commons, clan, feudal society, the Asian mode of production, or, with reference to Holloway's (2010a) account, the 'baker' who enjoys baking cakes for others.

As was already pointed out by Adam Smith (1976: Chapter 2) use-values are not produced to satisfy human needs directly. They are produced to satisfy the self-interest of what he calls the masters. They produce use-values for exchange, and the use-values therefore are of value to the masters only if they have value in exchange. A product that is not exchangeable is a failed commodity. It does not have a social use-value, and the labour that went into its production was spent unproductively and uselessly. Each individual labour process is a consumption process of social labour time and its validity as a socially necessary consumption of social labour is presented to it only post-festum in exchange. How much social labour time, then, did its private appropriation take; how long did it take to get the product ready for validation as a commodity that fetches a tidy sum of money, which more than covering the costs of its production yields a profit too? On the pain of ruin, there really is no time to spare to ensure, in competition with all other buyers of labour power, the social validity of the appropriated social labour on the basis of increased labour productivity. The threat of competitive erosion is constant. The individual capitalist has always to compare the social validity of his consumption of living labour with all other capitalists.

For Marx the two distinct qualities of capitalist labour, concrete labour, and abstract labour, belong to the same labour. There is only one labour and there is only one reality. Reality is not split into a concrete reality of production and an abstract reality of economic compulsion. Abstract labour is the valid social mode of concrete labour. What counts is exchangeability and what cannot be exchanged for money is socially speaking redundant, its unnecessary expenditure of concrete labour counts for nothing and as a consequence of its unnecessary expenditure, the noose tightens around the neck its employer, baker or brewer, as devaluation strikes.[2] Abstract labour is difficult to grasp because it is not a concrete labour—it is the exacting social form of the expended concrete labour, deeming it either valid or redundant. Abstract labour is an invisible labour, phantom like in its objectivity, unforgiving in its judgement, and spectral in its fateful movement. Against Adam Smith, Marx emphasizes that it is a labour that is 'forcibly brought about' by exchange (Marx, 1987b: 299). What Marx means here by exchange is not 'exchange with nature', as approaches that identify, like Finelli, Holloway and Vincent, abstract labour with the joyless, general character of concrete labour have it but the exchange of commodities for money in capitalist society. Money does not express their use-value. It expresses their exchange value. Value can therefore not be the substance of a single commodity. Rather, the value of a commodity is its social value. Expenditure of capitalist labour is either a socially valid appropriation of social labour by the dissociated producers, and therefore exchangeable, or it is not, in which case it does not posit any value at all, neither this nor that. Things that cannot be exchanged have neither a social use-value nor an exchange value. They are failed commodities, and the labour that went into them was expended unproductively. The consequences of the unproductive appropriation of social labour are most unpleasant, especially for the workers whose life hangs by the effective exploitation of their labour power. Bankrupt employers do not buy labour power. Rather, they shed labour.

The double character of capitalist labour entails a process of real abstraction, in which abstract labour figures akin to an automatic subject.

[2] Baker and brewer are a reference to Smith's Wealth of Nations, and to Holloway's (2010a) example of the baker who finds herself in alienation because she bakes for money. Whereas Smith's baker takes great enjoyment out of her role, Holloway's baker does not. She feels the pain of alienation. In either case, the social relations of productions are conceived of as relations of simple commodity production.

It is invisible, like a ghost (see Bellofiore, 2009), becomes visible, however fleetingly, in the form of money, and above all it is exacting and compelling. It 'cannot be either a geometrical, a chemical, or any other natural property of commodities. Such properties claim our attention only in so far as they affect the utility of those commodities, make them use-values' (Marx, 1990: 127). Indeed, no chemist 'has ever discovered exchange value either in a pearl or a diamond. The economists who have discovered this chemical element, and who lay special claim to critical acumen, nevertheless find that the use-value of objects belongs to them independently of their material properties, while their value, on the other hand, forms a part of them as objects. What confirms them in this view, is the peculiar circumstance that the use value of objects is realized without exchange, by means of material objects belongs to them independently of their material properties, while their value, on the other hand, forms a part of them as objects. What confirms them in this view is the peculiar circumstance that the use-value of a thing is realised without exchange, i.e. in the direct relation between the thing and man, while, inversely, its value is realised only in exhange, i.e. in a social process' (177). What, then, is specific about capitalism, is not abstract labour as such but the circumstance that concrete labour counts socially only as expenditure of abstract labour, as expenditure of a 'specific social form of labour' (Marx, 1987b: 278). As a 'purely social reality' (Marx, 1990: 139) it validates the appropriation of social labour by the dissociated producers as a socially necessary expenditure of labour. It does so through the exchangeability of their wares with money. Regarding those who expended socially unnecessary labour, its verdict is unforgiving.

As a real abstraction of social validation, abstract labour extinguishes therefore society's 'sensuous characteristics' (Marx, 1990: 128). It is the labour of social coldness. There is no freedom from economic compulsion; there is however the freedom to adjust to the movement of value in the form of the money subject. As the next section argues, what asserts itself in social coldness, in society as process of real abstraction, is the law of value as an abstraction of social time, a time without tangible content, yet variable and restless, and exacting to the point of madness.

On Value and the Time of Abstract Labour

The previous section argued that value is a 'perverse form of sociality based on the dissociation of private producers' (Smith, 2005: 176). Value is effected in exchange. It expresses the expenditure of concrete labour as a socially necessary expenditure of labour. The measure of socially necessary labour is socially necessary labour time. Value emerges as an 'abstraction of social time' (Bensaid, 2002: 75). This time, as Guy Debord (1992: 87) put it, 'has no reality apart from its exchangeability'. This section explores the time of abstract labour.

Marx developed the connection between the value producing labour and social labour time in his *Critique* of 1859. He quotes from his *Critique* in *Capital* volume one: 'As values, all commodities are only definite masses of congealed labour-time' (Marx, 1987b: 272; 1990: 130). In his *Critique*, he argues that '[o]n the one hand, commodities must enter the exchange process as objectified universal labour time, on the other hand, the labour time of individuals becomes objectified universal labour time only as a result of the exchange process' (Marx, 1987b: 286). When talking about value, we are therefore talking about the expenditure of 'definite masses of crystallized [social] labour time' (Marx, 1990: 297). That is to say, 'labour time is the living state of existence of labour…it is the living quantitative aspect of labour as well as its inherent measure' (Marx, 1987b: 272). Concrete labour takes place in its own time. In order for it to count as a valid expenditure of social labour, it has to appear as its opposite, as an exemplar of socially necessary labour time.

Capitalist wealth is haunted by the spectre of socially necessary labour time. It is 'the labour-time required to produce any use-value under the prevailing socially normal conditions of production and with the prevalent socially average degree of skill and intensity of labour' (Marx, 1990: 129). It is independent from the concrete temporalities of the individual expenditure of labour; and yet, results 'from the actions of the producers' (Postone, 1993: 191, also 215). The establishment of socially necessary labour time is an abstraction, which as such does not exist. Nevertheless, this 'abstraction…is made on a daily basis in every social production process. The dissolution of all commodities into labour-time is no greater an abstraction, but no less real than that of all organic bodies into air' (Marx, 1987b: 272). The dynamic of capitalist wealth comprises a 'social process that goes on behind the backs of the producers' (Marx, 1990: 135) and yet, it is their work.

On the one hand, then, concrete labour is 'actually expended' (Marx, 1990: 143) within its own time. Yet, on the other, each commodity 'objectifies general social labour time, [which as] a specific quantity of general labour time is expressed in its exchange value' (Marx, 1987b: 288). For the expenditure of the appropriated social labour to be valid as expenditure of the socially necessary labour, it cannot occur in its own good time. Rather, it has to occur within a time made abstract, this is the time of the socially necessary labour, of abstract labour. If it does not, it counts for nothing. The labour time that counts is the labour time of value, of exchangeability for money.

In sum, the value of a commodity is 'its social value; that is to say, its value is not measured by the labour-time that the article costs the producer in each individual case, but by the labour time socially required for its production' (Marx, 1990: 434). That is, 'only because the labour time of the spinner and the labour time of the weaver represent universal labour time and their products are thus universal equivalents, is the social aspect of the labour of the two individuals represented for each of them by the labour of the other' (Marx, 1987b: 274). In this sense, concrete expenditures of socially necessary labour are the expenditures of equally valid social labours (see 273–274). As Marx put it in his *Critique*, 'labour, which is thus measured by time, does not seem, indeed, to be the labour of different subjects, but on the contrary the different working individuals seem to be mere organs of this labour' (272). It is expenditure of objectified labour by an 'individual indistinguishable from all other individuals' (274, translation amended). Just as each capital is the capital, each expenditure of socially necessary labour is the social labour. In *Capital*, Marx therefore argues that 'the total labour power of society, which is manifested in the values of the world of commodities, counts here as one homogeneous mass of labour-power, although composed of innumerable individual units of labour power' (Marx, 1990: 129). Insofar as 'each of these units is the same as any other, to the extent that it has the character of a socially average unit of labour-power…the labour time which is…socially necessary' (ibid.). Social labour time 'is both the substance that turns [the use-values] into exchange values and therefore into commodities, and the standard by which the precise magnitude of their value is measured' (Marx, 1987b: 272). Socially necessary labour time is therefore the 'hidden secret under the apparent movement in the relative values of commodities' (Marx, 1990: 168). Price movements do thus not express the coincidence of selling and buying. Rather, 'in the midst of the accidental and every fluctuating exchange-relations between the products, the labour-time socially necessary to produce them asserts itself as a regulative law of nature' (168). The notion of an invisible hand of market regulation is therefore not untrue. Its truth 'has its origin...in the peculiar social character of the labour that produces them' (165).

Abstract Labour and the Sheer Unrest of Life

Socially necessary labour time is not fixed and given. It increases or falls with the increase or fall in social labour productivity. The 'labour time that yesterday was without doubt socially necessary for the production of a yard of linen, ceases to be so today' (Marx, 1990: 202). That is to say, whether the committed labour will turn out to be socially necessary can only be established post-festum. As was already argued, the labour that does not produce value in exchange is wasted with potentially ruinous consequences for both, the buyer of labour power and its sellers. For the labourer, turning her labour into profit is the condition of sustained access to the means of subsistence. Each labourer competes on the basis of a compelling dynamic of social necessary labour time with all other labourers on a world market scale for sustained wage-based employment. In explanation, the labour time that was effectively expended in a definite labour process might be inferior or superior to the existing conditions of socially necessary labour time. This private appropriator of social labour time, a commander over living labour, might struggle to make the cut while another might as well sell 'as less than its social value, even though he sells [above] its individual value' (Tomba, 2014: 142). Instead of throwing away the key and declaring his capital defunct, the inferior commander of living labour will try his upmost to reassert himself as a valuable exploiter of social labour, seeking to achieve greater labour productivity or by reducing the costs of labour, driving down conditions, etc. The struggle for competitiveness is constant and relentless. The dynamic of socially necessary labour time, this invisible, abstract form of economic compulsion, appears in competition as a seemingly 'external coercive [law]' whereas in fact it asserts 'the immanent laws of capitalist production' (Marx, 1990: 739). Socially valid labour exploitation makes money out of money. Socially invalid living labour processes represent no such thing. They represent defunct capital and redundant labour. Staying abreast of the competitors entails therefore a history of class struggle over the mastery of the labour process—the one trying to appropriate the living labour with werewolf-like hunger, the other desperate to preserve her living existence.[3]

The restless dynamic of socially necessary labour time is not limited to the exchange validity of actual labour processes. It also affects the social value of already produced and exchanged commodities. In relation to constant capital, Marx speaks about the risk of moral depreciation, which reduces retroactively the exchange value of, say, a machine that only yesterday established a competitive advantage. According to Marx (1990: 318) and drawing on Tomba (2014: 141), a machine loses exchange value, either because machines of the same sort are being produced more cheaply than it was, or because better machines are entering into competition with it. In either case, and however full of life the machine may still be, its value is not determined by the socially necessary labour time that it originally objectified, but by the social labour time necessary to produce it either anew or the better machine. Confronted by the lower socially necessary labour time, it has been devalued to a greater or lesser extent. Every capitalist might therefore find that a new piece of equipment that seemed to secure a competitive advantage, making his production process superior to the existing conditions of socially necessary labour time, only to find that shortly thereafter its value is drastically reduced by some further innovation. Its moral depreciation threatens the capitalist with a loss and spurs him into action to preserve his capital by frantically seeking to keep the machinery running without interruption, day and night, to secure the ready transfer of its value to new commodities before its value diminishes 'prematurely'.

For the labourer the implications are formidable, from the constant pressure to extend the working day through shift work, intensification of labour, increased density of work, cuts in down time, to other cost cutting measures such as cheaper workers to compensate for the potential loss of the value that has been sunk into the—depreciating—machinery.[4] Marx therefore argues that the fact that in capitalism every social progress

[3] I use mastery here with reference to Smith's definition of the capitalist as the master.

[4] The points raised here about moral depreciation reinforces the argument that value is fundamentally a social value and that, with reference to Marx (1990: 318), the value of a commodity is at any time 'measured by the labour socially necessary to produce them, i.e., by the labour necessary under the social conditions existing at the time'.

turns into a calamity has to do with the impact of enhanced labour productivity on the conditions of socially necessary labour time.[5] Every increase in social labour productivity increases material wealth but in its capitalist form cheapens the commodities leading to intensified competition for what is called market shares. Furthermore, every increase in labour productivity shortens the hours of labour but in its capitalist form, it lengthens them. The introduction of sophisticated machinery lightens labour but in its capitalist form, it heightens the intensity of labour. Every increase in the productivity of labour increases the material wealth of society but in its capitalist form cheapens the labourers, whose commodity, that is, labour power, falls in value as less socially necessary labour time is required for its reproduction. Most importantly of all, greater labour productivity makes labour redundant. But rather then shortening the hours of work and thus absorbing available labour into production based on a shorter working day, liberating social time from production for enjoyment, those in employment are worked more intensively, while those made redundant find themselves on the scrap heap of a mode of production in which time is money and in which therefore the satisfaction of human needs a mere sideshow.

Capital is thus 'the moving contradiction, [in] that it presses to reduce [social] labour time to a minimum, while it posits [socially necessary] labour time, on the other side, as sole measure and source of wealth' (Marx, 1973: 706). And then, without forewarning, '[s]ociety suddenly finds itself put back into a state of momentary barbarism; it appears as if famine, a universal war of devastation had cut off the supply of every means of subsistence; industry and commerce seem to be destroyed; and why? Because there is too much civilization, too much means of subsistence; too much industry, too much commerce. The productive forces at the disposal of society no longer tend to further the development of the conditions of bourgeois property; on the contrary, they have become too powerful for these conditions, by which they are fettered, and so soon as they overcome these fetters, they bring disorder into the whole of bourgeois society, endanger the existence of bourgeois property. The conditions of bourgeois society are too narrow to comprise the wealth created by them. And how does bourgeois society get over these crises? On the one hand by enforced destruction of a mass of productive forces;

[5] On the calamities of capitalist development see Marx (1990: 568–569).

on the other, by the conquest of new markets, and by the more thorough exploitation of the old ones' (Marx & Engels, 1997: 18–19). Overproduction is a false name for glutted market conditions. In the face of manifest social need, it is not the use-values that have been overproduced as such. What has been overproduced are the social use-values that as failed commodities cannot be converted into money as more money.

Conclusion

I have argued that abstract labour 'exerts an abstract form of compulsion' (Postone, 1993: 214). It compels the social individuals as personifications of a time made abstract. Work has to be performed not in its own good time, but within a time that is both invisible and exacting. Work that is not completed within the time of value, that is the time of exchangeability, is wasted, valueless, regardless of the social needs that its products might satisfy. That is, and in critique of capitalist wealth, 'the labour time expended must not exceed what is necessary under the given social conditions of production' (Marx, 1990: 295). How long a time did it take? Time is money and money is time. If then, capitalist wealth is a function of a socially necessary labour time that as such does not exist in the concrete labour processes and that therefore is dissociated from the concrete human circumstances and purposes which it measures in terms of their social value, then, really, time is everything. If 'time is everything, [then] man is nothing; he is, at the most, time's carcase' (Marx, 1976: 127).

In distinction to a substantialist labour theory of value, according to which the value producing abstract labour is embodied in commodities, one man's hour of labour is not worth another man's hour of labour. Rather, 'one man during an hour is worth just as much as another man during an hour' on the condition that each hour represents an expenditure of exchangeable socially necessary labour time (ibid.); or as Finelli (2007) puts it, this labouring individual is as good as any other, replaceable. What counts is value in exchange. What counts is money. Whether this concrete labour or that concrete labour, or both, expend socially necessary labour time is established in exchange, after the concrete labour has been committed under duress of the laws of exchangeability and measurability. There really is therefore no time to waste to ensure the social validation of this or that concrete labour as exchangeable abstract labours. Abstract labour is a ghost-like-labour. At the point of production, it feeds on living labour like a Vampire, sucking labour time for the sake 'profitable exchangeability'.[6] As the living means of wealth, the worker is really 'nothing more than personified labour-time' (Marx, 1990: 352–353)—a 'time's carcase' whose access to the means of subsistence is a function of the profitable exchangeability of her living labour in competition with all other living labour on a global scale. Labour that is unproductive of capitalist wealth represents the labour of a redundant time's carcase, that is, an economic zero whose access to subsistence lays in peril.

Finally, value-validity is the validity of labour time made abstract. Labour time is either money time or it is devalued time. On the pain of ruin, what counts is money—as more money. In his expansive critique of abstract labour, John Holloway argues that the capitalists benefit from the abstract labour that the labourers are 'forced to perform' (Holloway, 2010a, 2010b: 131) and he says that 'the worker can always refuse to obey' (169). Concerning the former I have argued that labouring in the abstract is quite impossible. Regarding the latter, there is one condition that is even worse than being an exploited worker, and that is, to be an unexploitable worker. Yesterday's profitable appropriation of some other person's labour buys another Man today, with the buyer seeking to make a profit to avoid bankruptcy by enriching himself; the seller seeking to monetise her labour power to make ends meet. What can the seller of redundant labour power trade in its stead—where to migrate to in search of income, and what is the price of a kidney? Nevertheless, and with Holloway, disobedience is the significant first step towards a society in which humanity is a purpose and not a means. Clearly, the working class struggles to make ends meet.

References

Adorno, T. (1990). *Negative Dialectics*. Verso.

Arthur, C. (2005). Value and Money. In F. Moseley (Ed.), *Marx's Theory of Money* (pp. 111–123). Palgrave.

[6] On the paradox of a profitable equivalent exchange, see Bonefeld (2016). On its crisis ridden dynamic, see Clarke (1994).

Backhaus, H. G. (1975). Materialien zur Reconstruktion der Marxschen Werttheorie 2. In *Gesellschaft. Beiträge zur Marxschen Theorie* (Vol. 3, pp. 122–159). Suhrkamp.
Bellofiore, R. (2009). A Ghost Turning into a Vampire. In R. Bellofiore & R. Fineschi (Eds.), *Re-reading Marx* (pp. 178–194). Palgrave.
Bensaid, D. (2002). *Marx For Our Time*. Verso.
Bonefeld, W. (2010). Abstract Labour: Against its Nature and on its Time. *Capital & Class, 34*(2), 257–276.
Bonefeld, W. (2016). Negative Dialectics and the critique of economic objectivity. *History of the Human Sciences, 29*(2), 60–76.
Bonefeld, W. (2020). Capital *Par Excellence*: On Money as an OBSCURE thing. *Estudios De Filosofía, 62*, 33–56.
Clarke, S. (1988). *Keynesianism, Monetarism, and the Crisis of the State*. Edward & Elgar.
Clarke, S. (1994). *Marx's Theory of Crisis*. Palgrave.
Debord, G. (1992). *Society of the Spectacle*. Rebel Press.
Finelli, R. (2007). Abstraction versus Contradiction. *Historical Materialism, 15*(2), 61–74.
Haug, W. F. (2005). *Vorlesungen zur Einführung ins Kapital*. Argument.
Heinrich, M. (1999). *Die Wissenschaft vom Wert*. Dampfboot.
Heinrich, M. (2004). *Kritik der politischen Ökonomie*. Schmetterling.
Holloway, J. (2010a). Cracks and the Crisis of Abstract Labour. *Antipode, 42*(4), 909–923.
Holloway, J. (2010b). *Crack Capitalism*. Pluto.
Horkheimer, M., & Adorno, T. (1989). *Dialectic of Enlightenment*. Verso.
Itoh, M. (1988). *The Basic Theory of Capitalism. The Forms and Substance of the Capitalist Economy*. Macmillan.
Kay, G. (1979). Why Labour is the Starting Point of Capital. In D. Elson (Ed.), *Value: The Representation of Labour in Capitalism* (pp. 46–66). CSE Books.
Marx, K. (1962). Randglossen zu Adolph Wagners Lehrbuch der politischen Ökonomie. In *MEW* (Vol. 19). Dietz.
Marx, K. (1973). *Grundrisse*. Penguin.
Marx, K. (1976). The Poverty of Philosophy. In *MECW* (Vol. 6). Lawrence & Wishart.
Marx, K. (1987a). Letter of Marx to Engels, 24 August 1867. In *MECW* (Vol. 42). Lawrence & Wishart.
Marx, K. (1987b). Contribution Toward a Critique of Political Economy. In *MECW* (Vol. 29). Lawrence & Wishart.
Marx, K. (1990). *Capital* (Vol. I). Penguin.
Marx, K., & Engels, F. (1997). *The Communist Manifesto*. Pluto.
Murray, P. (2005). The New Giant's Staircase. *Historical Materialism, 13*(2), 61–84.

Postone, M. (1993). *Time, Labour and Social Domination*. Cambridge University Press.
Reichelt, H. (2005). Social Reality as Appearance. In W. Bonefeld & K. Psychopedis (Eds.), *Human Dignity* (pp. 31–67). Ashgate.
Smith, A. (1976). *The Wealth of Nations*. Oxford University Press.
Smith, T. (2005). *Globalisation*. Brill.
Starosta, G. (2008). The Commodity-Form and the Dialectical Method. *Science and Society*, *72*(3), 295–318.
Tomba, M. (2014). *Marx's Temporalities*. Haymarket.
Vincent, J. M. (1991). *Abstract Labour: A Critique*. Palgrave.

CHAPTER 4

Class, Contradiction and Antagonism

Adrián Piva

Introduction

The classical Marxism of the Second International and the orthodox Marxism of the Third International had many elements in common, and one of them was to reduce class struggle to a shadow of the contradiction between productive forces and relations of production. Marxist structuralism, dominant since the 1960s in Western Marxism, questioned the simplistic base/superstructure model but to push to the limit the displacement of class struggle in its explanations of the reproduction and crises of capitalism.

In the face of this dominant tradition, since the 1920s, a lively and open Marxism has recovered the concept of *form* (Pashukanis, 1976; Rubin, 1976), developed negative dialectics (Adorno, 2008) and constructed a historicist interpretation of capitalism (Gramsci, 1992; Kellner, 1977; Korsch, 2008; Pannekoek, 2003). In the line opened by this effort, the concepts of *contradiction, antagonism* and *class struggle*

A. Piva (✉)
University of Buenos Aires, Buenos Aires, Argentina
e-mail: adrianpiva@gmail.com

A. García Vela and A. Bonnet (eds.), *The Political Thought of John Holloway*, Marx, Engels, and Marxisms,
https://doi.org/10.1007/978-3-031-34571-5_4

occupy the center of a thought that develops critique as a method and as a weapon.

Holloway's thought is inscribed in this tradition. He and Gunn (Holloway, 2002) opposed to *class* as classification, a sociological but dominant conception in Marxism, a concept of class as a social relation of antagonism and struggle. In this way, they escaped the aporias and inconsistencies that afflict the structuralist approach and that have their origin in the mysterious forms assumed by objective reality.

Open Marxism develops a critique of class as a datum, as immediate existence. In this way it unveils class as a process of reification and, therefore, of depersonalization of relations between people, which operates by classifying and fixing human beings to certain identities, transforming them into personifications of things (Holloway, 2002). Starting from its objectivity, from its reality as a constituted fact, it dissolves the class in the social relation that constitutes it, a social relation whose logic is the separation of producers from their conditions and results of production (means of production and products) and from their own activity (Bonefeld, 2002; Holloway, 2010).

However, the indistinction between contradiction and antagonism also characterizes the conceptualization of class in open Marxism. Already in his works of the '70s and '80s, in which he renewed Marxism by articulating the concepts of social form and class struggle, Holloway tended to erase that distinction and in *Crack Capitalism* he affirmed the indistinction between contradiction and antagonism as a specific difference *vis-à-vis* Postone's work (Holloway, 2010: 178).

In this chapter we recover the notion of class as an antagonistic social relation, but we try to show that its most fruitful development requires recovering the distinction between contradiction and antagonism. To this we will devote the first section. There we will raise, in the first place, the distinctions between contradiction and external opposition (or antithesis) and between external opposition and antagonism to then, in the second place, point out in what sense the relation of capitalist exploitation is objectively contradictory. In the third section, on that basis, we will present a conceptualization of class centered on the relation of exploitation, but which understands the wage relation as a mode of subordination of concrete labor to abstract labor, that is, as an essential moment in the subsumption of labor to capital. In the conclusions, we will briefly discuss some consequences of this conceptualization for the relationship between class struggles and struggles against other forms of oppression. We will argue that two possibilities follow from it: a more restrictive conception of class struggle that requires articulation and a broader one, as proposed by Holloway, that identifies them.

Contradiction and Antagonism

Why Distinguish Contradiction and Antagonism?

"The internal opposition between use-value and value, hidden within the commodity, is therefore represented on the surface by an external opposition, i.e., by a relation between two commodities such that the one commodity, *whose own* value is supposed to be expressed, counts directly only as a use-value whereas the other commodity, *in which* that value is to be expressed, counts directly only as exchange-value. Hence the simple form of value of a commodity is the simple form of appearance of the opposition between use-value and value which is contained within the commodity" (Marx, 1982: 153).

This distinction between internal opposition or immanent contradiction[1] and external opposition reappears in several other moments of

[1] The identity between internal opposition and immanent contradiction can be seen in the following paragraph: "There is an antithesis, immanent in the commodity, between use-value and value, between private labour which must simultaneously manifest itself as directly social labour, and a particular concrete kind of labour which simultaneously counts as merely abstract universal labour, between the conversion of things into persons and the conversion of persons into things; the antithetical phases of the metamorphosis of the commodity are the developed forms of motion of this immanent contradiction" (Marx, 1982: 209). Internal antagonism—external antagonism and immanent antithesis—external antithesis refers to the same conceptual distinction: *Innere/Inmanentegegensatz—Außerengegensatz* in the original German edition of *Capital*. There Marx treats as synonims innere/inmanente Gegensatz and inmanente Widerspruch and opposes both to Außerengegensatz: "*Der der Ware immanente Gegensatz von Gebrauchswert und Wert [...] dieser immanente widersprucher hält in den Gegensätzen der Warenmetamorphose seine entwickelten Bewegungsformen*" (Marx, 1962: 128). In the French edition revisaded by Marx "*Der der Wareimmanente Gegensatz...*" is translated as "*Les contradictions que recèle la marchandise...*" (Marx, 1872: 47). All these terms are, therefore, equivalent to the oppositions: contradiction and external opposition/antagonism, terms that we keep in order to give unity and clarity to the exposition. Unfortunately, the English translation of *Capital* does not adequately express these conceptual equivalences, which are clear in the German and French editions and in the Spanish translation of Pedro Scaron (Marx, 2010).

Capital and with a similar meaning.[2] In those paragraphs the contradiction immanent to the commodity, on the one hand, appears in the form of an external opposition, that is, it exists through it, that development is a necessary development, but, on the other hand, there is no opposition without contradiction. As Adorno points out—and we will develop this in a moment—this distinguishes the simply heterogeneous from the contradictory. The juxtaposition or even the inadequacy of the heterogeneous cannot be conceived of as contradictory and, therefore, neither as opposite. Contradiction, therefore, is the condition of possibility of—and at the same time structures—opposition.

But, in turn, in his usage, Marx also distinguishes external opposition from antagonism.[3] External opposition is the manifestation as external opposition of an internal opposition or immanent contradiction. Whereas antagonism refers to the irreconcilable character of that opposition. Money, as a social form, establishes—mediates—relations between people as relations between buyers and sellers (in its function as a means of circulation) or as creditors and debtors (in its function as a means of payment) (Rubin, 1976). However, per se these oppositions are not antagonisms, that is, irreconcilable oppositions, although, as we shall see, they are as forms of the capital relation. Marx points to this when he notes that Ricardo came to see the opposition between wage and profit but did not see in it more than a conflict of economic interests, the way in which classical political economy represented class opposition.[4] Marx reserves

[2] "But the antagonism between the relative form of value and the equivalent form, the two poles of value- form, also develops concomitantly with the development of the value-form itself" (Marx, 1982: 160); "Exchange, however, produces a differentiation of the commodity into two elements, commodity and money, an external opposition which expresses the opposition between use-value and value which is inherent in it" (Marx, 1982: 199). In German: "*Erproduziert eine Verdopplung der Ware in Ware und Geld, einenäußeren Gegensatz, worin sie ihren immanenten Gegensatz von Gebrauchswert und Wert darstellen*" (Marx, 1962: 119).

[3] In the German edition this distinction is reflected in the fact that in these cases Marx uses *Gegensatz* without any other adjective (see the citations in Notes 4 and 5 and compare with the German edition [Marx, 1962] in contrast to the citations of the Notes 1 and 2).

[4] "Let us take England. Its classical political economy belongs to a period in which the class struggle was as yet undeveloped. Its last great representative, Ricardo, ultimately (and consciously) made the antagonism of class interests, of wages and profits, of profits and rent, the starting-point of his investigations, naïvely taking this antagonism for a social

the use of the term antagonism for class relations[5] and usually uses the terms contradiction and antagonism as two distinguishable aspects of the capital relation.[6]

The purpose of this detailed reference to Marx's use of the terms is not to argue with authoritative quotations, but to point out the role of distinctions in such use. On the one hand, mere heterogeneity and even simple inadequacy do not imply opposition, they can coexist as juxtaposition or indifferent diversity, there must be contradiction for there to be antithesis; on the other hand, opposition, and therefore conflict, do not necessarily imply antagonism.

According to Adorno, what makes the relation between the concept and what is heterogeneous to it is the principle of non-contradiction that

law of nature. But with this contribution the bourgeois science of economics had reached the limits beyond which it could not pass" (Marx, 1982: 96).

[5] "On the other hand, the class struggle between capital and labour was forced into de background, politically by the discord between the governments and the feudal aristocracy gathered around the Holly Alliance, assembled in one camp, and the mass of the people, led by the bourgeoisie, in the other camp, and economically by the quarrel between industrial capital and aristocratic landed property. This latter quarrel was concealed in France by the antagonism between small-scale, fragmented property and big landownership, but in England it broke out openly after the passing of the Corn Laws" (Marx, 1982: 97). The context of this quote reinforces our interpretation of the distinction between external antithesis and antagonism, as it follows the previous one on Ricardo (see Note 3). But this apparently decisive victory of capital was immediately followed by a counter-stroke. So far, the workers had offered a resistance which was passive, though inflexible and unceasing. They now protested in Lancashire and Yorkshire in threatening meetings. The so-called Ten Hours' Act, they say, was thus mere humbug, a parliamentary fraud. It had never existed! The factory inspectors urgently warned the government that class antagonisms has reached an unheard-of degree of tension" (Marx, 1982: 405). "The control exercised by the capitalist is not only a special function arising from the nature of the social labour process, and peculiar to that process, but it is at the same time a function of the exploitation of a social labour process, and in consequently conditioned by the unavoidable antagonism between the exploiter and the raw material of his exploitation" (Marx, 1982: 449).

[6] "The contradictions and antagonisms inseparable from the capitalist application of machinery do not exist, they say, because they do not arise out of machinery as such, but out of its capitalist application!" (Marx, 1982: 568). "By the destruction of small-scale and domestic industries it destroys the last resorts of the 'redundant population', thereby removing what was previously a safety-value for the whole social mechanism. By maturing the material conditions and the social combination of the process of production, it matures the contradictions and antagonisms of the capitalist form of that process, and thereby ripens both the elements for forming a new society and the forces tending towards the overthrow of the old one" (Marx, 1982: 635).

structures the relation between the concept and its object: "The logical form of contradiction, however, adopts that distinction because whatever refuses to abide by the unity imposed by the principle of domination manifests itself not as something indifferent to that principle, but as a infringement of logic: as a contradiction" (Adorno, 2008: 167). This is due, as Adorno himself points out, to the "emphatic claim" of the judgment according to which $A = B$ that the concept and its object are "truly identical" (Adorno, 2008: 8). Or as he points out more precisely in *Negative Dialectics*: "It is precisely the insatiable identity principle that perpetuates antagonism by suppressing contradiction. What tolerates nothing that is not like itself thwarts the reconcilement for which it mistakes itself. The violence of equality-mongering reproduces the contradiction it eliminates" (Adorno, 2004: 142–143). In this second quotation in particular the role of the distinction between contradiction and antagonism is clear. There is antagonism because there is contradiction founded on the logic of identity. Without this "emphasis" on identity, proper to the principle of non-contradiction, the heterogeneous, the inadequate to the concept is only difference. And for Adorno this difference is inevitable because the identity between subject and object is an illusion; in turn, it is this same equalizing violence what renders the opposition irreconcilable.

The immanent contradiction—Adorno also uses this term[7]—does not correspond only to the concept, to thinking, but corresponds to the real, since both, practice and its reflection, are founded in the mode of domination over nature (Adorno, 2008: 10–11). And for both Marx and Adorno if we suppress contradiction we are left with only external opposition and, therefore, dualism. The subject/object relation and, ultimately, the human being/nature relation, are only representable as relations in which both poles mediate each other with reference to the contradiction that constitutes them. Only in this way can the hope of a transformation of the relation human being/nature be constituted as an emancipatory horizon. However, in Adorno there does not seem to be present that distinction that is glimpsed in Marx between antithesis and antagonism. This is because the structure of contradiction as Adorno presents it is the

[7] See for example Adorno (2004: 145).

same as that of the relation of capitalist exploitation.[8] Let us see, then, why the relation of capitalist exploitation is contradictory.

Why Is the Capitalist Relation of Exploitation Contradictory?

Laclau and Mouffe have pointed out that it is not enough to prove that the capitalist relation is a relation of exploitation in order to affirm that the relation between capitalists and workers is antagonistic. Let us put it in their terms:

> 'Serf', 'slave', and so on, do not designate in themselves antagonistic positions; it is only in the terms of a different discursive formation, such as 'the rights inherent to every human being, that the differential positivity of these categories can be subverted and the subordination constructed as oppression. (Laclau & Mouffe, 2001: 154)

For Laclau and Mouffe, relations of subordination are objective relations defined by the submission of one agent to the decisions of another. They refer to a system of differences between agents—positions that are only transformed into relations of oppression when they are the locus of antagonisms. For this, a discourse must intervene from the "outside" so that the relations of subordination can be interpreted as the negation of an "identity".

As Marxists, we tend to assimilate too easily the existence of relations of exploitation—and, therefore, of subordination—between capitalists

[8] This, however, is problematic, as it leaves no logical space between "indifferent diversity" and antagonism. For example, the relationship between parents and their children is contradictory and this contradiction gives rise to opposition and conflict, but it is not necessarily an irreconcilable opposition. The problem seems to lie in the mode of application of the principle of logical non-contradiction. If dialectical contradiction is considered to be compatible with the principle of logical non-contradiction—that is, dialectical contradiction involves a shift in point of view (synchronic) or in time (diachronic)—non-antagonistic opposition is representable and it depends on the structure of the contradiction whether or not it gives rise to antagonism. That seems to be Marx's point of view. This is relevant, as we shall see, to exchange. When exchange becomes generalized and becomes the means for the establishment of social relations, its logic unfolds as an antagonistic logic, insofar as it is transformed into the form of the capital relation. As we shall try to show, the thesis of the transformation of doing into abstract labor reaches its fullest development by retaining the distinction between contradiction and antagonism, but it also presupposes the distinction between antagonism and external antithesis.

and workers to the existence of antagonism, without questioning the link between the two notions. But there is no reason why exploitation—reduced to the exaction of surplus labor—should necessarily imply antagonism.

Let us start from the Marxist notion of exploitation in its most general form, the extraction of surplus labor from direct producers. It implies the division of the working day into necessary labor time and surplus labor time. It also assumes, therefore, that the increase of surplus labor has as a condition the reduction of necessary labor or the extension and intensification of the working day. In turn, since labor capacity is inseparable from the producers, such extraction presupposes direct or indirect compulsion as a means of obtaining the maximum possible effort from the workers. However, neither from the general conditions for the appropriation of surplus labor by the exploiters nor from the subjection of the direct producers demanded by it can the existence of antagonism be deduced. The fact that this relation presupposes the exclusion of direct producers from the economic ownership of the means of production does not change things much. Nor does the fact that there is interdependence, that is, that the capacity to appropriate surplus labor has as a condition the maintenance of the relation of exclusion and subjection of the workers.[9] All the rejection that these words produce in us comes from a certain normative perspective that has long since been naturalized. If this point of view comes from outside the relation, there is no longer *an objective (material) basis for the relation of antagonism.*[10] But what would happen if that point of view were internal—inherent—to the relation of exploitation? In that case, and only in that case, the capital/labor relation would be objectively constituted through an opposition between its formal (normative) character and its content in such a way that this "objective contradiction" would be the "locus" of an antagonism. We will try to show that this is so.

The relation of exploitation as we presented it in the previous paragraph, by its degree of generality, is applicable to any social form.

[9] See Wright (2015).

[10] This is the content of Laclau and Mouffe's (2001) critique of historical materialism, which they understand in the structuralist mode. The mere acceptance that the "superstructures" are necessary to construct the concept of exploitation suppresses de facto the "economic determination in the last instance". This would explain the aporias and logical inconsistencies of Marxist structuralism.

Therefore, it does not describe any particular relation of exploitation. It is a structure of differential positions which designates the places of the exploiters and the exploited in any exploitative society. But the *social form* of the exploitative relation cannot be reduced to any system, structure or space of differential positions (Gunn, 1987). If we abstract the relation of exploitation from its social forms, we only obtain the general formal conditions of all types of exploitation.

What specifies the capitalist relation of exploitation, differentiating it from all others, is the figure of the *free worker*[11]:

> For the transformation of money into capital, therefore, the owner of money must find the free worker available on the commodity-market; and this worker must be freein the double sense that as a free individual he can dispose of his labour-power as his own commodity, and that, on the other hand, he has no other commodity for sale, i.e., he is rid of them, he is free of all the objects needed for the realization of his labour-power. (Marx, 1982: 272–273)

In this paragraph we find the key to understanding why the capital/labor relation constitutes an *objective contradiction*. On the one hand, the worker is a free individual in the same sense that any person who owns commodities is free, including the capitalist. In this sense, the capital relation is de facto a relation between free and equal persons. This does not require any external determination, since it is a matter of the very *content* of the relation determined by the *form of mercantile exchange*:

> In order that these objects may enter into relation with each other as commodities, their guardians must place themselves in relation to one another as persons whose will resides in those objects, and must behave in such a way that each does not appropriate the commodity of the other, and alienate his own, except through an act to which both parties consent. The guardians must therefore recognize each other as owners of private property. This juridical relation, whose form is the contract, whether as part of a developed legal system or not, is a relation between two wills

[11] Marx refers on several occasions throughout the *Grundrisse* and *Capital* to "free labor" and the "free worker" as a logical and historical assumption of the capitalist relation. In most of them he emphasizes the contradiction equality/freedom—inequality/coercion that distinguished it and that is based on its separation (liberation) from the means of production.

> which mirrors the economic relation. The content of this juridical relation (or relation of two wills) is itself determined by the economic relation. (Marx, 1982: 178)

On the other hand, as a free individual (dispossessed) of the means of production, he is obliged to sell his labor power. And this coercive character of the capitalist relation is openly shown in the process of production:

> Capital developed within the production process until it acquired command over labour, i.e., over self-activating labour-power, in other words the worker himself [...] Capital also developed into a coercive relation, and this compels the working class to do more work than would be required by the narrow circle of his needs. (Marx, 1982: 424–425)

The figure of the *free worker*, therefore, summarizes the content of the capital relation: the separation of the direct producers from the means of production is the condition of their freedom (necessity) and of their equality (exploitation) *vis-à-vis* the capitalist. The relation of capital is contradictory insofar as it assumes and constitutes the opposing pairs equality—freedom/inequality—coercion as poles of the same relation, that is, to put it in Laclau's terms, insofar as it constitutes simultaneously the relation of subordination and the normative perspective (category) from which it *is possible to look at* it as a relation of oppression.

It is necessary to emphasize that equality and freedom are here objective categories that adequately describe specific types of interaction inherent to a given social form. Therefore, they are, *from this perspective*, independent of the respective legal categories, of the ways in which *people* represent their behavior and of their own identity. What matters is how one person behaves in relation to another. The legal fiction of the contract between free persons finds its foundation in the way in which flesh-and-blood persons behave toward one another when they exchange.

It can be seen that the structure of the relation of capitalist exploitation is the same as that of contradiction in Adorno. Its specific mechanism is the "equalizing violence" of the commodity. The antagonistic potential of the capitalist relation resides, in Adorno's view, in the fact that it is a conceptual reality: it imposes the coercion of surplus labor through a logic of identity. But it is not a process arising from the minds of individuals, it is a process of real abstraction, produced and reproduced through our "doing" in society. The reality of domination is "suppressed", "hidden" as a relationship between free and equal persons. But what is heterogeneous to the "concept" cannot fail to emerge. It does so as a difference of power at all levels of social life. And a world of free human beings cannot judge subordination except as oppression. The contradiction, therefore, must be repressed only to reappear as class antagonism. But two important consequences follow.

The first consequence is that in this same dialectic of equality—inequality/freedom—coercion lies the emancipatory potential:

> Once critical theory has shown it up [the barter principle] for what it is –an exchange of things that are equal and yet unequal- our critique of inequality within equality aims at equality too, for all our skepticism of the rancor involved in the bourgeois egalitarian ideal that tolerates no qualitative difference. (Adorno, 2004: 147)

The second consequence is that the relation of capitalist exploitation is the center from which, backward and forward in the exposition of the concept of capital, all moments of capitalist relations are transformed into the locus of antagonisms. In this sense, Holloway's critique of the tendency among Marxists to set aside the contradiction between concrete labor and abstract labor achieves its full power in the light of the distinction between contradiction and antagonism and between antagonism and antithesis.

Let us explain it better. In the *Grundrisse* Marx distinguishes between simple category and social form (Marx, 1993: 101–108). For example, commodity, money, wage, rent, etc., as simple categories, it is possible to find them in different historical epochs. But their meaning is transformed when we consider them as forms of capitalist relations. The commodity, where it occupies the interstices of society, constructs relations as an antithesis between buyers and sellers, but not necessarily as an irreconcilable opposition between oppressors and oppressed. It can bring into relation, for example, peasants of unequal wealth and needs or very diverse social formations with no more than quantitative inequality between them. But its generalization as a means of establishing social relations occurs where labor is subsumed to capital. The primitive accumulation is a double process of "liberation" of producers (separation from the conditions of production) and subsumption of their labor to capital: subordination of doing to abstract labor. This institutes the relation of exploitation as a relation of coercion mediated by the commodity (Cleaver, 2001). And, by this means, the contradiction concrete labor/abstract labor unfolds in an antagonistic logic, becoming an essential moment of this subsumption of labor to capital. In this process, the "wage form" occupies a central place and, as we shall see, structures the capital relation as class antagonism.

From Contradiction to Class Antagonism: Class as an Objective Social Relation

The Wage Relation as Mediation Between Contradiction and Antagonism

The wage is a social device—or mechanism—that structures the extraction of surplus value through a specific mode of payment of labor power. The mode of payment links remuneration and performance by presenting the payment of labor power as payment for labor. The result is the reification of the relation of exploitation and, at the same time, the subjectivization of "capital" and "labor" as poles of an antagonistic relation.

The various forms of wage payment are partial ways of solving the problems raised by the control of the labor force for the purpose of maximum extraction of surplus labor. The solutions to these problems are restricted/enabled by the specificity of the capital/labor relation: free labor excludes physical coercion in the productive process. The wage is usually paid once the labor power has been consumed, which in itself supports the idea of exchange of money for labor. But, as a general rule, all forms of wage payment seek to establish a link between remuneration and performance. Time and piecework wages are the basic forms and the ones Marx highlights in *Capital*, but a long list can be included, such as the collective performance bonus, wages for team production objectives, and a long etcetera. Thus, the payment of wages is firmly linked as remuneration for work and, consequently, the relation of exploitation is invisibilized. On this basic form the process of reification of the relations of exploitation unfolds.

To the extent that wage is presented as remuneration for labor, the latter—in its "natural" form, abstracted from any social form—appears as a resource capable of providing income. Wage labor, then, coincides with labor as a simple end-oriented activity, the general condition of the labor process. It is on this basis that capital is reduced to the means of production that embody it as a source of profit; and land, abstracted from property relations, as a resource that "generates" rent. Labor, capital and land are thus transformed into heterogeneous resources (assets) independent of each other.

On this foundation, *workers and capitalists* confront each other as *personifications of labor and capital* respectively.[12] It is in this minimum of subjectivation, as personifications of reified relations of production, or representatives of things (assets), that they are *classes*. *People* relate as exemplars of *classes* insofar as they confront each other as representatives of assets that produce goods and, therefore, generate appropriation rights (income) over a part of the product. On this basis, if conceived as classifications of individuals according to independent attributes (things), classes can proliferate alongside productive resources. However, it is the wage relation that structures relations between *people* as relations between exemplars of *classes*. From this perspective, *class* is an *objective social relation* and not a classification.

In turn, insofar as it is the product of the wage relation, the autonomous existence of the poles of "labor" and "capital" is nothing other than the objective capital/labor contradiction developed as an antithesis between external poles and, given the structure of that contradiction, a relation of antagonism. Despite the appearance of independence and exteriority, despite the fact that they seem to be defined by the relation between individuals and attributes (things) and despite the appearance of "possessing" particular conflicting but not antagonistic interests, capitalists and workers as classes, or exemplars of classes, subsist only in their mutually referenced relation as the personification of capital *vis-à-vis* labor and the personification of labor *vis-à-vis* capital. That is to say, class from the Marxist point of view is an objective and antagonistic social relation.

The wage relation, therefore, is neither simple revenue—wage as a simple category—nor mere monetary mediation in the act of buying and selling labor power. As a device that structures the subordination of concrete labor to the production of surplus value, it encompasses circulation and production and is an essential moment in the subsumption of

[12] We leave aside the landlords because their participation in the distribution of surplus value transforms them, as far as the relation of exploitation is concerned, into a fraction of the capitalists, like commercial capital or banking capital.

labor to capital, in Holloway's terms, of the subordination of "doing" to abstract labor. In fact, if primitive accumulation articulates two moments, separation and subjection, then wage—as a form of the capital relation—is the mode of subjection of liberated individuals. And it is in this condition that mediates the transformation of the contradiction immanent to the relation of capitalist exploitation into class antagonism.

On Intermediate Positions and Classes as a Collective Reality

But as capitalism develops and the tendencies toward concentration and centralization of capital unfold, the separation between ownership and management of the capitalist enterprise also emerges and develops. The owners, generally shareholders, are not necessarily at the head of the enterprises and those who exercise the tasks of management and control on behalf of capital are usually employees. The higher the position in the hierarchy of the company, the closer the employees are to the position of capitalist and, in general, the greater is the share of their income that corresponds to profit sharing. But the truth is that from the supervisors and foremen to the managers of large companies we have a series of individuals who confront each other as personifications of capital versus labor and, at the same time, as personifications of labor versus capital. This is where the fact that class is a social relation, a mode of relation of some people to others, becomes clearer. Therefore, there is no point where the working class ends and the bourgeoisie begins, that cut is the result of struggle. And this is true also for the mass of the sellers of labor power (unemployed, informal workers, formal wage earners) since "his or her feet remain mired in exploitation even while his or head (...) breathes in bourgeois ideological clouds" (Gunn, 1987: 23).

But along with the concentration and centralization of capital, the socialization of production is developing as well. With mechanization first and automation later, it becomes more and more difficult to attribute the contribution to production of each individual worker, as the product is increasingly the result of a collective worker. The difference between services, industry, agriculture, etc., and between productive and unproductive labor is also dissolved. In this way, what Marx put forward in the discussion on the way in which the rates of profit of the different branches of production tend to equalize becomes more and more a reality: the capitalists as a whole are partners in the exploitation of the workers as a whole. The class relation is established as a relation at the level of society as a whole.

Political (In)Conclusions

Throughout this paper we have tried to develop some elements for a concept of class that, taking up the contributions of open Marxism and, in particular, of John Holloway, restores the importance of the distinction between contradiction and antagonism. Starting from that distinction, we pointed out why the relation of capitalist exploitation is structured as an objective contradiction and why and in what way it unfolds as class antagonism. This allowed us to account for the specificity of the class form as a moment of the capital relation. But all this development is unimportant if we do not discuss, even briefly, some of its political consequences. Due to limits of space, we only point them out.

One of the consequences of the above is that, to the extent that the struggles of the workers are limited to the representation of the "structural libretto", that is to say, to the repetition of the structure or reified social relation, they have a reproductive function. Here there is a true element of the Leninist critique of syndicalism. But above all, as far as the interest of this volume is concerned, of Holloway's critique of the labor movement as a movement of abstract labor (Holloway, 2010: 151–161).

However, is there any other point of departure than class subjectivity? I intentionally use subjectivity rather than identity to point out the extent to which the subsumption of the whole of our social practices to capital shapes our most elementary dispositions. If class subjectivity meant only reproduction there would be no way out. But class is an objective social relation, between personifications or masks of reified relations, and, at the same time, an antagonistic relation, firmly founded on the contradiction of a relation of exploitation which is also the open door to subversion. Equality is "leveling violence" and simultaneously revolutionary aspiration. That is why Adorno can say that "If mankind is to get rid of the coercion to which the form of identification really subjects it, it must attain identity with its concept at the same time" (Adorno, 2004: 146). The struggle of the working class reproduces as antagonism that contradiction and, therefore, reproduces and subverts in every act. Hence its potency. In the very distance between the task prescribed by the company management and the real task, the distance between repetition and subversion that constitutes worker subjectivity arises.

The concept of class proposed, however, leaves pending the problem of the relation between class struggles and struggles against other forms of oppression, such as struggles against racism, against patriarchy, etc. From the above, two answers are equally possible. The validity of one or the other depends on the scope we give to the process of subsumption of social relations to capital. If this process unfolds to the point of internalizing contradictorily and antagonistically the whole of our social action, all struggle is class struggle. On the contrary, if the subsumption of certain relations which are not entirely deducible from—and reducible to—capital and which pre-exist it, such as patriarchy or certain forms of ethnic and religious oppression, does not suppress a certain radical exteriority of these relations with respect to capital; if capital and these other forms of oppression are relations which mediate one another without reducing one another, a certain articulation of these struggles, that would not be given simply by itself, is indispensable. I tend to think that this second formulation is the correct one, but I consider it an open and urgent question for the revolutionary struggle. In any case, respect for the autonomy of the different struggles and movements is a necessary condition for overcoming totalitarian practices that reproduce "equalizing violence" and, therefore, oppression.

References

Adorno, Th. W. (2004). *Negative Dialectics*. Routledge.

Adorno, Th. W. (2008). *Lectures on Negative Dialectics*. Polity Press.

Bonefeld, W. (2002). Labour, Capital and Primitive Accumulation: Class and Constitution. In A. C. Dinerstein & M. Neary (Eds.), *The Labour Debate*. Ashgate.

Cleaver, H. (2001). *Reading Capital Politically*. AK Press.

Gramsci, A. (1992). Analysis of Situations: Relations of Force. In Gramsci. *Selections from the Prison Notebooks*. International Publishers.

Gunn, R. (1987). Notes on Class. In *Capital & Class 2*. CSE.

Holloway, J. (2002). Class and Classification: Against, in and Beyond Labour. In A. C. Dinerstein & M. Neary (Eds.), *The Labour Debate*. Ashgate.

Holloway, J. (2010). *Crack Capitalism*. Pluto.

Kellner, D. (Ed.). (1977). *Karl Korsch: Revolutionary Theory*. University of Texas Press.

Korsch, K. (2008). *Marxism and Philosophy*. Monthly Review Press.

Laclau, E., & Mouffe, C. (2001). *Hegemony and Socialist Strategy*. Verso.

Marx, K. (1872). *Le Capital*. Maurice Lachatre et cie. [Source gallica.bnf.fr / Bibliothèque Nationale de France].

Marx, K. (1962). *Das Kapital. Kritik der politischen Ökonomie*, Buch 1, MEW Band 23. Dietz Verlag.

Marx, K. (1982). *Capital: A Critique of Political Economy* (Vol. I). Penguin.
Marx, K. (1993). *Grundrisse Foundations of the Critique of Political Economy*. Penguin.
Marx, K. (2010). *El Capital. Tomo 1*. Siglo XXI.
Pannekoek, Anton. (2003). *Lenin as Philosopher*. Marquette University Press.
Pashukanis, E. B. (1976). *La teoría general del derecho y el marxismo*. Grijalbo.
Rubin, I. I. (1976). *Ensayos sobre teoría marxista del valor*. México: Cuadernos de pasado y presente—Siglo XXI.
Wright E. O. (2015). *Understanding class*. Verso.

CHAPTER 5

An Eighteenth-Century Ancestor of Crack Capitalism: How Rousseau's Radical Democracy Helps Us Open Cracks in Capitalism

Yiorgos Moraitis and Vasilis Grollios

Introduction

There are studies that connect Open Marxism, as a separate strand in Marxism, with Marx's philosophy. However, our study aspires to connect it with a former philosopher than Marx, Jean-Jacques Rousseau. Hopefully, this will broaden our understanding of Open Marxism and *Crack Capitalism*, more specifically, and enrich the content of its frame of thinking.

Y. Moraitis (✉)
National Center of Social Research (EKKE), Athens, Greece
e-mail: gimoraitis@yahoo.com

V. Grollios
Independent Scholar in Political Philosophy, Athens, Greece

A. García Vela and A. Bonnet (eds.), *The Political Thought of John Holloway*, Marx, Engels, and Marxisms,
https://doi.org/10.1007/978-3-031-34571-5_5

For mainstream readings of Jean-Jacques Rousseau's philosophy, the most important problem in society concerns how individuals, as bearers of specific social interests, create stable political societies at peace and without conflicting class interests among individuals. In this reading, the general will is merely a means by which state policy minimizes social inequalities and cares for the financially weakest members of the society. Similarly, the conceptual content of the "political" is exhausted in the context of state policy. As a result, the plane on which the most fundamental human needs are met, that of people interacting in their everyday lives and working to sustain their livelihood, almost disappears, and thus the political loses its materialist content. According to the mainstream reading of Rousseau, in his philosophy social forms, such as the state or bourgeois forms of democracy, are closed, fetishized, and finally attain validity as natural phenomena. People fail to think or imagine themselves, their lives, and daily actions apart from them.

In contrast, we see Rousseau as a thinker who cast light on the inherent social contradictions that lie veiled under the cover of social forms and who sought to open and denaturalize them. This text re-evaluates Jean-Jacques Rousseau's concept of the general will to show the connection between its critical character and Open Marxism. According to our interpretation, Rousseau elaborates a materialist method that reaches for an alternative organization of social relations, in which our most basic human needs will be satisfied. Rousseau's concept of the general will should not be analyzed simply in terms of state public policies, as usually happens in traditional bourgeois-liberal theory. In other words, the general will does not merely describe one of several ways of creating socio-political institutions that will produce a more effective capitalist mode of production; it offers a different method of fulfilling our most basic human needs and desires while we attempt to sustain a livelihood. As a result, his theory can be constructive in forming a theory of how cracks can open in capitalism, and that is why he can be considered as a forerunner of the critical theory found in John Holloway's *Crack Capitalism*.

The Open Marxism Path of Thinking

For Marx, critique is radical and "ad hominem" at the same time (Marx, 1975: 182).[1] Marx means that economic categories and socio-political forms are wrongly accepted as fetishes since they are produced by people's historical and social practice. These forms express themselves as the relation between essence/content and appearance/form. Content describes the individual's real or concrete labor or how individuals can use their corporeal and intellectual force to fulfill their most basic needs within society and nature. Form indicates how essence appears in different historical moments. In this instance, capital, contrary to traditional theory, is not hoarded wealth created by those who adopt the values of honorable industriousness and hard work. Instead, capital is not simply a thing or a relation, but, more specifically, the perverted form that our doing takes, that is to say, abstract labor. Capital is not something external to us; to the contrary, we are capital to the extent that we consent to the subordination of everything we do in the effort to produce the fruits of abstract labor, that is, money.

The most important question for Open/Critical Marxism is how it is possible for individuals to be the only real subjects of this world while, at the same time, they are enslaved by abstractions and socially fetishized forms created by those abstractions. The world takes a perverted or inverted form. While people attempt to make a living amid the fierce antagonisms of capitalism, they create a world that alienates them and turns them against each other, forcing them to compete for the maximum production of profit. In this alienated world, most people are so focused on their struggle for survival that they cannot imagine a different manner of fulfilling their most basic human needs (Marx, 1996: 187).

Marx's answer to mainstream and traditional political theory is that the way our life is organized under capitalism appears to be through closed and trans-historically valid social forms that are wrongly considered as unavoidable traits of human nature. In contrast, they are products of a specific historical contingency. Marx's critique is a critique of the appearance, of the fetishism, of economic and political categories. A critique of political economy must reveal people's social practice as the basis of

[1] For Marx's theory of critique and its connection to democracy and materialism, see the first two chapters of Grollios, Vasilis (2017) *Negativity and Democracy: Marxism and the Critical Theory Tradition*, Routledge, New York.

any social and political form. Thus, a theory of de-fetishization and de-naturalization must take place for the human content of the seemingly autonomous categories to come to the surface.

Marx's materialism becomes dialectical only because present reality is formed by a key contradiction. On the one hand, people must survive the fierce competition of capitalism and produce profits incessantly, while on the other hand they must live in solidarity and peace with their fellow human beings. According to Marx, dialectics is not found in nature but in an "enchanted, perverted, topsy-turvy world" (Marx, 1998: 817), where the real subjects of history, people, are dominated by the social forms they produce.

In Marx's thought, essence and form are mediated by each other. Essence always appears but in capitalism this takes place in an inverted or perverted form. While Marx attributes this phenomenon chiefly to commodities, we hold that it can also be considered as something widespread throughout all capitalistically organized society. As Holloway asserts, "social antagonism runs through each of us" (Holloway, 2010: 221). Because of this, "we are all permeated by this antagonism, we are all self-contradictory, torn internally" (Holloway, 2010: 221). According to this analysis, we face capitalism as a process that is validated and reproduced by people themselves each time they follow the logic that "time is money."

According to Holloway's *Crack Capitalism*, the determining factor that gives cohesion to capitalist society is neither the state nor the economy, but the way our doing is organized or, in other words, submitted to the dictates of abstract labor, to the incessant money accumulation. Thus, social cohesion becomes a power that cannot be controlled by anyone. It appears to have its own dynamic, although this dynamic exists because our daily existence is organized in such a way that we give life to its autonomy. What appears, though, is not an illusion; it is real. Fetishism is real, not product of a false consciousness. This totality has its own logic, that of capital, and has only one goal: the creation of money by money.

The negation of the subordination of our everyday activity in this totality is the dialectic element within the Marxian concept of dialectical materialism. Negative dialectics is that of our misfitting, or, as Holloway contents, "the negative restlessness of misfitting" (Holloway, 2010: 85) that unfolds in "the power of No" (Holloway, 2010: 19). Cracks can be opened in the capitalist totality only by comprehending that the logic of capital is constituted by our distorted doing, that is, by abstract labor, by labor time, by the subordination of our time to the demands of socially necessary labor time and consequently by our denial of this process.

We generate class struggle every time we refuse to accept the logic of profit maximization. In Open Marxism, the key notion is fetishism as a process. This relates to how people's concrete labor or creative activity is continually transformed into abstract labor, which only produces commodities for exchange in a competitive market with the ultimate goal of money accumulation. We participate in class struggle and promote it every time we refuse to let money determine our practice and our whole existence; class struggle, contrary to what traditional Marxism accepts, is related to our everyday doing, to our most common activities. Anti-capitalist struggle is taking place when we come out of shadows, when we make "our doing-in-against-and-beyond-capital" visible, when we deny "the mask of abstract labour" (Holloway, 2010: 212).

In the following, we will attempt to connect this particular strand of Marxism, promoted by *Crack Capitalism*, with Rousseau's social and political theory to demonstrate how Rousseau's theory continues to be relevant today, especially in our struggle, taking place in the context of Open Marxism, against contemporary capitalism.

Materialism and Alienation in Rousseau's Political Thought

Rousseau states in the *Social Contract* that people possess a multi-faceted nature that seeks self-preservation and can be either a selfish and antagonistic *amour-propre* or a more cooperative *amour de soi-meme* (Rousseau, 1968: 50). He clarifies that there is a relationship between justice and utility that can be read as a relationship between common and personal interest (Rousseau, 1968: 49).

Rousseau's philosophy is far from traditional/bourgeois thinking when he states that "Each one of us puts into the community his person and all his powers under the supreme direction of the general will; and as a body, we incorporate every member as an integral part of the whole" (Rousseau, 1968: 61). He further clarifies that "this act of association creates an artificial and corporate body composed of as many members as there are voters in the assembly, and by this same act that body acquires its unity, its common ego, its life and its will" (Rousseau, 1968: 61). According to the traditional/bourgeois understanding, freedom for the individual is freedom from the state and the rest of the society. In contrast, in Rousseau, individual freedom does not conflict with the whole community or seek protection from it but must be fully incorporated to it.[2]

Rousseau contends that alienation and authoritarianism originate in how people have collectively organized their livelihood and not by their individual morality. He makes this point clearly when he writes that:

> Man was born free, and he is everywhere in chains. Those who think themselves the masters of the others are indeed greater slaves than them [...] the social order is a sacred right which serves as a basis for all other rights. And as it is not a natural right, it must be one founded on covenants. (Rousseau, 1968: 49–50)

Rousseau connects both the general will and sovereignty with the need for the people to fulfill their livelihood in a new way that is not exclusively focused on state policy.[3] He believes that state policy in his era proves that people already live in an alienated society. So, most of the people not only reproduce alienation, but they have also lost any will to change their living conditions (Rousseau, 1968: 52).[4] Chiefly, people experience a vicious circle of alienation which has not been imposed on them from

[2] Rousseau's idea of freedom, as something positive and collective, is relevant to what John Holloway describes, mostly in the *Change the World without Taking Power*, as "social flow of doing." By this, Holloway means that: "Doing is inherently social. What I do is always part of a social flow of doing, in which the precondition of my doing is the doing (or having done) of others, in which the doing of others provides the means of my doing. Doing is inherently plural, collective, choral, communal" (Holloway, 2010: 26).

[3] In *The Confessions*, Rousseau comments that: "The justice and uselessness of my complaints left a seed of indignation in my soul against our foolish civil institutions in which the true public good and genuine justice are always sacrificed to some apparent order or other, in fact destructive of all order, and which does nothing but add the sanction of public authority to the oppression of the weak and the iniquity of the strong" (Rousseau, 1995: 274).

[4] In the Second Discourse *Rousseau* notes that "the extreme inequalities in ways of life, the excess of idleness among some, the excess of work among others, the ease with which our appetites and our sensuality are aroused and satisfied, the excessively exotic dishes of the rich, which fill them with inflammatory humors and wrack them with indigestions, the bad food of the poor, which most of the time they do not even have, and the want of which leads them greedily to overtax their stomachs when they get the chance, the late nights, the excesses of every kind, the immoderate transports of all the passions, the fatigues and exhaustion of the mind, the innumerable sorrows and pains that are

some external source but is reproduced by people themselves (Rousseau, 1997: 163).

According to Rousseau, exit from the currently prevailing alienated situation can only be achieved if people have access to everything they might need to meet their basic daily needs. In relation to that, he writes that "[w]here wealth is concerned [...] no citizen shall be rich enough to buy another and none so poor as to be forced to sell himself" (Rousseau, 1968: 96).

Rousseau's materialism comes to the fore in a double sense. The concepts of democracy and sovereignty have a material content that is not only related to how people access the elementary goods for their preservation but is also chiefly related to how they plan the fulfillment of their livelihood (Rousseau, 1997: 161).

Rousseau's materialism makes us aware of how he moves beyond the classical distinction found in social contract theories between rational and passionate persons who reproduce virtues and vices, respectively.[5] Rousseau is against an approach that focuses on individual morality in the context of empty moralizing theory, so he assesses virtues and vices according to the extent to which people succumb to the core bourgeois values of hard labor and seeking the maximization of profit.[6] In this regard, he especially condemns the Swiss for having absorbed the logic of capital and financialization:

> They debased themselves and were no longer but mercenaries. The taste for money made them feel that they were poor; disdain for their station insensibly destroyed the virtues that were its work and the Swiss became five-penny men, as the French are four-penny ones. (Rousseau, 2005: 135)

experienced in every station of life and that constantly gnaw away at men's souls; such are the fatal proofs that most of our ills are of our own making" (Rousseau, 1997: 137–138).

[5] This distinction can be found in Thomas Hobbes who is the most well-known proponent of it. See, Thomas Hobbes (2001: 69–75).

[6] In the fifteenth chapter of the third book of the *Social Contract*, Rousseau contends that "It is the bustle of commerce and crafts, it is the avid thirst for profit, it is the effeminacy and the love of comfort that commute personal service for money. Men give up a part of their profits so as to increase the rest at their ease. Use money thus, and you will soon have chains. The word 'finance' is the word of a slave; it is unknown in the true republic. In a genuinely free state, the citizens do everything with their own hand and nothing by means of money [...] The better the state is constituted, the more does public business take precedence over private in the minds of the citizens" (Rousseau, 1968: 140).

Rousseau's vision does not include the accumulation of profit but instead points toward a different evaluation of "happiness." In the *Social Contract*, he supports the idea that in a politically well-ordered society "the sum of the public happiness furnishes a larger proportion of each individual's happiness, so there remains less for him to seek on his own" (Rousseau, 1968: 140). People do not pursue their private happiness in opposition to the state's sphere, as traditional/liberal theory supposes, but through it. It must be stressed though that in the next lines he clarifies that the people's involvement in politics takes the form of participation in the assemblies, and not in a bourgeois democracy. So, the state he refers to is not what is found in bourgeois democracy. Moreover, in the *Considerations on the Government of Corsica*, Rousseau connects this happiness either with the development of agriculture or with moderate industrial production, both of which aim at the satisfaction of the most important human needs, and not at the maximization of profit and constant transformation of money into capital.[7]

Thus, the notion of progress should not involve the goal of making profit for its own sake but the effort of organizing daily life to fulfill basic needs without being forced to act as a personification of abstract economic categories or being haunted by the logic of money accumulation. He explains this idea by contrasting the primitive with the civilized man:

> Primitive and civilized man differ so much in their inmost heart and inclinations that what constitutes the supreme happiness of the one would reduce the other to despair. The first breathes nothing but repose and freedom, he wants only to live and to remain idle [...] By contrast, the citizen, forever active, sweats, scurries, constantly antagonizes in search of ever more strenuous occupations: he works to death, even rushes toward it in order to be in a position to live, or renounces life in order to acquire immortality. (Rousseau, 1997: 186–187)

Freedom consists in the ever-present potential to abolish alienated and perverted living conditions under capitalism. Laws are not imposed on

[7] Rousseau notes on that: "Even if they wanted to, the Corsicans could not carry on trade abroad without buying superfluities; thus even in such a case money would not be necessary for them for commerce, since it is the only merchandise that they would go looking for. It follows from this that, in these relations of nation to nation, Corsica has no need of money" (Rousseau, 2005: 139–140).

people from above, from state officials, but originate from the general will, which is the authentic expression of people's desire to arrange common affairs in solidarity and equality. The general will is based on a law:

> the most important of all, which is inscribed neither on marble nor brass, but in the hearts of the citizens, a law which forms the true constitution of the state, a law which gathers new strength every day and which, when other laws age or wither away, reanimates or replaces them. (Rousseau, 1968: 99)

The idea of materialism appears throughout Rousseau's work. It can be traced not only in the *Two Discourses* and the *Social Contract* but also in his later work, mainly in the *Letters Written from the Mountain* and the texts about the constitutions of Corsica and Poland. Specifically, he maintains that the general will or sovereignty do not carry a steady and transhistorical content but are formed by people's daily struggles under capitalist competition. The idea previously found in the *Social Contract* that alienation is not something imposed by a corrupt elite that holds state power but originates in how people interact to sustain a livelihood and as a result create their own enslavement can also be found in the *Letters Written from the Mountain* (Rousseau, 2001: 246).

At the beginning of the *Letters Written from the Mountain*, Rousseau accuses the rulers, members of the Small Council of Geneva, of not considering in their decisions the general will (Rousseau, 2001: 238–239). Later in the same work, he mostly criticizes ordinary citizens because they adopt the logic of capital, of profit accumulation, which causes alienation.[8] Specifically, he argues that the citizens of Geneva are "completely absorbed in their *domestic occupations and always cool about the rest*, [and] consider the public interest *only when their own is being attacked*" (Rousseau, 2001: 293). These ideas show Rousseau's materialism. He does not pity Geneva's citizens for falling victim to a corrupt elite but argues that they deserve to lose their own freedom because of

[8] Rousseau comments about the citizens of Geneva that: "They are Merchants, Artisans, Bourgeois, always occupied with their private interests, with their work, with their trafficking, with their gain; people for whom even liberty is only a means for acquiring without obstacle and for possessing in safety" (Rousseau, 2001: 293).

how they have arranged their common affairs in everyday life (Rousseau, 1968: 141).

In the case of Geneva, Rousseau cannot specify any effective reaction against alienation. He supports the claim that it is always difficult to address situations where citizens themselves create their own fetters, since their only concern is to hoard wealth (Rousseau, 2001: 299). Citizens should not focus their struggle for a better world on changing state policy because that would reiterate the logic of representative government, which is one of the social forms that the capitalist mode of production takes.[9]

The central question that can now be posed is how a world of equality and justice may be possible because people themselves are responsible for reproducing the abstract social forms and categories that restrain their freedom. In our reading, this question is mostly addressed by Rousseau in his texts about the constitutions of Corsica and Poland, where the abolition of alienation presupposes a new way of satisfying human needs.

The Role of Money and Assemblies in Rousseau's Philosophy

In the *Social Contract* Rousseau considers the Corsicans as the only people that deserve to live according to a new kind of freedom.

[9] In the *Second Discourse*, Rousseau connects the appearance of the state with the inequalities and miseries that were formed in the antagonistically organized society in the capitalist mode of production:

> The rich, above all, must soon have sensed how disadvantageous to them was a perpetual war of which they alone bore the full cost, and in which everyone risked his life while only some also risked goods [...] [and so] at last conceived the most well-considered project ever to enter the human mind; to use even his attackers' forces in his favor, to make his adversaries his defenders [...] To this end, after exhibiting to his neighbors the horror of a situation that armed all of them against one another, that made their possessions as burdensome to them as their needs, and in which no one found safety in either poverty or wealth, he easily invented specious reasons to bring them around his goal: "Let us unite," he told them, "to protect the weak from oppression, restrain the ambitious, and secure for everyone the possession of what belong to him". (Rousseau, 1997: 172–173)

> There is still one country in Europe that is fit to receive laws, and that is the island of Corsica. The valour and fidelity with which this brave people have recovered and defended its freedom entitle it to be taught by some wise man how to preserve that freedom. (Rousseau, 1968: 96)

Along the same line of thinking, the Polish are also regarded equally worthy for such a freedom. With these two examples, Rousseau insists that productive relations different from those of the capitalist mode of production are feasible, and he opposes the dependence that workers, who are forced to sell their labor power to owners of the means of production. experience. “Anyone who depends on someone else and does not have his resources in himself cannot be free” (Rousseau, 2005: 124).

Rousseau’s analysis also includes a discussion of the logic of the immediate economy, of primal production, which creates powerful individuals and is not subject to trade agreements (Rousseau, 2005: 125–126). Rousseau argues that Corsicans:

> have to make use of their people and of their country as much as possible; to cultivate and gather together their own forces, to depend upon them alone, and to think about foreign powers no more than one would if none of them existed. (Rousseau, 2005: 125)

This quote may be general in its meaning and thus not reveal Rousseau’s anti-capitalist character, but it should be read in connection with the following:

> in order to multiply men, it is necessary to multiply their means of existence, hence agriculture. By this word I do not understand the art of talking about agriculture in a sophisticated way [...] I do understand a constitution that leads a people to spread itself out over the whole surface of its territory, to settle there, to cultivate all its places, to love the country life, the labors that relate to it, to find the necessities and embellishments of life so well in them that it does not at all desire to leave it (Rousseau, 2005: 126). ‘[T]he administration more favorable for agriculture is the one whose force, not being at all united in some point, does not involve the unequal distribution of people, but leaves it evenly dispersed over the territory; such is democracy. (Rousseau, 2005: 127)

He also clarifies that “the only means for maintaining a state in independence of other is agriculture. Even if you have all the wealth in the world, if you do not have anything with which to nourish yourself you are dependent on others" (Rousseau, 2005: 127). According to Rousseau, a well-ordered society, the one which will have developed the general will, creates relations of production capable of fulfilling elementary human needs.

> The Island of Corsica ought to try to get richer in men. The power that comes from the population is more real than one that comes from finances and produces its effect more certainly. Not being able to hide itself, the use of men's arms always reaches the public destination, it is not the same for the use of money: it slips away and melts into private destinations; one heaps it up for one purpose one gives it out for another; the people pay in order to be protected and what they give serves to oppress them. *That is why a state rich in money is always weak, and a state rich in men is always strong* (our emphasis). (Rousseau, 2005: 125–126)

Rousseau contrasts a society that prioritizes the cultivation of agricultural products with one that is focused on money accumulation through the finance sector. When agriculture becomes a means to promote commerce class polarization is amplified:

> It is necessary to establish as a definite maxim that everywhere that money is of the outmost necessity the nation detaches itself from agriculture in order to throw itself into more lucrative profession; the station of plowman is then either an object of commerce and a sort of manufacture for the big farmers, or the last resource of poverty for the crowd of peasants. When they have earned enough, those who get rich by means of commerce and industry place their money in landed estates which other cultivate for them; the whole nation thus finds itself divided into rich sluggards who possess the land and wrenched peasants who do not have enough to live on while cultivating it. (Rousseau, 2005: 13)

Every time the farmer is forced to sell his products, he loses his freedom to the merchant.

> I look at every system of commerce as distractive of agriculture so much so that I make no exception even of commerce in commodities that are the product of agriculture. For it to be maintained in this system, the profit would have to be capable of being divided equally between the merchant and the cultivator. But this is what is impossible because the trade of the one being free and that for the other forced, the first will always give the

> law to the second, a relation which [...] cannot form a solid and permanent condition. (Rousseau, 2005: 139–140)

Rousseau brings to the reader's attention the corrupting role of money. Chasing profit makes society insecure. We can also find in Rousseau a first distinction between use value and exchange value that was later developed by Marx:

> Your neighbors can give your money whatever value they please because they can wait; but the bread we need has an indisputable value for us and in every sort of commerce it is always the least hurried person who gives the law to the other. (Rousseau, 2005: 127)

Similar to Marx's argument that "The wealth of those societies in which the capitalist mode of production prevails, presents itself as 'an immense accumulation of commodities'" (Marx, 1996: 45),[10] Rousseau argues that:

> It must not be imagined that the Island will be richer when it has a lot of money [...] a nation is neither richer nor poorer for having more or less money [...] Not only is money a sign, but it is a relative sign which has a genuine effect only by the inequality of its distribution [...] and since it is useful only as a sign of inequality, the less of it that circulates in the Island, the more real abundance will reign there. (Rousseau, 2005: 140)

Rousseau continues along similar lines when he states that "[i]t is necessary to see whether what is being done with money cannot be done without money; and assuming that it can be, it is necessary to compare the two means relatively to our object" (Rousseau, 2005: 140). The best possible way of fulfilling the most essential human needs is by providing access to the necessary means of subsistence. In our view, here we can find a strong connection between Rousseau and John Holloway's call to oppose the rule of money (Holloway, 2012: 201), which is the logic that destroys every aspect of our life that does not bring profit.

The anti-capitalist and radical character of Rousseau's philosophy is obvious when we read that his ideal would be the abolition of money.

[10] See the excellent analysis of John Holloway, Read Capital: The First Sentence, Capital Starts with Wealth, not with the Commodity, *Historical Materialism*, v.23, n. 3, 2015, pp. 3–26.

However, since he holds that this is not feasible, he does not propose that money be prohibited but instead seeks to gradually minimize its role in people's daily practice:

> the Corsican people could continue to exist comfortably and independently with very little trade, how this little that will be necessary for it the greatest part can easily be made by exchanges [...] From that it is seen that if the use of money and currency cannot be absolutely annihilated in the affairs of private individuals, at least it can be reduced to so small a thing that it will be difficult for abuses to arise, that no fortunes at all will be made by this way, and that if they could be made they would become almost useless and would give little advantage to their possessors. (Rousseau, 2005: 146–147)

It must be stressed, that in his text on Corsica, Rousseau does not focus on changes at the level of the state, because fulfilling his demands for equality and freedom does not depend on state action. In contrast to traditional/bourgeois political theory, he calls for a new way in which people will interact to satisfy their daily needs, without following the logic that "time is money." In this context, people's activity cannot be measured according to the rule of money. Rousseau's social theory also includes a reduction in the duration and intensity of labor[11]; against the core bourgeois values of labor intensification and wealth accumulation, Rousseau preached "disinterestedness and poverty in good grace" (Rousseau, 1995: 303). He also confesses that at a personal level:

> I renounced forever every project of fortune and advancement. Determined to pass the little time I had left to live in independence and poverty, I applied all the strength of my soul to breaking the irons of opinion, and to doing courageously everything that appeared good to me, without bothering myself in any way about the judgement of men. (Rousseau, 1995: 303–304)

[11] In the ninth book of *The Confessions*, Rousseau contends that: "even though I was lazy, [...] my laziness was less that of a sluggard than that of an independent man who likes to work only on his own schedule. Two thousand francs that I had left from the yield from the Village Soothsayer and my other Writings gave me an advance so I would not be in financial straits, and, even without fleecing the publishers, several works that I had on the loom promised me sufficient supplements for me to be able to work at my ease without wearing myself out, and even while turning my leisure walks to advantage" (Rousseau, 1995: 337–338).

Rousseau notes that "In every country the people do not notice that one is attacking its liberty *until one attacks its purse*" (Rousseau, 2001: 243). Rousseau refers to changes in the state not because that is where popular sovereignty, equality, and freedom can be located but because the citizens of Geneva have already adopted the logic of capital and maximization of profit. If they react only after their purses have been attacked, their reaction can take only an institutional form, as the fetishization of the capitalist mode of social organization prevents the citizens of Geneva from demanding changes to state policy (Rousseau, 2001: 244–245) This connection had already been described by Rousseau in the *Second Discourse*, where he noted that representative governance is just the means of exploitation that the rich oppressors imposed on the vast majority of the population to secure their arbitrarily seized property (Rousseau, 1997: 172–173).

In Rousseau's thought, people's political participation in the formation of common affairs should not take place through a bourgeois democratic, representative system. Rousseau does not describe in detail an alternate plan of managing common affairs, yet he lays out constructive thoughts that reveal his radical theory. In the *Social Contract*, he calls for participation in the decision-making process through the formulation of councils and assemblies:

> [T]he assemblies of the people, which are the shield of the body politic and the brake on the government, have always been the nightmare of all magistrates; hence the latter spare no effort in raising objections, problems, promises to turn the citizens against assemblies (Rousseau, 1968: 139).

It is of crucial importance to consider that despite that Rousseau retains the concept of the state, it is not functionally similar to the state in bourgeois political theory, bearing in mind that in Rousseau state officials only implement the decisions that assemblies make.

> Sovereignty cannot be represented, for the same reason that it cannot be alienated; its essence is the general will, and will cannot be represented – either it is the general will or it is something else; there is no intermediate possibility. Thus the people's deputies are not, and could not be, its representatives; they are merely its agents; and they cannot decide anything finally. Any law which the people has not ratified in person is void; it is not law at all. (Rousseau, 1968: 141)

In Rousseau's philosophy assemblies are unpopular in modern societies not because politicians are corrupt but rather because citizens "are avaricious, cowardly, pusillanimous and love repose more than freedom [and] they do not hold out against the redoubled efforts of the government" (Rousseau, 1968: 139).

One of the best quotes to prove that Rousseau celebrates the ideal of assemblies is the following:

> The sovereign, having no other force than the legislative power, acts only through the laws, and since the laws are nothing other than authentic acts of the general will, the sovereign can act only when the people is assembled. The people assembled, it will be said- what an illusion! It is indeed an illusion today; but two thousand years ago it was not. Has human nature so much changed? (Rousseau, 1968: 136)

Bearing in mind the above, it would be no exaggeration to say that Rousseau is closer to the council communism and anarchism traditions than is usually thought.

Unfortunately, we are unaware of other scholars who have attempted, like us, to directly connect Rousseau's democracy with councils. Kevin Inston has written a non-materialistic approach to Rousseau's democracy, according to which:

> The immense change effected by the lawgiver highlights how the founding of a democracy cannot come from his directly transmitting the people's will, since that will has no essential or pre-existent form, and if it did, it would exclude the necessity of both the lawgiver and the contract. The people therefore needs the lawgiver's mediation for its constitution. The legislator cannot merely have a neutral connection to the people but must actively create the feeling of unity among individuals in their disunity. (Inston, 2010: 403)

Yet, in our opinion, the role of the legislator in Rousseau is not so important, bearing in mind that the general will is created by people during peaceful and solidaristic daily interactions that reject the logic that time is money. Therefore, before the legislator intervenes unity is formed in people's daily activity. Inston's approach has a bourgeois character because he claims social unity does not originate in people's ordinary activities but in the legislator's decisions. Social change in Rousseau, according to Inston, has a non-materialist character, since it come from above, without presupposing an overturning of the logic of the system, that is of capitalism.

Alessandro Ferrara, in contrast, connects Rousseau with the critical theory tradition. Unlike us, Ferrara does not read in Rousseau an attempt to show the irrational manner in which people come into contact with each other to satisfy their basic needs under capitalism. His non-materialist analysis focuses on the concept of authenticity and connects it to the notion of identity: “identity can be a source of normativity and […] such potential rests on its capacity for being authentic” (Ferrara, 2017: 1). For Ferrara:

> the education for autonomy does not suffice. Also *authenticity* is needed – a general term by which I understand a capacity to distinguish the aspects of a person’s inner world which are crucially constitutive for the identity of the person from those which are expendable […] and the courage to follow one’s moral intuitions. (Ferrara, 2017: 8)

In his study, Ferrara focuses exclusively on Rousseau’s ideas on individual morality and personal behavior.

> Rousseau’s remedy for the ills of societal competitive reproduction […] required the strengthening of the individual’s immunity defense against the corrupting influence of competition for divisive rewards. Such strengthening […] can be understood as a program for an education to autonomy. (Ferrara, 2017: 6)

Contrary to Ferrara’s approach, critical thinkers must examine the content of normativity and authenticity bearing in mind that we live in a world that is ruled by the logic that time is money. And critical thinkers should question if we can lead an authentic life while we are constantly being forced to act as personifications of economic categories.

Ferrara’s reading ignores the materialist element in Rousseau’s analysis, which casts light on the most important social relation, that is how people’s elementary needs are fulfilled in the capitalist mode of production. In Ferrara’s analysis, both autonomy and authenticity attain a totally abstract character since they lead to a claim of empty moralizing that is exhausted at the level of individual moral behavior. He draws attention to Rousseau’s claim that “the overall psychological outcome of individual growth is going to manifest very different nuances […] depending on whether the individual has been allowed to respond *autonomously* to the various challenges or [has] had to conform to ready-made solutions" (Ferrara, 2017: 7). His analysis is trapped in the context of traditional/liberal/bourgeois philosophy that does not attempt to bring to the fore Rousseau's revolutionary criticism and democratic radicalism.

Conclusion

Rousseau may protect private property, but it should not escape our attention that this takes place only under the presupposition that he refers to independent, small producers. They are not forced to sell their labor to the owners of the means of production, that is to owners of more property than they themselves can use. As a result, they do not have the incentive to hire other's people labor power. At the same time, he entertains the idea that people's struggle for democracy should not be focused on changes at the level of state policy or on the choices state officials make but on a new way with which people will approach each other to make a living. As a result, his criticism is focused on the first stages of the development of the financial system, the stock market and the industrialization found in his time, which aimed at making a maximum profit.

His references to alienation and the mass character of culture are not written as an abstract and empty moralizing theory that targets individual morality, as some readers may believe, but alienation and mass culture originate in the inherent contradictions of the capitalist mode of production. In capitalism, instead of people satisfying their needs, they seek to satisfy the need for money that is accumulated at the expense of their everyday needs. These ideas are later developed by the socialist tradition and more specifically by the critical/autonomist/open Marxism met in John Holloway's *Crack Capitalism*. Rousseau's references to the need to form assemblies and make decisions through them is radically important even for us today. His social and political theory may appear from a cursory reading to belong to the distant past, yet, if it is read carefully, it can help us crack capitalism in the twenty-first century.

References

Ferrara, A. (2017). *Rousseau and Critical Theory*. Brill.

Grollios, V. (2017). *Negativity and Democracy: Marxism and the Critical Theory Tradition*. Routledge.

Hobbes, T. (2001). *Leviathan*. Cambridge University Press.

Holloway, J. (2010). *Crack Capitalism*. Pluto Press.

Holloway, J. (2012). Rage Against the Rule of Money. In F. Campagna & E. Campiglio (Eds.), *What We Are Fighting for: A Radical Collective Manifesto*. Pluto Press.

Inston, K. (2010). Representing the Unrepresentable: Rousseau's Legislator and the Impossible Object of the People. *Contemporary Political Theory, 9*(4), 393–413.

Marx, K. (1975). *Contribution to the Critique of Hegel's Philosophy of Law, Collected Works* (Vol. 3). International Publishers.

Marx, K. (1996). *Capital, Collected Works* (Vol. 35). Lawrence and Wishart.

Marx, K. (1998). *Capital* (Vol. 37). Lawrence and Wishart.

Rousseau, J.-J. (1968). *The Social Contract* (M. Cranston, Ed.). Penguin.

Rousseau, J.-J. (1995). The Confessions. In C. Kelly, R. D. Masters, & P. G. Stillman (Eds.), J.-J. Rousseau, *The Confessions and Correspondence Including the Letters to Malesherbes. The Collected Writings* (Vol. 5). Dartmouth College Press.

Rousseau, J.-J. (1997). *The Discourses and Other Early Political Writings* (V. Gourevitch, Ed.), Cambridge University Press.

Rousseau, J.-J. (2001). Letters Written from the Mountain. In C. Kelly & E. Grace (Eds.), J.-J. Rousseau, *Letter to Beaumont, Letters Written from the Mountain, and Related Writings. The Collected Writings* (vol. 9). Dartmouth College Press.

Rousseau, J.-J. (2005). Plan for a Constitution for Corsica. In C. Kelly (Ed.), J.-J. Rousseau, *The Plan for Perpetual Peace, on the Government of Poland, and Other Writings on History and Politics. The Collected Writings* (vol. 11). Dartmouth College Press.

PART II

Negativity, Cracks, and Emancipation

CHAPTER 6

Ontologizing Negativity: The Political Consequences of the Tension Between Doing and the Cracks

Edith González Cruz and Panagiotis Doulos

The Irrationality of Revolution Today

It is clear that we are no longer in 2010. This was the year when *Crack Capitalism* by John Holloway became one of the most influential theoretical references globally. *Crack Capitalism* appeared at the threshold of the insurrections that characterized the end of the twentieth century and the beginning of the present one and made it possible to place emancipation at the centre of the debate. In *Crack Capitalism*, the author maintains

E. González Cruz (✉)
Instituto de Ciencias Sociales y Humanidades, Benemérita Universidad Autónoma de Puebla (BUAP), Puebla, México
e-mail: goned.20@gmail.com

P. Doulos
IxM-CONAHCYT/Benemérita Universidad Autónoma de Puebla (BUAP), Puebla, México
e-mail: panagiotis.doulos@conahcyt.mx

A. García Vela and A. Bonnet (eds.), *The Political Thought of John Holloway*, Marx, Engels, and Marxisms,
https://doi.org/10.1007/978-3-031-34571-5_6

an open dialogue with the mobilizations and uprisings of *los de abajo*, from the zapatistas to the Argentinean *piqueteros* (see Bonnet, 2002), the insurrections in Bolivia (see Gutiérrez , 2009), Greece and Oaxaca (see Nasioka, 2017), the Arab Spring, etc. It is no coincidence that he refers to these mobilizations as *cracks*, in the sense that they are processes of breaking capitalist totality. To render tribute to a text by reviewing it would not be worth the effort if the text had nothing more to say or offer. However, *Crack Capitalism* contains in its very name the urgency of the reflection that continues to torment us: how can we curb the dynamic that is leading us to our own annihilation? (Holloway, 2019).

A tribute that repeats the words of an author and does not debate the text is devoid of content. The heart of a tribute is in the critical dialogue through which the text itself remains alive. In this article we intend to highlight Holloway's contributions to revolutionary theory, as well as enter into dialogue with the aspects that fuel the debate. Many of these aspects were already criticized by different authors when the problematics of some of its theoretical positionings still seemed distant. Reality today appears more challenging. If *Crack Capitalism* was published at a time of enthusiasm about the uprisings taking place around the world, today's dystopian image of capitalist brutality forces us to shift the focus of the analysis. The more the brutality, the more urgent the need for radical change. However, we have observed the emergence of a growing fetishism of the concrete (Postone, 2003; Scholz, 2015) and of an immediate praxis which negates the importance of critical theory and self-reflection. For, paradoxically, a revolutionary praxis without the *act of seeing*, without theory,[1] becomes blinded.

The analysis of *Crack Capitalism*, as of any other text, demands that we place the author within his own historical constellation; that is, in his debates and disputes with other schools of thought which inspire him and/or which he aspires to overcome. We witness how Holloway's entire work is a defence of the contributions of Marxism as a theory of struggle that must be emancipated from the orthodox readings of traditional Marxism. He does this through a reinterpretation of Marxist theory that is imbued by a particular reading of Theodor W. Adorno's *Negative Dialectics* (2004), which allows him to establish a dialogue between the meaning of revolution as a struggle in everyday life, with categories

[1] "The word 'theory' contains in itself the act of seeing, theory means contemplation, consideration" (Bloch, 1980: 97).

such as *negativity* and *anti-identity*. A challenge that involves the conciliation of Adorno's critique of immediacy with Vaneigem's (2012) concept of the "revolution of everyday life". That is, keeping in mind Adorno's critique of immediacy, Holloway attempts to reclaim the revolution of everyday life without falling into the trap of the immediate experience that captured the situationists and different currents within *operaismo*; however, his reading of Adorno serves him precisely to reclaim the immediacy of the negative, rather than to theorize the social mediations that characterize capitalist totality (Kurz, 2017).

Despite the abovementioned, the concept of the revolution of everyday life strongly echoed the concerns voiced by the autonomist, situationist, and anarchist struggles, as well as the multiple theoretical interpretations that emerged from the threshold of the uprisings of those years. The image of the girl sitting on a bench in the park reading a book is the expression of this proposal, and it is perhaps the most criticized one. It is the image of the *ordinary*, rebellious people that allows him to reflect on radical transformation "as a multiplicity of interstitial movements running from the particular" (Holloway, 2010: 11). The girl in the park is the image of irreverence and irrelevance that seeks to challenge the true militants, the revolutionary leaders, the partisan academics, and all those who cannot imagine a concept of revolution without the idea of the vanguard. These elements of insolence, sarcasm, and provocation are precisely what allow us to continue debating *Crack Capitalism* ten years after its publication.

The goal of this essay is to highlight the ontological foundation of Holloway's concept of *doing*, which is characteristic of human beings and is in constant tension with the idea of the *crack*. While cracks appear as a deterritorializing process against the different forms of domination, *doing* tends to be the common denominator of any social resistance, a movement that codifies struggles under one sole principle. That is, despite his effort to reflect on revolution through anti-identity, he tends to enclose it within the logic of the identity and the ontology of concrete labour. The ontology of *doing* becomes entrapped within the constellation of the concept of labour and, therefore, considers the other spheres of domination as deriving from it. In this sense, we argue that the *cracks* contribute to rendering visible the negation of domination as a constellation of spheres of power. If interstitial movements are presented as a multiplicity, it is because they express the negation of capitalism as a fragmented totality.

In the first section we will approach the relation between the twofold nature of labour and concepts as masks of struggle. We trace the importance of returning to the duality of labour as the axis of Marxist critique, which will allow us to better understand what Holloway refers to with the process of opening up categories in order to find living antagonism. In the second section, titled "*Doing* and the *Cracks*: a latent tension", we begin to approach the political consequences of reducing the multiplicity of the *cracks* to *doing* as their raw material. This contradiction was already present in Marx's work and informs Holloway's proposal. In the fourth section we review Holloway's subject, the "we", and how it relates to his concepts of anti-identity and concrete *doing*; we then go on to ask ourselves who "we" are and reflect on the consequences of this subject. Finally, in our last section, "Cracks or Barbarity", we elaborate a brief reflection on the reductionism of the dimension of gender in Holloway's critical theory and on the potentiality of the *cracks* to render visible the different dimensions of capitalist domination.

Concepts as Masks of Struggle

The struggles of *doing against labour*,[2] referred to by Holloway as *cracks*, have marked the critique of labour deployed during the events of May '68, sharpened by the crisis of orthodox Marxism and the Fordist model of production. In this sense, Holloway's argument is in constant debate with the concept of autonomy as the creation of spaces of exodus suggested by Hardt and Negri (2000, 2004, 2009) and with the critiques of value articulated by Postone (2003) and Grupo Krisis (1999).[3] Why return to the twofold nature of labour? For Holloway, the duality of labour as the axis of critique involves an opening up of the categories and the unveiling of the living antagonism located at their core, suggesting that human activity is not completely subsumed under the grammar of capital. The red thread of *Crack Capitalism* is that abstract labour is the process that weaves all social relations: time, space, class relations, gender, etc. It is a process of classification and identification that synthesizes society as a

[2] The Spanish edition includes the subtitle *doing against labour*, which presumably sums up the argument of the book.

[3] In none of these cases is this debate taken to its ultimate consequences; it rather constantly appears as a subtext that opens up different questions and problematics that crack the argument (see Day, 2005; Dinerstein, 2012; Scholz, 2010; Stoetzler, 2012).

totality, granting it a cohesive character that drags us towards its reproduction. Holloway argues that the central importance given by Marx to the twofold character of labour is an aspect that has been, until recently, almost forgotten within Marxism (Holloway, 2010: 88).

One of the most notable readings on this issue is that of Moishe Postone (2003), for whom the dialectical contradiction between *concrete labour* and *abstract labour* structures capitalist relations; therefore, he presents class struggle as an epiphenomenon of capitalist totality. In Holloway, the dual character of labour unfolds as a living antagonism that allows him to conceptualize totality as an incomplete process; for totality as a *fact*, alien to human practice, reproduces the very fetishization of social relations (Holloway, 2010: 92–96). That is why Holloway (2005, 2010) perceives totality as a process whereby constitution and existence are not separated; an antagonism between the processes of totalization and detotalization[4] that will allow him to link the *cracks* to the crisis of abstract labour.

Now then, returning to the duality of labour as the central axis of the critique of political economy requires reclaiming Marxism as a theory of struggle. This reclaiming is important for Holloway in that it underpins the rejection both of the transformation of Marxism into an academic paradigm and of the perception that identifies it as an "ideology of the state" (Holloway, 1991).[5] These perspectives rendered the Marxist language more sophisticated, he claims, but they were unable to eliminate the determinism that characterized the communist parties (Holloway, 1991: 10). The result of both perspectives has been catastrophic for Marx's critical theory. As Holloway argues, for decades "the struggles against the state [and against *academic language*] have taken the form not of struggles inspired by a 'truer Marxism' (…) but of struggles against Marxism as such" (Holloway, 1991: 9). Struggles for which the critique of value, the fetishism of the commodity and the twofold nature of labour belong to an old language that is no longer valid.

The evolutionist and determinist dimensions of the Marxist tradition, based on the primacy of the economic sphere, led contemporary struggles to go beyond the Marxist categories and find new theoretical referents

[4] On the concept of detotalization, see Tischler (2012).

[5] Such was the case of the Regulation School or the state theory of Poulantzas, whose influence on the contemporary left can still be felt today.

that completely abandoned Marxism as a point of reference. The tendency of Marxism to consider the rest of the spheres of domination as epiphenomena of class struggle, such as the patriarchate or racism; or the Marxist cult of hierarchy, discipline, and the organization of the Leninist party as a sine qua non for revolution are elements that undeniably justify this rejection (see Federici, 2021). However, it must be stressed that this rejection is shaped by a traditional reading of Marx's critical theory; that is, a reading that is bound to a vision of the world as it is.

To *emancipate* Marx[6] from these determinist approaches that separate theory from praxis was the explicit task undertaken by various authors linked to *Open Marxism*, amongst them John Holloway. In the Introduction to *Open Marxism III*, the authors argue that, for the orthodox perspective, "the specific contribution of Marxism to the comprehension of our social world is understood as the analysis of the objective conditions of social practice" (Bonefeld, 1995: 2). It follows that social antagonism was perceived as a product of the very contradictions of capital as an *automatic subject*, which rendered Marxism a theory of capital and not of struggle. The particularity of *Open Marxism* is that, while it distances itself from the tradition of historic materialism, it reflects on Marxian categories not as instruments of a "scientific" analysis but as a critique that rearticulates the relation between theory and praxis. To perceive the categories as imbued by antagonism is an attempt against so-called orthodox Marxism, which understood the relation between theory and praxis, between the logic of capital and human practice, as an external one.

Holloway revisits Marx's early writings to stress the fact that, in capitalist society, the products of human practice appear as autonomous entities that determine social activity; this leads to the emergence of idols of the social becoming that dominate their creators under the form of god, law, state, money, etc. In societies conceived religiously, metaphysical entities appear as the creators of human beings and not as creations of social activity. It is a process of constant mystification of social relations through which domination is reproduced (Marx, 2009). As Marx argued, the same occurs in capitalism: classic political economy interpreted the world on the basis of categories that are presented as *subjects* that determine the social mode of existence of the human being and its practice.

[6] See Volume 3 of *Open Marxism* (Bonefeld, 1995).

It is no coincidence that, in *Capital* (1982), Marx constantly offers allegories between political economy and theology. Therefore, to open up the categories is to revisit Marxian critique *ad hominem*, which wishes to reveal the inversion between subject and object in capitalist society.

Marxian critique *ad hominem* presupposes examining social phenomena not as things but as *forms-processes* that are historically determined by social activity. On this basis, *Open Marxism* suggests understanding experience as constitution and negation, as opposition and resistance, as the attempt to theorize this experience as the starting point and substance of critique (Bonefeld, 1995: 3). This way, *Open Marxism* tries to distance itself from the classic category of consciousness that imbued all revolutionary theory during the past century. It shows that, although experience is mediated by the processes of domination, this does not mean that it is completely trapped within them, but rather that it must be considered as an antagonistic field that expresses class struggle. Furthermore, under the reading of *Negative Dialectics*, Holloway argues that opening up the categories entails seeing within them "non-identity under the aspect of identity" (Adorno quoted in Holloway, 1991: 13). To open up categories such as labour, commodity, money, or the state is an attempt to find within them the human practice which constitutes them but, at the same time, negates them.

From this point of view, the concept of class must not remain bound to the chains of the positivist thinking reproduced by Marxism (Gunn, 1987). For *Open Marxism*, as for Holloway, class does not amount to a concept with sociological pretensions that describe a social group and its structural position, whose characteristics, as well as objectives, motivations, demands, etc., can be classified (see García Vela, 2017). Class is considered a constant process that reduces human activity to a closed identity through which capitalist relations are reproduced (Holloway, 2010: 114–118). Class, race, and gender are masks imposed by the processes of identification of a society mediated by abstract labour.[7] However, they appear with an ontological status, independent from the capitalist relations that mediate them and constitute them as concrete forms of an abstract domination. If they are not presented as such it is because, to paraphrase Marx (1982: 719), *fictio juris* [legal fiction] maintains the appearance of freedom and equality guaranteed by law.

[7] Although, as we shall see in Holloway, there is a hierarchy amongst them.

The refusal of *Open Marxism* to think in terms of static structures suggests a reflection that is based on antagonistic processes and unveils the immanent relation between class and class struggle. That is why Holloway (2005: 144) insists that the working class is more than the personification of capitalist relations. Class suggests a process of struggle against our classification, against the processes that reduce human creative activity to abstract labour and its identification with totality. Through his concept of *anti-identity*, Holloway tries to find the lines that interrupt the blind force of totality. Even if the untrue capitalist Whole is preserved through the antagonism that individuals experience, as Adorno (2004: 311) suggested, for Holloway there is the intrinsic capacity to negate and overcome capitalist domination—expressed subjectively under the form of the *scream* or the *crack*. Thus, to return to the twofold character of labour is to return to the central antagonism that characterizes capitalist society, which Holloway crystallizes in the formula of *doing in-against-and-beyond abstract labour*.

Doing and the *Cracks*: A Latent Tension

Antagonism creates *cracks*. This is the starting point for Holloway's theorizing. *Cracks* explain the flow of *doing*, an excess that creates ruptures in the totalizing processes of capitalist domination (Holloway, 2010). The concept of the *crack* is part of a *new anticapitalist grammar* with which to refer to the social experiments of the last three or four decades. In general terms, the emergence of this new grammar can be understood as a reaction to the failed attempt of Marxism as a theory of struggle and as part of a growing consensus that the critique of value is unable to grasp the different dimensions of capitalist power.[8] In this context, a vast array of concepts emerge which try to update Marxist critique, although what can be more broadly observed is the abandonment of all ties to Marxism, relegated to a footnote in the history of struggles.

[8] On the patriarchate that produces commodities and the split of value, see Scholz (2015). An interesting analysis that at the same time points out the limits of the critique of value for the analysis of gender and/or racism as well as discusses the immanent relation between the patriarchate and capitalism. This is a relation which, we believe, is discussed only superficially in Holloway's argument (2010).

Thus, while the proletariat has lost its status as the revolutionary subject, new subjectivities have become the analytical axes of contemporary critical thought: the *multitude*, the indigenous peoples, the subaltern classes, women, etc. Something similar can be said of the category of revolution, which has lost its central character and has been displaced by concepts such as the defence of the commons, autonomy and direct democracy as forms of organization alternative to capitalism. This implies that the idea of universal social transformation has been replaced by territorialized and fragmented social changes; that is, changes that do not go against capital or the state but are reduced to a logic of defending what exists as something that can still be improved. According to Holloway (2010), these categories are characterized by an increasing tendency towards positivization, which is characteristic of the analyses that eliminate the dialectic between totality and struggle. This tendency became clear in so-called identity politics, where resistance unfolds within the logic of democracy and respect for the law,[9] but it can also be found within other, more radical forms of struggle. In this case, the positivization is revealed when the social experiments of resistance are perceived as spaces of exodus or alternatives to the capitalist dynamic that tend to be territorialized or articulated through the identification of the struggles with their militants, stress the primacy of practice, and produce absolute truths that become self-referential.

Social synthesis presupposes an active field of classification that allows for the reproduction of capitalist relations. That is, the existence of capital as a specific mode of social organization imposes the identification of human practice with specific roles and/or functions such as housewife, patriot, woman, working class, etc. (also see Federici, 2004). That is why Holloway (2005) insists that the struggle must be conceptualized as an act of negation of these modes of identification. It follows that what appears as an existence already established by the *phantasmagorical world of commodities* must be questioned on the basis of the non-separation between the constituted and the constituent; as a constant antagonism that runs through the very categories of thought and praxis. In this sense, the *cracks* do not say that the time of struggle is determined by the contradiction between the productive forces and the relations of

[9] It is no coincidence that Mouffe (1993: 77) argued that the stake for *pluralist and radical democracy* was the creation of *chains of equivalence* between the different struggles for equality.

production, as if we were before a quasi-automatic process, neither by a revolutionary subject that is the product of this contradiction. Capital depends on the dominated for its reproduction (Holloway, 2005). Thus, there is a dialectical relation between totality and struggle, and at the core of this relation lies the very fragility of the domination (Holloway, 2017: 140).

However, the particularity of the capitalist social synthesis is that, while it fragments, it is also constituted as a unity-in-separation. Guy Debord (2014: 3) and the situationist referred to this process with the concept of *spectacle*, in the sense that it is the unfolding of the fetishism of the commodity under late capitalism. For Debord (2014: 2), "everything that was directly lived has receded into a representation" that holds the world together. The result of this process, which follows the rhythms of the division of labour, is the constant fragmentation of the world: between production and consumption, between working hours and free time, and so on and so forth. According to Debord (2014: 8–9), the fragmentation of the world creates in subjects the impossibility of an immediate experience. For, in the society of the spectacle, the image of the world that the subject perceives is that of a shattered mirror or a kaleidoscope: the image of a fragmented whole. The problem of conceptualizing reality as a spectacle is that the fetishism of the commodity is presented as a nearly finished process against which there is no point in fighting. That is, totality and struggle remain two separate spheres.

For Holloway (2010), the theorization of the experience of resistance and negation under the form of the *cracks* suggests two things. On the one hand, that antagonism is immanent in capitalist society and, on the other, that struggles are unfinished processes that are constantly abused or coerced by social synthesis. Inspired by an image by Edgar Allan Poe, Holloway (2010: 8) portrays capitalist totality as walls that are closing in on us and are "threatening to crush us all to death". Theoretically, the *cracks* are an allegory of the movement against the fragmentation caused by categories of thought through which domination is reproduced: citizenship, the individual, the people, the nation, representative democracy, and the state, amongst others. They are categorizations referring to a specific type of social cohesion that emerge from the process of abstraction of the social relations that constitute them (Holloway, 2010: 58–59) and reflect the long process of the positivization of thought. That is why he insists on analysing social becoming on the basis of the concrete mode in which negation is expressed, at times as struggles against class, racism, or gender-based violence. The *crack* calls upon the diversity of horizontal experiments as schizoid and multidimensional practices of resistance which, even if not always visibly, are linked through lines of continuity (Holloway, 2010: 73–75).

Holloway (2010: 220) translates these lines of continuity as the antagonism between *doing* and *abstract labour*. This antagonism becomes the line of continuity between the girl in the park, zapatismo, and the great uprisings, and shows that "Hope lies in the dual, self-antagonistic character of human doing" (Holloway, 2010: 86). From this perspective, both small everyday actions and the greatest insurrections and uprisings express what does not fit into the classifications imposed by *abstract labour*, that is, anti-identity. This is an attractive conceptualization that echoes the famous phrase by Vaneigem that "people who talk about revolution and class struggle without referring explicitly to everyday life, without understanding what is subversive about love and what is positive in the refusal of the constraints, such people have a corpse in their mouth" (Vaneigem, 2012: 14). The *cracks* are expressions of the *social flow of doing* that resist being subordinated to the classifying dynamic of *abstract labour*, the foundation of the axiom "*we are the crisis of capital*" (see Holloway, 2019). Paradoxically, this formulation suggests two dimensions of the concept of labour that stop mediating each other. The result is the confrontation of a "capitalist being" and a "non-capitalist being": *Being* against *Being*. The ontology of *doing* against the capitalist ontology. In fact, all conceptual pairs that are derived from the confrontation of *abstract labour* and *concrete doing*, that is, fetishization/defetishization, power-over/power-to, positivization/negation, express a separation that is necessary if we are to find hope.

It follows that *abstract labour* becomes the alienated and alienating form of *doing*, while the latter is the anti-identitarian force[10] that overflows the totalizing dynamic of the former (Holloway, 2010: 84). As we can see, *doing* as the *push towards self-determination* is the metonymy of *concrete or useful labour* referred to by Marx. Therefore, *doing* is the *conscious and free vital activity* that characterizes the human being as a *generic being* but is negated by the alienated labour of the capitalist form (Holloway, 2010: 87–88). It is clear that Holloway follows the

[10] Holloway's (2009) reading of *Negative Dialectics* is an effort to politicize the concept of negativity through anti-identity, which is not necessarily the same as the non-identity found in Adorno.

line of argumentation of Marx's *1844 Manuscripts*, who, aligned with Aristotelian logic, argues that what separates *men* from animals is their *conscious and free vital activity*.

Insofar as social relations are mediated by alienated labour, the result is the alienation of the product from its activity, from its own activity, which is at the same time the alienation from itself and from others; that is, the alienation from its own nature as a social being and its relegation to an *animal* life (Marx, 2009: 28–35). This ontological conception of concrete labour reappears in *Capital*, particularly in passages such as the following: "Labour, then, as a creator of use-values, as useful labour, is a condition of human existence which is independent of all forms of society; it is an eternal natural necessity which mediates the metabolism between man and nature, and therefore human life itself" (Marx, 1982: 133).

The emphasis put on labour as "independent of all forms" or as a "condition of human existence" and a "natural necessity" gives labour a transhistorical character which is problematic. This is an assertion that not only clashes with the specific character of labour in capitalist society, as Marx himself contradictorily affirms later on, but also, above all, has grave consequences for thinking of radical change.

Holloway tries to eliminate the transhistorical character of the concept of labour in Marx by arguing that what is "*common* in all forms of society" is useful or concrete labour, but that it is a "historical concept" given that "useful labour changes in each historical epoch and can only be understood in its historical context" (Holloway, 2010: 91). If this is so, it is not clear what should be understood as the "historical character of labour". For, if labour is common in all social formations even if its specific form depends on the historical context, there must be an underlying common *essence* in labour, independent from the social form, which allows it to exist in different *forms* in different historical periods. An *essence* that characterizes human becoming as a *generic being*. Therefore, this is not simply a language issue.[11] Holloway's attempt to clarify the Marxian concept of *useful labour* does not solve the problem. Neither does substituting *doing*

[11] Ana C. Dinerstein (2012) also interprets *doing* as a metonymy of *concrete* or *useful labour*. That is why in her article *doing* sometimes appears as *concrete doing* and others as *useful doing*. Holloway affirms that, following an observation made by Engels in a footnote in *Capital*, he prefers to use the word *doing* instead of work to refer to the social activity that creates use values (Holloway, 2010: 272). Therefore, concrete labour (work) and *doing* appear as interchangeable terms.

for *concrete* or *useful labour* change the fact that an ontological aspect prevails in the same concept.[12]

In both Marx's *concrete labour* and Holloway's *doing* there is an underlying prime essence that determines the mode of existence of the social form as the main social mediation between human beings and nature. The full realization of *doing* presupposes the unfolding of the *generic being* as a force whose realization is obstructed by the existing social totality (also see Holloway, 2017). The emancipation of *doing* from *abstract labour* would imply setting in motion the realization of the true potential of humans as social beings. Capitalism is a mode of abstract domination, a constant process of abstraction that presupposes that *doing* amounts to a non-alienated mode of labour. Thus, *doing* is the key category for understanding the processes of subordination as well as of insubordination in capitalist totality.

Despite how attractive this suggestion might seem to certain expressions of struggle, it unveils a latent tension between Holloway's *cracks* and *doing*. While the *cracks* refer to heterogeneous forms of the negation of domination as totality—that is, to the negation of the different spheres that make up the power weave—*doing* homogenizes them. While the concept of *crack* describes a movement that walks down different paths, *doing* reduces it to one direction. To think of *doing* as the common denominator of the *cracks* is problematic. If *cracks* refer to the negation of domination as a constellation of abstract spheres of power (see Adorno, 2005), we assume the *cracks* do not have a centre and are created in a schizoid fashion. However, if we emphasize the *doing*, all these *cracks* are reduced to concrete or useful labour as a prime essence, for which all other expressions of domination become secondary categories. With this we wish to highlight the complex connection between the different spheres of power that constitute capitalist totality; otherwise, we can

[12] Marshall Sahlins (2013) criticizes the axiom of historical materialism that labour is the primary determination in any social formation, given that it implies that instrumental rationality prevails in any historical period. In this sense, the point made by Postone on the difference between the young and the old Marx is pertinent. It is not the separation made by Althusser. Postone suggests that the early Marx is essentialist and proposes a transcendent critique, whereas the older Marx assumes the stance of a more immanent critique. However, it appears that Postone does not completely escape the ontology of labour either, when he argues that some type of labour will continue to exist in any social formation.

see the orthodox scheme that separated the base from the superstructure entering through the back door. This perspective reduced struggles to the issue of labour and considered other forms of resistance a mere product that derived from it. For example, the patriarchate was reduced to a secondary category that obeyed the "relations of production". This tension between the *crack* and *doing* is being weaved and is expressed through paradoxes that revolutionary theory must confront, as we shall see in what follows.

Who Are "We"?

We have approached some central aspects of Holloway's work in order to understand how it reclaims Marxist theory as a theory of struggle. We see that *doing* is the key category for understanding the dialectic between the processes of subordination and insubordination to capitalist totality, but we have also begun to outline some of the tensions that can be found in his proposal. In this section we propose a dialogue and a going deeper into the problematics that exist in Holloway's argument on the basis of certain important aspects that have been previously pointed out by Roswitha Scholz (2010) and Marcel Stoetzler (2005, 2012). As we shall see, these critiques focus on the fact that Holloway: (a) tends to lose sight of the strength of totality, (b) allows a binary, non-dialectical taxonomy that tends to fetishize anti-identity, and (c) ontologizes concrete *doing*. As a whole, these critiques point towards the danger of echoing conservative screams that also claim to be anticapitalist.

According to Scholz (2010, s/p), in Holloway's work there is, above all, an effort to "criticize the fetish in a way that it becomes adequate for empiricism and susceptible to practice". According to the author, in doing so, Holloway reduces the critique of the fetish to a subjective dimension that turns its back on the objective moment of the dialectical relation subject/object. Scholz (2010) argues that, in conceptualizing the fetish as a process, Holloway strips the commodity *form* of its very character which renders it "de facto externally opposed to the human being", even though it is made by the latter. In other words, in the concept of fetishism as fetishization there is a dissolution of the objective structures in action (*doing*); consequently, it is difficult to conceive the way in which totality mediates subjectivity (*the scream*),[13] for it avoids the question of how the abstract spheres of power configure the particular subject. Although Holloway argues that the subject is schizophrenic to the extent that it negates the forms of capitalist domination but also reproduces them, his emphasis on the moments of negation suggests that social emancipation underlies subjective power itself, consciously ignoring how totality scars the individual.

Besides the abovementioned, Scholz (2010) claims that, while Holloway tries to reconciliate critical theory with the elements of *operaismo* or (post)*operaismo*, he distances himself from the reflexive moment which was characteristic of Adorno. That is, Holloway translates Adorno's thinking into the language of instrumentality, which the latter so opposed. Holloway "'acts' and behaves completely within the logic of identity without mediation" and, in doing so, he inverts Adorno's negative dialectics (Scholz, 2010, s/p). It follows that, in the non-identity referred to by Holloway, there is an underlying "ontologized dimension of 'doing', of everyday life and of praxis, a dimension that ultimately must bear no relation to capitalism"[14] (Scholz, 2010, s/p). Identity and non-identity are analyzed as a "Zero or One" circuit (Scholz, 2010, s/p), in which identity is identified with capital and abstract labour, while non-identity is identified with the "we" and with *doing*. This presupposes that, as we said in the previous section, the nature of the human being is inherently "innocent" but is alienated by capital (Kurz, 2017; Scholz, 2010, s/p). Scholz has a point here: the act of defining non-identity as something emancipating per se turns it into something positive. That is why, against all attempts to avoid the positivization of his formulations by pointing out that non-identity is the content that does not fit into the *form* (identity),[15] these critiques emphasize that, in Holloway, non-identity is positivized under the guise of negativity or anti-identity. The

[13] Surely, Scholz's critique is linked to the passages in which Adorno approaches *objectivity and reification*, where he claims that "The thinker may easily comfort himself by imagining that in the dissolution of reification, of the merchandise character, he possesses the philosophers' stone" (Adorno, 2004: 190).

[14] Also see García Vela (2019) and Schäbel (2019).

[15] Holloway claims that (2010: 85) "we start from that which does not fit in, that which overflows, that which is not contained, that which exists not only in but also against-and-beyond. We start not from the stillness of identity but from the moving of non- or, better, anti-identity. We start dialectically, but not with a dialectic understood as interaction but rather as the negative restlessness of misfitting, of insufficiency".

latter becomes a formula defining the subjects and struggles that come close or distance themselves from the context of negativity. Anti-identity is presented as if it were the identifying principle.

Firmly following Adorno,[16] Scholz (2010) argues that non-identity is not something that leads us to emancipation in itself. This is the presupposition on which her critique of the *dissociation of value* lies, according to which, although non-identity is the Otherness that is excluded by the very capitalist administrative rationality, its existence is at the same time necessary for the reproduction of the same capitalist rationality (Scholz, 2015). Therefore, we understand that non-identity and identity are two poles of the same relation that constitutes capitalist barbarity. The non-identical is the opposite pole of identity, they both constitute one same relation as a fragmented totality. As the following passage suggests,

> The world spirit, a worthy object of definition, would have to be defined as permanent catastrophe. Under the all-subjugating identity principle, whatever does not enter into identity, whatever eludes rational planning in the realm of means, turns into frightening retribution for the calamity which identity brought on the nonidentical. (Adorno, 2004: 320)

Thus, identity and non-identity constitute the principle of identity. That is, the process of defining the non-identical defines the identical and vice versa.[17] According to Hegel (1977: 472), in the principle of identity, identity and non-identity must be seen as a relation-in-motion and not as isolated elements with a priori properties. Its own antithetical movement constitutes the character of the two poles and not its existence per se. Unlike the aforementioned, for Holloway the very existence of the subject-doer acquires an anti-identitarian character.

However, if Hegel focuses on the identity of the identity and of the non-identity as a dialect that shapes the Whole, Adorno (2005: 50) counters that "The whole is the false". With this, he substantiates his negative dialectics that refers to the non-identity of identity and non-identity. That is, while Hegelian dialectics points towards the reconciliation of subject and object, for Adorno, the dialectics between the identical and the

[16] Adorno (2004: 158) says: "The nonidentical is not to be obtained directly, as something positive on its part, nor is it obtainable by a negation of the negative".

[17] The principle of exchange is based on this dialectic between identity and non-identity. This text does not intend to go deeper into this relation for lack of space.

non-identical is what reproduces capitalist brutality. Therefore, he denies the possibility of reconciliation in capitalist totality without negating the existence of antagonism. However, Adorno sees in antagonism what is immanent in totality. As the following passage suggests,

> Civil society is an antagonistic totality. It survives only in and through its antagonisms and is not able to resolve them. In the work by Hegel that is most notorious for its restorationist tendencies, its apology for the status quo, and its cult of the state, the Philosophy of Right, that is stated bluntly. (Adorno, 1993: 28)

The dialectics between the identical and the non-identical permeates all mechanisms of domination, as expressed in racism, sexism, and classism. That is why Adorno (2004: 362) claims that "Auschwitz confirmed the philosopheme of pure identity as death". With this affirmation, he is telling us that fascism is not simply the brutal implementation of identitarian thought but the more violent expression of the dialectics between identity and non-identity that led to the . For that reason, Critical Theory must not fall into the trap of an untroubled and simplifying thinking, whereby critique is reduced to easy—and, above all, dangerous—dualities. Holloway is, precisely, often criticized for tending to grant a priori properties to identity and to non-identity, as if each pole were predetermined. This eliminates the dialectic between the two poles, turning negation into a theology (Chrysis, 2009: 58).

That is why Scholz points out that Holloway's theory falls into a duality between "Zero or One", whereby *doing* does not only have an "ontologized dimension" but is also itself identified with anti-identity. This, following Scholz (2010), makes him abandon the perspective of concrete totality and hurls him into an immediate praxis that rejects "all requirements of a rational foundation", the use of an emotionally attractive language (doing, done, scream, everyday resistance, dignity, etc.), and the inversion of Adorno's negative dialectics. At this point, we would like to express our disagreement with Scholz regarding the rejection of all intellectualism by Holloway. There is no such rejection "of all intellectualism". In any case, there is genuine concern for offering a revolutionary theory at moments when thinking of revolution has become more difficult (González, 2019). Holloway's work is an attempt that risks falling into contradictions which allow us to open up the dialogue. Using these critiques as a starting point, we would like to point out that not all negations of capital amount to a search for social emancipation, not all represent a threat to capitalism, neither are they all interested in radical change, as Stoetzler suggests (2012: 197).

In this sense, Stoetzler (2005, 2012) argues that neither *Change the World Without Taking Power* nor *Crack Capitalism* offer a theory of fascism that explains to what extent anticapitalist movements—to which Holloway refers as *screams* or as the unfolding of a *social flow of doing*—can be considered starting points for communism and not the confirmation of the more terrifying spectres of capitalism. Stoetzler considers that neither the *scream* nor *doing* refer simply to the negation of capitalism, perhaps even less so to the construction of communism. The problem for Stoetzler lies in that in both the *scream* and in *doing* a certain ambiguity prevails, one which is not resolved by branding struggles and movements as "anticapitalist". Fascism was also anticapitalist, he claims, as were other nationalist movements of the past which played a functional role in the overcoming of capitalist crises (Stoetzler, 2012: 196). Stoetzler goes further in saying that a revolutionary theory should also renounce the adjective "anticapitalist", for it does not have much to offer to critical theory. The author argues that anticapitalism has only resulted in the updating of "endless discussions about class and non-class movements" which prevailed within Marxism for decades (Stoetzler, 2005: 195).

It follows that Holloway's work deploys a much more abstract theory of the subject. A theory that refers to the old concept of the proletariat under the more inclusive figure of "we". The problem is that the more abstract the concept becomes, the easier it is for it to turn into an identifying force. Or, rather, the more abstract the *scream/doing* becomes, the easier it is for it to fall into an ideology (Scholz, 2010; Stoetzler, 2012). Who is that "we"? Everything seems to indicate that he refers to the zapatistas, the anarchists, to the girl in the park and to cooperatives that sell coffee in mugs with Che Guevara's image on them. But does it also include the voters of the far right and the nationalist groups that seek to put a stop to the abstract dynamic of capital? Let us recall Postone's (1980: 114) words: "Auschwitz was a factory to 'destroy value,' that is, to destroy the personifications of the abstract. Its organization was that of a fiendish industrial process, the aim of which was to 'liberate' the concrete from the abstract". Therefore, if Auschwitz represented the culmination of the fetishism of concrete labour, how much of the motto "work sets you free" does not echo the *scream* against *abstract labour*?

It is no coincidence that Stoetzler (2005) arguments that the ambiguity of the *scream/doing* can lead to movements and/or subjects that scream and who, with their *doing*, might reject the more harmful aspects of capital but, at the same time, be indifferent towards racism, sexism, antisemitism, etc. If the significant core of Holloway's subject is human creativity, are the holocaust, the atomic bomb, and genocides not the product of this very creativity? How can we be sure that the fetishizing dimensions that characterize *abstract labour* are not present in concrete labour or in *doing*?

Cracks or Barbarity?

We have argued that the effort to find a line of continuity between diverse social experiments that pursue emancipation leads to the reduction of this diversity to an identifying principle: productive activity. Concrete or useful *doing* turns into a parameter that hierarchizes and classifies struggles on the basis of a productivist element that presents profound similarities to the practices that characterized traditional Marxism; or one that serves to point out the identitarian or anti-identitarian elements of other expressions of rebelliousness. It is a contradiction in terms of a theory that aims at defying the principle of identity that prevails in the critical thinking of the left. Furthermore, we have pointed out that to speak from the viewpoint of *doing* can lead to disregarding different manifestations of domination such as racism, sexism, antisemitism, etc. That is why Scholz (1992, 2015; also see Kurz, 2017) argues that an androcentric perspective prevails in all critical theory of value; the same occurs with the theory of *doing*.

The anthropocentric image of capitalist modernity of the man who creates, the man who creates the world and himself (Echeverría, 2010: 226), presupposes the domination of Otherness. It he is presented as a human being in the sense of a neutral entity, this is because it is a symbolic transfiguration of the patriarchate. In this image, the man-creator is a productive, dynamic, and spiritual subject; while woman (or the slaves or the indigenous) are presented as an object, identical to nature and to an untouched territory which must be dominated. That is, as territories-bodies ready to be conquered. Holloway's attempt to analyse gender relations reveals the difficulties facing Marxism and the critical theory of value in approaching them in depth. While the critique is based on the *generic being* as an abstract subject, the gender-based dimensions that run through this concept are not questioned.[18] The creating subject or the doer is reasserted as a male or masculine subject, while the concept of the *generic being* bears the masculine mark that emanates from Aristotelian philosophy.

It follows that the primacy of productive activity or concrete *doing* reproduces the androcentric perspective where the patriarchate seems to be a product of alienated labour. Holloway emphatically argues that gender relations emanate from labour, as the following passage suggests:

> It is not that gender conflict, say, must be added to class conflict to understand society: it is rather that the very concept of binary gender divide between men and women is the product of the abstraction of doing into labour. *In this sense, the conflict between doing and labour is prior to other conflicts*. (Holloway, 2010: 222–223. Italics added)

This argument avoids touching upon the way in which capitalist society reconfigures gender relations. This reconfiguration is central in that it becomes one of the foundations for the reproduction of the mode of capitalist organization.

The uprisings of recent years, where gender has become one of the parameters for radical transformation, have revealed that political correctness is not enough to analyse the dialectic between the patriarchate and capitalism (see Kurz, 2017). If *cracks* are the allegory for the movement against the fragmentation that certain categories of thought entail and through which domination is reproduced (citizenship, individual, people, nation, representative democracy, amongst others), as we have pointed out, these categories must necessarily question the gender relations that produce the concepts man/woman. For, as Richard Gunn suggests:

> The suggestion may be hazarded that the only possible line of critical questioning which seems fertile is that which asks whether the capital-labour relation is the sole such relation of struggle which, in all its richness, structures our lives. And here there can be no question of supplanting Marx:

[18] The political animal of Aristotle already presupposed the exclusion of women and slaves: his definition referred to a society that separated the private sphere (*oikos*-home) from the public sphere (*agora*-market). Under this argument, the free citizen occupied himself with the political sphere, while the woman, as a "failed case of essential nature" (see Sanabria, 1987: 23; see also Scholz, 1992) was relegated to the private sphere.

other such relations (sexual and racial relations, for example) are mediated through the capital relation just as, for its part, it exists as mediated through them. (Gunn, 1987, Note 16)

Perhaps the paradoxes in Holloway's argument respond to the moment of urgency we are experiencing. As the barbarity grows, so does the anguish to act against it, to stop it, to transform it. However, the more urgent it becomes to develop a revolutionary theory, the more the time comes to place the thinking of the left under scrutiny. As Holloway (2020) recently manifested "critical thinking does not have the right to get comfortable". Today, more than ever, capitalism has shown that it has not only come to the world "dripping from head to toe, from every pore, with blood and dirt" (Marx, 1982: 926), but that its existence depends on the reproduction of the dynamic of terror that characterizes it. Capitalist domination must be understood as a fragmented totality, constituted by a weave of abstract spheres of power that feed off each other. There can be no primacy of one sphere over the other. So yes, let us think of *cracks* as the unfolding of experiments that try to break with capitalist barbarity in its multiple dimensions. We find ourselves at a moment in which we must face the imperative: *cracks* or barbarity! It becomes more and more evident that Holloway's work reflects this dilemma.

References

Adorno, T. W. (1993). *Hegel: Three Studies*. MIT Press.

Adorno, T. W. (2004). *Negative Dialectics*. Routledge.

Adorno, T. W. (2005). *Minima Moralia: Reflections on a Damaged Life*. Verso.

Bloch, E. (1980). *Abschied von der Utopie?* Suhrkamp.

Bonefeld, W., Gunn, R., Holloway, J., & Psychopedis, K. (1995). *Open Marxism, Volume III: Emancipating Marx*. Pluto Press.

Bonnet, A. (2002). Que se vayan todos: Crisis, insurrección y caída de la convertibilidad. *Cuadernos del Sur, 18*(33), 39–70.

Chrysis, A. (2009). *On the Dialectic of Power and Revolution: Reflections on John Holloway's work Change the World Without Taking Power* [Για την διαλεκτική εξουσίας και επανάστασης: Σκέψεις με αφετηρία το έργο του John Holloway ας Αλλάξουμε τον κόσμο δίχως να καταλάβουμε την εξουσία]. Editions KPSM (Greek edition).

Day, R. J. (2005). *Gramsci Is Dead: Anarchist Currents in the Newest Social Movements*. Pluto Press.

Debord, G. (2014). *The Society of Spectacle*. Bureau of Public Secrets.

Dinerstein, A. C. (2012). Interstitial Revolution: On the Explosive Fusion of Negativity and Hope. *Capital & Class, 36*(3), 521–540.
Echeverría, B. (2010). *Definición de la cultura*. Ítaca/Fondo de Cultura Económica.
Federici, S. (2004). *Caliban and the Witch*. Autonomedia.
Federici, S. (2021). *Patriarchy of the Wage: Notes on Marx, Gender, and Feminism*. PM Press.
García Vela, A. (2017). El *open marxism* y la clase como lucha. In M. Modonesi, A. García Vela, & M. Vignau Loría (Eds.), *El concepto de la clase social en la teoría marxista contemporánea* (pp. 121–140). UNAM, ICSyH BUAP, Ediciones La Biblioteca.
García Vela, A. Objectivity and Critical Theory: Debating Open Marxism. In A. C. Dinerstein, A. G. Vela, E. González, & J. Holloway (Eds.), *Open Marxism 4: Against a Closing World* (pp. 47–62). Pluto Press.
González Cruz, E. (2019). From Revolution to Democracy: The Loss of the Emancipatory Perspective. In A. C. Dinerstein, A. G. Vela, E. González, & J. Holloway (Eds.), *Open Marxism 4: Against a Closing World* (pp. 155–167). Pluto Press.
Gunn, R. (1987). Notes on Class. In *Common Sense* (No. 2). https://libcom.org/library/notes-class. Consultado 5 Feb 2021.
Gutiérrez Aguilar, R. (2009). *Los ritmos del pachakuti: levantamiento y movilización en Bolivia (2000–2005)*. ICSyH-BUAP, Bajo Tierra Ediciones, Sísifo Ediciones.
Hardt, M., & Negri, A. (2000). *Empire*. Harvard University Press.
Hardt, M., & Negri, A. (2004). *Multitude: War and Democracy in the Age of Empire*. Penguin Press.
Hardt, M., & Negri, A. (2009). *Commonwealth*. Belknap Harvard.
Heinrich, M. (2004). *An Introduction to the Three Volumes of Karl Marx's Capital*. Monthly Review Press.
Hegel, G. W. F. (1977). *Phenomenology of Spirit*. Oxford University Press.
Holloway, J. (1991). In the Beginning Was the Scream. *Common Sense, 11*, 69–78.
Holloway, J. (2004). ¿Dónde está la lucha de clases? Holloway J. (comp.) *Clase= Lucha. Antagonismo social y marxismo crítico* (pp. 85–102). Ediciones Herramienta, Instituto de Ciencia Sociales y Humanidades "Alfonso Vélez Pliego"de la BUAP.
Holloway, J. (2005). *Change the World Without Taking Power: The Meaning of Revolution Today*. Pluto Press.
Holloway, J. (2009). Why Adorno? Negativity and Revolution: Adorno and Political Activism. In J. Holloway, F. Matamoros, & T. Tischler (Eds.), *Negativity and Revolution: Adorno and Political Activism* (pp. 12–17). Pluto Press.

Holloway, J. (2010). *Crack Capitalism*. Pluto Press.
Holloway, J. (2017). *Una lectura antiidentitaria de El Capital*. Herramienta Ediciones, Sísifo ediciones, Bajo Tierra Ediciones, Instituto de Ciencia Sociales y Humanidades "Alfonso Vélez Pliego"de la BUAP.
Holloway, J. (2019). *We Are the Crisis of Capital: A John Holloway Reader*. PM Press.
Holloway, J. (2020). *¿Todavía hay debates?* http://comunizar.com.ar/todavia-hay-debates. Accessed 3 Jan 2021.
Krisis Group. (1999). *Manifesto Against Labour.* https://www.krisis.org/1999/manifesto-against-labour/. Accessed 11 Apr 2021.
Kurz, R. (2017). *We Are Everything: The Misery of (Post)-operaismo*. Palim Psao. http://www.palim-psao.fr/2017/01/we-are-everything.the-misery-of-post-operaismo-by-robert-kurz-negri-tronti-holloway-cie.html. Accessed 11 Apr 2021.
Laclau, E., & Mouffe, C. (2001 [1985]). *Hegemony and Socialist Strategy: Towards a Radical Democratic Politics*. Verso.
Marx, K. (1970). *Introduction: Critique of Hegel's Philosophy of Right*. Oxford University Press.
Marx, K. (1982). *Capital: A Critique of Political Economy* (Vol. 1). Penguin Books.
Marx, K. (2009 [1844]). Estranged Labour. In *Economic and Philosophical Manuscripts of 1844. First Manuscript* (pp. 28–35). Progress Publishers.
Mouffe, C. (1993). *The Return of the Political*. Verso.
Nasioka, K. (2017). *Ciudades en insurrección: Oaxaca 2006/Atenas 2008*. Universidad de Guadalajara.
Postone, M. (1980). Anti-Semitism and National Socialism: Notes on the German Reaction to "Holocaust." *New German Critique, 19*, 97–115.
Postone, M. (2003). *Time, Labour, and Social Domination: A Reinterpretation of Marx's Critical Theory*. Cambridge University Press.
Sahlins, M. (2013). *Culture and Practical Reason*. University of Chicago Press.
Sanabria, J. R. (1987). *Filosofía del hombre: antropología filosófica*. Editorial Porrúa.
Schäbel, M. (2019). Is Open Marxism an Offspring of the Frankfurt School? Subversive Critique as Method. In A. C. Dinerstein, A. G. Vela, E. González, & J. Holloway (Eds.) *Open Marxism 4. Against a closing world* (pp. 76–91). Pluto Press.
Scholz, R. (1992). Der Wert ist der Mann. Thesen zu Wertvergesellschaftung und Geschlechterverhältnis. In *EXIT! Krise und Kritik der Warengesellschaft*. https://www.exit-online.org/textanz1.php?tabelle=autoren&index=35&posnr=25&backtext1=text1.php. Accessed 4 July 2021.

Scholz, R. (2010). Forma social e totalidade concreta. Na urgência de um realismo. Traducido al portugués por Boaventura Antunes e Virgínia Saavedra. http://www.obeco-online.org/roswitha_scholz12.htm. Accessed 3 Jan 2020.

Scholz, R. (2015). Das warenproduzierende Patriarchat. Thesen zu Kapitalismus und Geschlechterverhältnis. In U. Isop, V. Ratkovic, & W. Wintersteiner (Eds.), *Spielregeln der Gewalt* (pp. 151–170). transcript Verlag. https://doi.org/10.14361/9783839411759-010

Stoetzler, M. (2005). On How to Make Adorno Scream: Some Notes on John Holloway's Change the World Without Taking Power. *Historical Materialism, 13*(4), 193–215.

Stoetzler, M. (2012). On the Possibility That the Revolution That Will End Capitalism Might Fail to Usher in Communism. *Journal of Classical Sociology, 12*(2), 191–204.

Tischler, S. (2012). Revolution and Detotalization: An Approach to John Holloway's Crack Capitalism. *Journal of Classical Sociology, 12*(2), 267–280.

Vaneigem, R. (2012). *The Revolution of Everyday Life*. PM Press.

CHAPTER 7

Emancipating Our (Lost) Bodies in the Pandemic Era

Katerina Nasioka and Marios Panierakis

What beautiful nights!
The nights when we meet again, with no identities.
The nights when our glances meet, clear,
away from the shadows of money.
The nights when our glances become full,
Walking–perhaps under compulsion–down a different path.
We met after so long a confinement
yet the problem is not that we were confined in our homes.
The problem is that we are confined
as objects within social relations.
And objects do not breathe (...)

K. Nasioka (✉)
Independent Scholar in Marxist Theory, Aegina, Greece
e-mail: katerinaenasioka@gmail.com

M. Panierakis
Instituto de Ciencias Sociales y Humanidades, Benemérita Universidad Autónoma de Puebla (BUAP), Puebla, México
e-mail: mariopsoc@gmail.com

A. García Vela and A. Bonnet (eds.), *The Political Thought of John Holloway*, Marx, Engels, and Marxisms,
https://doi.org/10.1007/978-3-031-34571-5_7

We met, and we meet, at the fall of the old,
inside the storm.
At times when the social relations of capital are left inactive.
Let us walk this space,
let us walk towards a different direction,
let us walk into the storm (…)
We bloom; we bloom at night;
in the nights of the storm, our storm.
And if we want our days to bloom,
all we must do is fill them with hours of rebellion.
With a doing as simple as these encounters,
a doing as daily as our night-time encounters.
(Pikralides, May 2020)

Greece, May 2020.

After many months of confinement, people leave their homes and meet in the neighbourhood squares. This coming together is perceived by the state as a public health risk, and the mechanisms of repression are immediately deployed. More specifically, at 2 a.m. on Saturday the 9 of May 2020, in Ag. Georgiou sq. in the Athenian neighbourhood of Kipseli, police forces launch an organized attack with no previous warning or recommendation against the crowd that is concentrated there. The surrounding streets become the setting for further pursuit. On another occasion, on Sunday the 17 of May 2020, at noon, the square of Kallithea in the Ano Poli neighbourhood of Thessaloniki is surrounded by the forces of repression. Their presence increases at midnight, and riot police attack the crowd using stun grenades and chasing people as far as 1 km. away. The public sphere is generally characterized as disease-ridden, and bodies are repelled. The living human presence is abolished. The sanitary body is born in its own absence, it is the abstraction of the body.

The Monologue of the Sanitary Crisis

For the past two years, our ears have been bombarded with the *language of total administration* (Marcuse, 1991: 88–107) and of science. Pandemic politics—a set of disperse discourses through which the intertwining interests of knowledge and power become increasingly obvious—converge in one main target: to regulate, correct, define what is normal and permissible on the basis of biological criteria: What is normal?

What is pathological?[1] It is a discourse that commands, organizes, urges people to follow the instructions of the experts and leaves no room for tension. The effort to explain the pandemic and the transformation of social relations is, perhaps, the first step of the critique: it is crucial that the focus of attention be directed to the expansion of biopolitical control and to the responsibilities of the capitalist mode of production in the extraction of the different microorganisms threatening the health of humans. In any case, however, the social relations that are being consolidated under the presence of Covid-19 are perceived by the social majority as given, as a new normal.

Consequently, we feel the need to rethink the discussion of the pandemic in terms of the notion of the cracks deployed by John Holloway in his book Crack Capitalism (2010), precisely because it goes against the "normality" of our social experience and focuses on its overturning. The method of the cracks is to read capitalist society from the viewpoint of its fragility. To assume the Cracks as our starting point in a world where more and more people "overflow" is to begin from the viewpoint of the dialectics of all those who feel they "do not fit" into the commands of capital (see Holloway, 2010: 8–9). The conceptualization of capitalism through the prism of its overcoming brings the notion of crisis to the forefront. Crisis is not perceived, according to Holloway (1992: 146), as a notion referring to hard times; it rather underlines the discontinuity of time and stresses the uncertainty of history (ibid.).[2] Beyond their attributes such as economic or political, crises are a much deeper expression of the overall instability of capitalist social relations (Holloway, 1992: 159–160; 1987: 56; Holloway & Picciotto, 1979: 1). Their existence places capital within the specific historical context; that is, it acknowledges its mortality and, therefore, conveys a message of hope (Bonefeld & Holloway, 1995: 225; Holloway, 2002: 203; 2012). That is

[1] The analysis in terms of the distinction between the "normal" and the "pathological" belongs to Georges Canguilhem (1991). The emphasis on the intertwining interests of power, scientific knowledge and biopolitics stem, of course, from Foucault. See, for example, 2003.

[2] That is why Marxism is a theory of crisis (Holloway, 1992: 147) and not a theory of capitalist rule and repression. We do not need a theory that reveals that we are oppressed, that tells us the obvious, that we live in a oppressive society. Marxist theory is more necessary than ever because it shows we can overcome this oppression (Holloway, 1990: 52).

why Holloway (2002: 204) suggests that revolutionary processes be read as an intensification of crises.

The openness of history and the absence of certainty with regard to the outcome of crises open up a field of contingencies, both on the side of social emancipation and on that of domination, as a possibility for the rearticulation of social relations. According to Philippidis (2020: 20) "crises are opportunities for the state and capital; opportunities to rearticulate social relations, promoting new ways of conceptualizing the self, new forms of (re)production and new forms of social control". More specifically today, in the name of the pandemic, capital occupies new social territories, encloses them, and creates a new normality which it does not intend to question after the withdrawal of the disease. The new regulations, the laws, and the norms of confinement and disciplining in the context of the sanitary crisis do not aim at the eradication of the pandemic but, above all, at the consolidation of the social relations that are being rearticulated. For Philippidis (2020: 49), this is a process that marks "a freezing of the time of social movements and a simultaneous acceleration of the time of power".

In the following analysis we will try to look into two questions. The first is to what extent the period of the pandemic is a time devoid of cracks, a period during which social resistance freezes in the time of the past. The second has to do with the relation between the cracks and the possibility of an all-embracing social transformation. Do the dispersed, uncoordinated, and diverse refusals have the power to converge, meet, and acquire the momentum that will carry away the social organization of capital? Can they become the fast and frenetic dance which will not only silence the military marches of the state but also entrain all those who try to prolongate the reproduction of capital, even if with less violent ways? These two questions, as well as the very category of the cracks, inevitably direct the focus of attention on the category of subjectivity and the processes of its constitution.

Following the foundation of Holloway's theoretical position that the world "is" and "is not" (see Holloway, 2002, 2010)—in other words, that it is in constant motion—we attempt to read the social relations in times of Covid-19 from the viewpoint of the antagonism between what exists and the "not-yet"; that is, emphasizing the clash between the relations that try to impose themselves and those that struggle to emerge from the storm. And if, indeed, the crucial field in the breaking of capitalist normality is the convergence and coming together of the cracks, then we are trying to feel the sounds of a melody which might make our bodies dance without, however, bearing the sign of a happy ending: only our restlessness and our need to ask questions; our restlessness and our need to once again set the agenda ourselves.

The Covid-19 Pandemic: A Time and Space Without Cracks?

The pandemic clearly showed that more and more people are being thrown out of the labour market and thrust into poverty. The public health crisis accelerated this process and created an entire "reserve army of labour". This condition is no longer an "exception", a discardable "immiseration thesis" (see Endnotes, 2014), as considered after World War II; it is now the norm. While proletarization increases, labour seems unable to serve as the unifying element of any revolutionary subject; on the contrary, it constitutes a decisive division between those who can be normally employed in the labour market and those who enter and exit the ranks of the reserve army. *Proletarization-without-labour* is spreading. However, it is not a condition that relates to labour in a positive way; all the more so, it does not outline a revolutionary process based on the subject of the worker. On the contrary, it states that the proletariat is being reproduced as an unwanted, cursed surplus "within" the capitalist condition (see Nasioka, 2020).

The expansion and normalization of the stagnant, surplus population would, according to Endnotes (2014) "tendentially lead to the reproduction of the proletariat becoming contingent to that of capital. If the post-war settlement had formalised the reciprocal but asymmetrical relation in which the reproduction of the working class is necessary to that of capital, with the end of that settlement and the rise in surplus populations, those who are surplus are effectively reproduced as a sort of 'side-effect' of capitalist production". Thus, the proletariat can confirm its existence as a class (that is, become subjectified) in a liminal way; and mainly in its fragmented pieces, which struggle against each other according to their social status and degree of access to the labour market, to the repression, oppression, and exclusion they suffer.[3]

[3] This process is perceived by Endnotes (2014) as "abjection", that is, a loss of the identity characteristics of the subject and the adoption of a decadent or contingent character. From another theoretical perspective, in his conceptualization of the state of

In the pandemic, exclusions spread to every aspect of social life. This new harsh norm targets all those who, for example, do not fulfil the criteria of sanitary safety defined by the state or are stigmatized as a public health hazard; the immigrants whose paths simply crossed with those of the border police, treated as filthy and homeless bodies whose life does not matter (Kotouza, 2020); those displaced from their land due to large development projects such as the construction of a railway, a wind farm, or a mining project; the femininities that cannot breathe in the context of heavy-handed patriarchy. The enclosures and exclusions reveal an ever-repeating process of class-ification which takes place within capitalist social relations (Holloway, 2002: 142). However, this class-ification acquires today a deviating character: it does not lead to the confirmation of the class condition of labour as a unified identity but rather highlights the divisions of capital. Therefore, how can we conceptualize class struggle today? We must find new conceptual tools that will reflect the processes of today's resistances, or else we should better stop talking about forms of class struggle.

We believe the present-day social condition can be linked to Holloway's position on class struggle (Holloway, 2002: 143) that "the existence of classes and their constitution cannot be separated: to say that classes exist is to say that they are in the process of being constituted".[4] Therefore, to talk about non-class forms of struggle is out of the question. The working class is a constantly open concept: "Struggle arises not from the fact that we are working class but from the fact that we-are-and-are-not working class, that we exist against-and-beyond being working class" (2002: 144). For Holloway, "we all exist within that conflict, just as the conflict exists within all of us" (2002: 147). Class struggle is the continuous everyday antagonism (visible and non-visible) between alienation and de-alienation, definition and anti-definition. In this sense, "we do not struggle *as* working class, we struggle *against* being working class, against being classified" (2002: 144).

emergency and of exclusion, Agamben refers to "ecstasy-belonging" (1998, 2005), the "being-outside", and yet belonging (2005: 35) whose main characteristic is the lack of distinction between the "inside" and the "outside" and which creates a space within which deviation is legitimized.

[4] At this point it should be noted that the notion of reproduction creates the image of a process that occurs effortlessly. On the contrary, Holloway suggests that the existence of capitalist relations is constantly at issue (Holloway, 2002: 144).

Holloway (2010: 10–13, 63) claims that revolution is a process of radically changing the world that takes place in the interstices of capitalism, in the individual instances. That is where we create cracks, when we seek the dignity that the social organization of capitalism does not provide us. Therefore, social change is not something produced by professional revolutionaries but rather the result of everyday activities. Cracks carry the philosophical load of a negative dialectic. They condense the moments of refusal and creation of subjects. Refusal might be the foundation of the cracks, but refusal is not enough. "The break begins with refusal", Holloway mentions (2010: 17), and he adds that the true force of the crack is revealed when, through our negation, we are led to a different *doing*, "in a movement of refusal and creation" (2010: 6). Those who do not fit in and do not adapt are forced to make their lives in different ways, to turn their initial "no" into "an opening to a different activity, the threshold of a counter-world with a different logic and a different language" (Holloway 2010: 19).

This creative dimension of struggle was put to practice with particular force in the social struggles of the global Occupy movement (2011 onwards) before they began to withdraw. Today, in certain cases of long-lived struggles, such as Rojava or the Zapatistas, a high degree of organization and autonomy has been attained. In other cases, and in a broad spectrum of the proletarian struggles in the western world, those who live in the margins of society do not converge in the emergence of a unified, collective class subject. However, their actions are imbued by the dialectic of refusal-and-creation; such is the case of the immigrants who—if they manage to cross the Aegean Sea and do not die trying—occupy empty buildings in Athens and turn them into their homes; or of those who unite in the streets of the metropolises of the world to express their rage for the worsening of their living conditions within the bankrupt neoliberal model (such is the case of the *gilets jaunes* in France); to oppose authoritarian regimes (such as the student clashes in Hong Kong); protest against the measures and the policies for the handling of the pandemic through clashes, injuries, and deaths, such as in Chile (see Jimenez, 2021) and Colombia; or demonstrate against the gender-based experiences in patriarchy (metoo) and the racialized police violence that murders black people on a daily basis in the USA (Black Lives Matter) (see Palencia, 2020).

The period of the pandemic is not a one-dimensional continuous time of capitalist composition which goes by uncontested. On the contrary, the handling of the pandemic underlines the fact that the contradictions of capital have become so acute that the reproduction of the capitalist relation without the imposition of a military field for the administration of the entirety of social relations and the submission of social reactions and demands seem impossible. The pandemic is being "used" as an instrument of militarization tailored to the needs of the western crisis-ridden "democracies", whose permanent characteristics include potential hotbeds of social unrest, political destabilization in the face of the ever-increasing impoverishment and the ample production of excess life which threatens the "security" of the social construct of capital, crisis of capitalist valorization, and crisis of commodity-producing labour, that is, crisis of the class relation itself. The social relation (capital) clashes today with its own limits, internal and external.

As for Greece, police arbitrariness in the Covid era has skyrocketed. The imposition of militaristic measures, limitations, and prohibitions is reminiscent of times of war: "the imposition of a state of emergency and the de facto overriding of the Constitution, the suspension of rights and the limitation of liberties, the curfews and the bans on public gatherings, the closing of borders, the transformation of the economy into an economy of war (unleashing, of course, a global recession commensurate with those occurring in times of war), the digital surveillance of the movement of citizens and the tracing of their contacts, the activation of antiterrorist laws, the criminalization of counter-information and partly of the public criticism of the prevailing medical discourse, the use of drones to control gatherings, the beatings, arrests, incarcerations, even murders by agents of law enforcement as a response to the violation of restrictions" (Philippidis, 2020: 39).

The direct consequence of the state crowd management policies is that the *encounters* of the proletariat are inevitably limited. To appear in the public space is considered toxic, the bodies automatically retreat in the sight of the other. The measures are clearly a form of "education" for the future. The curfew and the ban on public gatherings, the characterization of any form of physical encounter in spaces of social antagonism and social demands as *antisocial behaviour* expresses the curtailing of the time and space of communication and interaction of the proletarians. The redesigning and rearticulation of the social body and the overall social territory is an effort to preserve the capitalist composition in the context of an ever-intensifying crisis, to create subjects who adapt. The body becomes a field of antagonism not only in labour but, much more intensely, outside of it. The body is attacked, banished, it resists, it comes together.

Body,[5] Crack, Encounters

The pandemic has provided the side of the counter-rebellion an opportunity for further enclosure. Enclosures appear not only in the field of labour but also in every sphere of life, causing exclusion and intensifying the segregations of capital. The process is never concluded; it is a continuous questioning, inscribed in each subjectivity. The privileged locus of this inscription is the body, both as the immediate sensorial receptor of the exclusion and, as we shall show, the bearer of our power. Our bodies are imprisoned, controlled, disciplined, self-confined, they become bodies where the exploitation and oppression are inscribed, but also the conflict, the rupture. The state handling of the pandemic reveals the fact that it targets the physical body; it aims at disciplining it and controlling it. The body in the pandemic is a space of enclosure; it becomes alien, it does not belong to us, it is the object of surveillance, control, and repression.[6]

Thus, the state manages to mutilate dimensions of everyday life, discipline bodies even more to the command of productivity, render them "operative" for capital by legitimizing the ban on any non-lucrative activity. The experience of the metropolis where the bodies crowd together is abolished, it becomes a nostalgic memory. Desires are banished to a space outside of what is possibly the only physical trajectory allowed today: workplace-home-workplace. To find ourselves outside this enclosed space of political inactivity—as reflected in the two images at the beginning of the text—to find ourselves in spaces of unexpected encounter, we must thread our way through the labyrinth of prohibitions or face repression. In times of pandemic, emotions are trapped in front of a screen, desires remain in the realm of phantasy, and the body itself is absent from any social activity. The penetration of our bodies by capital

[5] We would like to thank the people who took part in the collective reading of the text "To Be Done with the Massacre of the Body" which was organized in the squat of Rosa Nera in September 2021, as well the small group of collective reading which was created by the students of the ICSyH and which studied this text (amongst others).

[6] For the immaterial, virtual body of post-Fordism, see Hardt and Negri (2000). For the body as a "desiring machine", see Deleuze and Guattari (2009).

acquires at the same time a dimension of guilt. Control turns into self-control. The desire for play, for coming together with others, is nipped in the bud.

In his provocative essay "To Be Done with the Massacre of the Body", Guattari (1973) opens up an important issue regarding the conceptualization of the body and its materiality within the enclosed capitalist reality. Guattari (1973) claims that capital enters our body "using every available access route into our organisms, it insinuates into the depths of our insides its roots of death. It usurps our organs, disrupts our vital functions, mutilates our pleasure, subjugates all lived experience to the control of its condemning judgments. It makes of each individual a cripple, cut off from his or her body, a stranger to his or her own desires".

The author manages to focus the clash between life and survival—also introduced by Vaneigem (2001) in *The Revolution of Everyday Life*—on the body and, in this way, place the question of self-determination within the sphere of the body. Following Guattari's train of thought, the body is revealed as the field where lived experience is embedded, as it is the foundation on which desire, emotions, and social relations are developed. The body is perceived in its relational dimension, as the result of social relations. On the other hand, it is tortured, tamed, oppressed into becoming a useful force and a vessel for capital in everyday life.[7] Guattari's thinking is valuable because it allows us to politicize the body—and, by extension, everyday life—and transform it from a field of victimization to the locus of liberation and emancipation: "We want to see frigid, imprisoned, mortified bodies explode to bits, even if capitalism continues to demand that they be kept in check at the expense of our living bodies" (ibid.). Guattari thus reflects his own dimension of class conflict. The body as conflict expressed by Guattari echoes the perception of struggle not only as an "external"[8] but also an "internal" relation, which is also one of the main lines of analysis of the current of *Open Marxism*. At the same time, the body as the agent of the overturning of the capitalist condition places

[7] "We can no longer permit our nervous system to serve as a communications network for the system of capitalist exploitation, for the patriarchal state; nor can we permit our brains to be used as instruments of torture programmed by the powers that surround us" Guattari (1973).

[8] The identity of the body is the locus of class consciousness *par excellence* for the bourgeoisie. It is quite telling that the bodies of immigrants and refugees, of the poor and the socially marginalized, or of political dissidents have always been considered repulsive and stigmatized as a public health hazard.

the force of *resistance-and-revolt* in the processes of subjectification and inscribes the revolutionary refusal in the field of everyday life.

In this sense, the body is the foundation of a new dimension of class struggle, a different approach to struggle: it is, at the same time, the most direct material agent of our submission, the field in which repression takes root, but also the material foundation of our liberation (in the here and now). The most interesting point of this approach is that, to Guattari, the body is not a passive field, subject to repression, in which oppression is embedded; it is a field of antagonism where the struggle of capital is organized "in order to rivet to our subconscious its mechanisms for reproducing this system of enslavement" (ibid.) and, at the same time, the movement of the more direct physical space of freedom unfolds as the physical foundation of resistance. We are not before two structurally separate worlds; on the contrary, the body constitutes a dialectic space which encompasses encounter and conflict. It is through the body that we will strive for the liberation of society (ibid.).

However, Guattari challenges the notion that the body expresses something individual and, therefore, places the collectivization of our bodies on the agenda: "This desire for a fundamental liberation, if it is to be a truly revolutionary action, requires that we move beyond the limits of our 'person', that we overturn the notion of the 'individual', that we transcend our sedentary selves, our 'normal social identities', in order to travel to the boundaryless territory of the body, in order to live in the flux of desires that lies beyond sexuality, beyond the territory of the repertories of normality" (ibid.). Guattari invites us to break the limits of the individual body, to break identities, collectivize desire, to proceed with a collectivization of the body. Therefore, the notion of conflict in this specific text is not completed with the individual body. On the contrary, escaping the individual boundaries of the body is an integral part of the struggle.

The body as rupture or crack brings to the surface of the pandemic the notion of encounter, whose importance is not limited to the coming together of individual bodies. The encounter is a conflict-ridden process which attempts, by repelling the relations of exchange, to open up spaces of autonomy, solidarity, self-organization, and self-determination in the interstices of capitalist articulations. Through this prism, encounters—not only as interclass celebrations but also as a reverse process of class-ification—inevitably preserve an imponderable and contingent spontaneous character which underlines the historical discontinuity of events of resistance (see Nasioka, 2017). In this ambiguous space of encounter, the (lost) body can produce its own liberation, be emancipated, clash with what exists, and reflect new social relations. We try to hear the wall breaking, to spread the cracks, to extend our hands to each other. As Guattari (1973) says, "we want to open our bodies to the bodies of other people, to let energies circulate, allow desires to merge, so that we can all give free reign to our fantasies, to our ecstasies".

In the actual conditions of the pandemic, the theoretical meeting of Guattari's "body" and Holloway's "cracks" offer—to those of us who conceive capitalism through the prism of its overcoming and still seek ways to achieve this—two points of affirmation. First, affirms the class struggle as a class-ification fluid-process by rejecting the idea of class struggle as an external conflict between opposed groups. Second, affirms that struggle is placed in our everyday doing, in the cracks that our somatic/subjective experience creates; without, however, finding its horizon there, as in order to open and spread the crack, the collectivization of our worries and desires is required.

Beyond these affirmations, Guattari's perception can enforce the argument of "Crack Capitalism". The breaking of the limits of our person and, thus, the collectivization of bodies, compose an invitation to an encounter of cracks. From the standpoint of cracks, it composes a passage towards the search for all those bodies that resist, perhaps individually, perhaps silently; and this is how the decision to embark on a small boat and cross the Atlantic Ocean becomes meaningful. However, "Cracks are vulnerable to the gelatinous suction of capitalist synthesis" (Holloway, 2010: 51) for facing at least three challenges: the state, the rule of value, and the isolated/fragmented individual. In the pandemic era, these challenges have as their primary (material) base the body. This shift is significant in the actual social conditions, where the body is subject to discipline, control, and punishment of the state. Correspondingly, the body becomes a carrier of the social cohesion of capital; it is no coincidence that the working process is changing form in order to keep the body productive. Again, it is no coincidence that the body, according to epidemiological data, is not dangerous when it produces "value", but becomes dangerous when it produces "encounters" with "others". Thus, Guattari's interpretation not only helps us to extend the cracks inside the subject, but more than that gives focus on the connectivity of struggles that Holloways proposes by joining our hand to the other (Holloway, 2021) with the encounter; with the collectivization of our concerns. To do so, the body is being recognized not just as a medium of sovereignty, but at the same time as a principle of resistance; a moving crack.

Therefore, emancipation is not an individual matter, neither is the body perceived here in its individual and sensorial dimension. The political stake is the historical body, that is, the body that is bound by its historical weave to specific functions and social relations. In the present pandemic era, the collective body emerges as a political stake not only in its unity with state power—that is, legitimizing it as "the people" or "civil society"—but in its confrontation with it. And this is so because the medicalization-biologization of life makes it clear that the policy responses to the pandemic guarantee a borderline legality of life, and even that refers only to certain population groups. The creation of exclusive sanitary zones based on the body, as well as the dichotomizing performed on the grounds of the "bodies of the healthy", are the ultimate expression of life as survival, paving the way for new categorizations and leading to the assimilation of surveillance and, above all, of self-surveillance and mutual surveillance.

The somatization of the social is based on common experience. The commonly lived experience today renders survival a collective/common ground and leaves the social body exposed to normalization, segregation, and biopolitical management technologies. It is, therefore, crucial to crack the segregated zones and reclaim the encounter as a social and physical experience that defies "the homogenizing sweeping of bodies to the level of living matter" (Antitriage, 2021). However, it is better to not speak as much of a "common" experience through the encounter but rather of the unexpected encounters of different bodies, with different mediations of experiences that clash with the social forms of capitalism, creating cracks in which social relations change unpredictably at different levels of coexistence. This can be seen as a disorder dance of dignity which tunes into the rhythm of the bodies of "the others". The social body is subjectified (not individually as an end in itself) in conflict, in class struggle, and in the encounter.

According to Holloway (2010: 35), "Our cracks are not self-contained spaces but rebellions that recognise one another, feel affinities, reach out for each other". This encounter, the collectivization of the social body, is the element of hope that we must fertilize in order to keep the candle of the total transformation of society lit.

References

Agamben, G. (1998). *Homo Sacer: Sovereign Power and Bare Life*. Stanford University Press.

Agamben, G. (2005). *State of Exception*. Chicago University Press.

Antitriage Collective. (2021). «Από την καραντίνα στην "ελευθερία". Σημειώσεις για το υγειονομικό κράτος, την επιστήμη και τους εμβολιασμούς» [From quarantine to "freedom". Notes on the sanitary state, science, and vaccinations]. https://sinialo.espiv.net/wp-content/uploads/2021/07/antitriage_final_mail.pdf

Bonefeld, W., & Holloway, J. (1995). Money and Class Struggle. In W. Bonefeld & J. Holloway (Eds.), *Global Capital, National State and the Politics of Money* (pp. 210–227). Macmillan Press.

Canguilhem, G. (1991). *The Normal and the Pathological*. Zone Books.

Deleuze, G., & Guattari, F. (2009). *Anti-Oedipus: Capitalism and Schizophrenia*. Penguin Classics.

Endnotes. (2014, October). An identical abject-subject? In *Endnotes* (Issue 4). https://endnotes.org.uk/issues/4/en/endnotes-an-identical-abject-subject

Foucault, M. (2003). *Society Must Be Defended: Lectures at the Collège de France 1975–1976*. Picador.

Guattari, F. (2012/1973). *To Have Done with the Massacre of the Body*. https://Thefunambulist.Net/Editorials/Philosophy-to-Have-Done-with-the-Massacre-of-the-Body-by-Felix-Guattari

Gunn, R. (1987). Notes on Class. *Common Sense, 2*, 15–25.

Hardt, M., & Negri, A. (2000). *Empire*. Harvard University Press.

Holloway, J. (1987). A Note on Fordism and Neo-Fordism. *Common Sense, 1*, 52–59.

Holloway, J. (1990). The Politics of Dept. *Common Sense, 9*, 51–57.

Holloway, J. (1992). Crisis, Fetishism, Class Composition. In W. Bonefeld, R. Gunn, & K. Psychopedis (Eds.), *Open Marxism—Volume 2—Theory and Practice* (pp. 145–170). Pluto Press.

Holloway, J. (2002). *Change the World Without Taking Power: The Meaning of Revolution Today*. Pluto Press.

Holloway, J. (2010). *Crack Capitalism*. Pluto Press.

Holloway, J. (2012, March 18). *Left Forum, Closing Plenary Lecture*. Pace University, New York. https://www.youtube.com/watch?v=wU_e1IBaC7c&ab_channel=DeepDishTV

Holloway, J. (2021, May 20). The Zapatistas' Surreal Struggle for Life—And Against Capitalism. *Roar Mag*. https://roarmag.org/essays/zapatista-journey-for-life/

Holloway, J., & Picciotto, S. (1979). Introduction: Towards a Materialist Theory of the State. In J. Holloway & S. Picciotto (Eds.), *State and Capital: A Marxist Debate* (pp. 1–31). University of Texas Press.

Jimenez, P. (2021). La revuelta social en la región chilena en el contexto de la crisis del valor. *Revueltas, 3*, 103–126.

Kotouza, D. (2020). Whose Lives Matter? Nationalism, Antifascism, and the Relationship with Immigrants. In J. Holloway, K. Nasioka, & P. Doulos (Eds.), *Beyond Crisis, After the Collapse of Institutional Hope in Greece, What?* (pp. 138–170). PM Press.

Marcuse, H. (1991). *The One-Dimensional Man*. Routledge.

Nasioka, K. (2017). *Ciudades en insurrección: Oaxaca 2006/Atenas 2008*. Editorial Cátedra Jorge Alonso.

Nasioka, K. (2020). The Proletariat Versus the Working Class: Shifts in Class Struggle in the Twenty-First Century. In A. C. Dinerstein et al. (Eds.), *Open Marxism 4. Against a Closing World* (pp. 125–141). Pluto Press.

Palencia, S. (2020). *Black Lives Matter: del coronavirus a la revuelta social en Nueva York*. https://www.no-ficcion.com/project/black-lives-matter-nueva-york-revuelta-social

Philippidis, C. (2020). *Είμαστε σε πόλεμο με έναν αόρατο εχθρό* [We Are at War with an Invisible Enemy]. Futura.

Πικραλίδες. (2020). «Τι όμορφες αυτές οι νύχτες!» [What beautiful nights!] https://pikralides.noblogs.org/post/2021/08/17/%cf%84%ce%b9-%cf%8c%ce%bc%ce%bf%cf%81%cf%86%ce%b5%cf%82-%ce%b1%cf%85%cf%84%ce%ad%cf%82-%ce%bf%ce%b9-%ce%bd%cf%8d%cf%87%cf%84%ce%b5%cf%82-%ce%bc%ce%ac%ce%b7%cf%82-2020/

Vaneigem, R. (2001). *The Revolution of Everyday Life*. Rebel Press.

PART III

Holloway and Critical Theory

CHAPTER 8

Holloway and Marcuse: The Foundations of Antagonistic Subjectivity

Alfonso García Vela

John Holloway has pointed out the importance of reflecting on the issue of revolution and has taken a closer look at rebelliousness and at the struggle of subjects in present-day capitalism, in a historical context marked by the large changes of the end of the twentieth century. Changes which have cast doubts on the capacity of the subject to emancipate itself and to radically transform society. However, in his work, Holloway has sought to lay the foundations for a theory of antagonistic subjectivity and understand the subject not as "a weak messianic power" but as a "volcanic power" that screams, rebels and causes the crisis of capitalism. Holloway considers the revelation that we are the crisis of capital as vital, for our own survival as a species within a mode of social life that is increasingly violent and destructive, as is contemporary capitalism, depends on it. To avoid destruction and attain an emancipated world is, undoubtedly, an

A. García Vela (✉)
Instituto de Ciencias Sociales y Humanidades, Benemérita Universidad Autónoma de Puebla (BUAP), Puebla, México
e-mail: galileo.vela@correo.buap.mx

A. García Vela and A. Bonnet (eds.), *The Political Thought of John Holloway*, Marx, Engels, and Marxisms,
https://doi.org/10.1007/978-3-031-34571-5_8

urgent task for humanity. His writings and reflections have attracted a lot of attention and captivated activists, social movements and intellectuals, as well as led to considerable discussion and criticism.

Holloway's work can be considered an effort to reappropriate and update the critical theory of the Frankfurt School, although it has also been linked to contemporary autonomist Marxism.[1] In recent years, Holloway has shown special interest in the thinking of Theodor W. Adorno and in his most important work, *Negative Dialectics*. However, his reappropriation of Adorno and his anti-identitarian perspective have been largely questioned,[2] and many recognize a strong influence of Herbert Marcuse in Holloway's theory. Karl Reitter (2012) was the first to acknowledge that Holloway's *Crack Capitalism* can be interpreted as a perspective in favour of Marcuse's Great Refusal (2007: 66): the Great Refusal is "the protest against that which is".

According to Reitter, *Crack Capitalism* portrays a way of rebelling which refers to the Great Refusal that tries to break and recreate social existence. However, for Reitter, Holloway does not manage to go beyond the abstract approach of Marcuse's Great Rejection and stops at the desire to quit partaking in the madness of capitalism. Likewise, in his book *Negativity and Democracy* (2017), Vasilis Grollios highlights the similarity between Holloway's notion of interstitial revolution and the concept of interstices in the critical theory of Marcuse.[3]

However, it was Mario Schäbel (2018) who set out to analyse in more detail the relation between the theory of Marcuse and that of Holloway in his doctoral dissertation titled *Open Marxism and the Legacy of the Frankfurt School*. Generally speaking, Schäbel (2020) tried to show that Holloway's thinking, and that of Open Marxism in general, is closer to the critical theory of Herbert Marcuse than to that of Theodor W. Adorno.

Why is this relevant? Precisely because Holloway and Open Marxism have ultimately remained anchored to a subjective idealism that, to a certain point, is constitutive of the thinking of Herbert Marcuse. Thus, to overcome this falling back into idealism, one must seriously think of

[1] See Alex Callinicos (2005), Robert Kurz (2007) and the contribution of Marcel Stoetzler in this book.

[2] On this, see Schäbel (2018, 2020), García Vela (2020a, 2020b) and the contributions of Alberto Bonnet, Edith González Cruz and Panagiotis Doulos in this book.

[3] A more detailed discussion of the perspectives of Karl Reitter and Vasilis Grollios can be found in Schäbel (2018).

the idea to open Open Marxism itself through the theory of Adorno; this is a perspective that I share with Schäbel and which I believe is crucial if the limits and weaknesses of Open Marxism and of Holloway's theory are to be overcome. From my viewpoint, Adorno's critical theory is the most important effort, within the Frankfurt School, to overcome the idealism that has remained latent in modern thinking as a whole. Although one can reasonably wonder: is an Open Marxism without a latent idealism indeed possible?

In this chapter, I look into an aspect that is highlighted by Schäbel's research and which I consider fundamental in Holloway's theory of praxis: his anthropological core, a characteristic he shares with the critical theory of Herbert Marcuse and also with the theory of communicative action of Jürgen Habermas. However, unlike Marcuse and Habermas, this anthropological nature is not part of Holloway's self-understanding of his own theory. Furthermore, as we shall see later on, it has implications for a theory of praxis which aspires to be anti-identitarian, such as the theory of Holloway; its anthropological character causes it to relapse into the identity it wishes to overcome.

At this point, we will focus mainly on the relation between Holloway and Marcuse, for they both have revolutionary subjectivity as their central subject matter, while the backdrop and leitmotif of the theory of Habermas is democracy. I am interested in trying to understand why both Marcuse and Holloway reconstruct the foundations of antagonistic subjectivity on anthropological grounds, which means that this subjectivity remains rooted in an affirmative idea of nature or of the human essence. Unlike Marx, who, in *Capital*, grounded the possibilities for the emancipation of the proletariat on the fabric of society itself and not on an alleged human nature. In his early writings, however, and especially in the *Economic and Philosophic Manuscripts of 1844*, Marx assumed an approach that could be called anthropological and which focused on a generic conception of the human being.

The impact of *Economic and Philosophic Manuscripts* on the theories of Marcuse (1973, 2007) and of Holloway (2010b) is well-known. However, according to Adorno (1980) and Alfred Schmidt (2014), the work of Marx from his writings against Feuerbach negates the anthropological intention that was present in his early texts. More specifically, from Marx's sixth thesis (1998: 570), where he posits that "the essence of man is no abstraction inherent in each single individual. In its reality it is the ensemble of the social relations". Marx's critique of Feuerbach aspires to prove that, deep down, human beings are socially constituted.

The theories of praxis articulated after Marx, such as those of Lenin, Rosa Luxembourg, or Gramsci, focused mainly on the antagonism between capital and labour, as well as on the political organization and tactics of the proletariat, without however questioning or drastically transforming the foundations of the classical theory of revolution that Marx elaborated in the nineteenth century. However, there is a significant change in Marcuse's theory, one which is present in Holloway's theory of praxis and, arguably, also in the theory of communicative action of Habermas. From my viewpoint, Marcuse's concept of the one-dimensional society is crucial in the understanding of the anthropological orientation of the theory of the mentioned authors. The objective of this chapter is not only to discuss the idea of a theory of praxis with anthropological foundations, but also to try to examine the impact of historical transformations on the constitution of the theories of Marcuse and Holloway.

Philosophical Anthropology and the Frankfurt School

Philosophical anthropology was a project that emerged during the Weimar Republic and whose main representatives were Max Scheler, Helmuth Plessner and Arnold Gehlen; the latter greatly influenced the thinking of Habermas, who reappropriated the theory of Gehlen to develop his own theoretical project.[4] Philosophical anthropology reflected on the human nature and tried to propose a concept of man through a theory of the human being, a theory that would explain his most essential nature (Johannssen, 2018; Marquard, 2007).

The discussion of human nature and the reception of philosophical anthropology was not a minor matter within the Frankfurt School; in fact, it arguably divided its main representatives. Horkheimer and Adorno were sceptic and reluctant towards the idea of a human nature perceived positively, while Marcuse and Habermas related to philosophical anthropology. Dennis Johannsen (2013, 2018) superbly portrays the different postures and critiques in relation to philosophical anthropology within the

[4] On this, see Honneth (1993).

Frankfurt School, and clearly describes how one of the main problems in this discussion was whether it was possible to answer the question of what the human being is in a context of reified social relations. In this sense, Adorno (2007: 124) opposed philosophical anthropology and argued in *Negative Dialectics* that "if the essence of humanity were deciphered from its contemporary constitution, then this would sabotage its possibility".

Adorno (2006, 2007) criticized ontologies of a naturalist type, such as philosophical anthropology, for developing a relation between nature and history that is characterized by a primacy of nature. In the anthropological perspective, human nature constitutes the fundamental structure of historical processes, it is presented as what is essential and expressed through different historical forms. In an anthropological approach with a revolutionary meaning, human nature is asserted as the biological foundation that is repressed by history and must be liberated; human nature acquires the meaning of what must be and has been negated by history. In this perspective, praxis and critique are founded on a human nature that must be realized and must bring about an emancipated world.

However, as Johannsen (2013) has pointed out, Adorno (2008) remained open to an idea of anthropology, albeit one with a dialectical and not affirmative character; unlike philosophical anthropology, which is based on an idea of human nature that does not vary, in the sense that human nature becomes immutable through historical change. Adorno thought of the possibility of a dialectical anthropology that would not posit human nature in a positive way and, furthermore, would be able to reflect on the problematics of the proletarian revolution and its failure, according to Adorno (2008: 45) "we simply cannot think any more as Marx thought, namely that the revolution was imminent".

We have already mentioned that the main representatives of the Frankfurt School did not respond to philosophical anthropology in a homogeneous way. Herbert Marcuse was very interested in this philosophical school; according to Martin Jay (1972), this interest began when he was a student of Martin Heidegger at the end of the 1920s. Marcuse's theory is not a philosophical anthropology in the strict sense, such as the theories of Helmut Plessner, Max Scheler and Arnold Gehlen (Bundschuh, 2004); nevertheless, he does retain its fundamental idea, namely that history lies on natural grounds.[5]

[5] On the meaning of philosophical anthropology, see Habermas (1981).

Marcuse's theoretical project sought to develop a social philosophy with a concrete character, that is, to understand human existence and the possibilities of emancipation on an ontological and anthropological basis. That is why we can say that Marcuse's critical theory takes a turn towards human nature, a nature that provides the foundations for the possibilities and forces of revolution; this turn will be kept up in the theory of communicative action formulated by Jürgen Habermas and in his reappropriation of the phenomenological concept of the lifeworld.[6]

The publication of the *Economic and Philosophic Manuscripts* in the 1930s was for Marcuse (1973: 3) "a crucial event in the history of Marxist studies". In the essay titled "The foundation of Historical Materialism", which is dedicated to the analysis of the *Manuscripts*, Marcuse (1973) points out that what must be seen and understood in the *Manuscripts* is that Marx tries to capture the essence of man, an aspect that the bourgeois political economy did not see, and formulates an idea of this essence and of its historical realization which is the basis for the theory of revolution.

For Marcuse, capitalism has not only led to economic and political crises; it is also a catastrophe for human nature, for the species being. It is my understanding that, in this essay, Marcuse moves between ontology and anthropology through the *Manuscripts*. If Heideggerian ontology focuses on reflecting on the being and on the foundation of the world, a concrete, ontological philosophy such as the one that Marcuse aspires to, which tries to understand human existence, will focus on the basis of the species being; that is, on the nature of man.

The anthropological approach of Marcuse's social theory was not a perspective of his youth; he continued to develop in his work the anthropological idea that history, the becoming of human existence, lies on natural grounds. In his now classic *Eros and Civilization*, published in the mid-1950s and more than twenty years after his comment on the *Manuscripts*, Marcuse presents on the basis of his reappropriation of Freudian theory the natural or biological foundation of human beings in terms of a historically dynamic instinctive structure with the potential for revolution.

According to Marcuse (2015: 7 and 107) "Freud developed a theory of man" with ontological implications because "Freud's theory contains

[6] Bundschuh (2004) argues that German philosopher Odo Marquard defines philosophical anthropology as a philosophy of man which is rendered possible with the turn towards a lifeworld and becomes fundamental with the turn to nature.

certain assumptions on the structure of the principal modes of being" from a psychology of the human genus that reveals the basic biological structure behind society. In *Eros and Civilization*, Marcuse recovers the Freudian hypothesis that civilization begins with the methodical repression of instincts and formulates a dialectic between the foundation of the instinctive structure and civilization in terms of the antagonism between Eros and alienated labour. The latter lay the foundations for the material basis of civilization and keeps Eros subordinated to Thanatos.

Furthermore, alienated labour is the absence of gratification and, therefore, the renouncing of "the freedom of the libidinal subject-object which the human organism primarily is and desires" (Marcuse, 2015: 46). While Eros as a force of gratification struggles against alienated labour, this negativity that is inherent in instincts has an emancipating potential for the species. According to Marcuse, Freud's critique of civilization moves from the mystified forms of the individual through regression until it discovers the basic negativity of the hidden biological foundations of these forms. The antagonism between Eros and labour is fundamental and allows for the understanding of the antagonism between capital and labour. The latter shall be analysed by Marcuse in the context of the advanced industrial society of the mid-twentieth century in his most important work, *The One-Dimensional Man*. An outstanding book which, together with *Negative Dialectics*, is among the most important works of the Frankfurt School to be published in the 1960s.

In 1969 *An Essay on Liberation* is published. Marcuse (1969) revisits the subject matters of *Eros and Civilization* and tries to approach the possibilities of revolution and of socialism through the biological foundation of human beings. And in his last work, *The Aesthetic Dimension*, human nature continues to develop as the foundation of history (1978: 16–17; 2007: 69):

> The emergence of human beings as "species beings"—men and women capable of living in that community of freedom which is the potential of the species—this is the subjective basis of a classless society. Its realization presupposes a radical transformation of the drives and needs of the individuals: an organic development within the socio-historical. Solidarity would be on weak grounds were it not rooted in the instinctual structure of individuals.

A model can be outlined based on Marcuse's critical theory which is characteristic of his theory of negative subjectivity. It is an anthropological model with an antagonistic character whose main features will be repeated in the theory of Jürgen Habermas and of John Holloway. The basic idea of the Marcusian model is that there exists an antagonism between human nature and the social–historical world; the development of the latter is affected by the negativity of its ontological basis, human nature with a potential disposition towards emancipation.

Thus, a positive negativity is postulated in the model that characterizes the theory of Marcuse, in the sense that human nature struggles to assert itself and can only be realized within an emancipated world. It is my belief that this model originates in the interpretation of *The Phenomenology of Spirit* by Marcuse. According to the latter's reading (2015) of this work, Hegel preserves the tension between the ontological and the historical content in the different states of civilization.

Although the central theme in the theories of Marcuse and Habermas is radically different—in the former it is revolution and, in the latter, the democratic organization of society—the influence of the Marcusian model can be found in different works by Habermas, such as *The Reconstruction of Historical Materialism* and *The Theory of Communicative Action*. In the second, his most important work, Habermas (2015a, 2015b) tries to anthropologically substantiate action and reason in the human ability for language. Language and its communicative potential are colonized in capitalism by the instrumental reason that dominates modern society, which implies a pathological misfitting between the lifeworld and the system. However, communicative reason, anthropologically rooted in language, has the potential to rebel against the social pathology caused by instrumental reason. Likewise, the author argues, communicative reason is the normative foundation and the possibility of a democratic society.[7]

Two main aspects stand out in the Marcusian model[8]: the first one refers to factual dualisms that are constituted by one part that is capitalist and another that is potentially non-capitalist; the interaction of both parts is antagonistic. Eros and alienated labour (civilization) is the dualism existing in Marcuse's own theory; the lifeworld and the system constitute

[7] On Habermas and his relation to ontology and anthropology, see García Vela and Longoni (2020).

[8] This theoretical perspective is in debt to the critical theory of Theodor W. Adorno and of Moishe Postone.

the—not necessarily antagonistic—dualism that characterizes the theory of communicative action of Habermas[9]; and, as we shall see further one, doing and labour is the dualism that is implicit in Holloway's theory of praxis.

Secondly, there is a shift in the locus of antagonism: it is no longer located in the fabric of society itself, where it was to be found according to the classical theory of revolution. For Marx, the subject and the recipient of this theory was the proletariat, a class with unique characteristics and with the potential to radically transform society and bring about human emancipation. Arguably, Marx's conception of the proletariat as the subject of the radical transformation of society emerged from a double analysis: on the one hand, the political and social "discovery" of a class on a historical rise which experiences directly and intensely the oppression and exploitation that characterize modernity.[10]

On the other hand, in *Capital*, Marx derives the theoretical foundations of the proletariat as a potential negation of capitalism from his immanent critique of capitalist society. According to Marx, this society is itself contradictory, and its negation is intrinsic to the specifically capitalist labour process.[11] Marx did not substantiate the possibility of the emancipation of the proletariat anthropologically; the condition of possibility of emancipation was the inherently contradictory character of society.

On the contrary, in the Marcusian model, the condition of possibility of antagonistic subjectivity moves within a level that he considers fundamental: the anthropological level, the locus of a potential inclination towards the negation of capitalism. Thus, fundamental antagonism is reformulated as the antagonism between human nature and society, a society with a qualitatively different character from the one analysed by Marx in the nineteenth century. According to Marcuse (2007), the advanced industrial society of the twentieth century has a one-dimensional character.

Beyond Marcuse's ontological approach, the concept of the one-dimensional society—which I will analyse in what follows—is key to understanding the anthropological direction of his critical theory of

[9] On dualism in the social theory of Habermas, see Honneth (1993).

[10] On the theory of revolution in the young Marx, see Löwy (2005).

[11] On this, see Cohen (1982) and Postone (2003).

society. The changes affecting capitalism in the first half of the twentieth century are directly linked to the emergence of this concept and to the path taken by the critical theory of society.[12] The concept of one-dimensional society in Marcuse's critical theory is rooted in the theory of Friedrich Pollock.

The Concept of the One-Dimensional Society

It is known that Herbert Marcuse and the other members of the Frankfurt School shared the historical experience of the failure of the German revolution of 1918–1919 during the Weimar Republic, the 1929 crisis, and, years later, the rise of fascism and its military defeat in the 1930s and 1940s.[13] Furthermore, the Soviet Union was revealed as an authoritarian state and as a revolution that did not achieve the radical transformation of society; and the proletariat did not fulfil the historical mission it had been entrusted with by Marx's classical theory: to perpetrate revolution in the more advanced industrialized societies and to realize human emancipation. In this sense, theory was in crisis and there was a need to question its foundations and understand the historical changes that determined the new phase of postliberal capitalism and the new form of society that was emerging in the twentieth century.

Friedrich Pollock was one of the main representatives of the Frankfurt School, and his theory of postliberal capitalism greatly influenced the idea of society which would later on be developed by Horkheimer, Marcuse and Adorno. At the core of Pollock's analysis (1989) on state capitalism, which is the mode that characterized the postliberal social order of the first half of the twentieth century, lies the idea that capitalism can be completely managed and directed through a political state-run plan, which would replace the primacy of economics with the primacy of politics; this was decisively different from the previous phase of free-market capitalism, characterized by the primacy of economics (Marramao, 1975; Postone, 2003).

The complexity and clarity of Pollock's theory, which he deployed mainly in his articles "State Capitalism" and "Is Social Nationalism a New

[12] On this, see Postone (2003).

[13] On this, see Maiso (2018, 2020).

Order?", exceed the scope of this chapter. However, I would like to highlight a hypothesis regarding his social theory which was articulated by Giacomo Marramao in his essay "Political Economy and Critical Theory" and was later analysed in more detail by Moishe Postone from a different theoretical standpoint. According to Marramao (1975), Pollock's analysis displays a tendency to strip society of its contradictory elements, even if Pollock claimed that social contradictions in the politically administered capitalist had not been overcome. However, his theory failed to posit the inherently contradictory nature of society in the new phase of development of capitalism.

Postone (2003) concurs with the latter, and his detailed analysis of the theory of state capitalism clearly states that, for Pollock, there is no immanent contradiction in the new phase of capitalist development. That is, for Pollock, contradiction stopped being intrinsic in the basic structure of society; it is extrinsic, and it is the contradiction between production and distribution. The analysis of state capitalism results in the notion of a one-dimensional social totality that is completely managed and integrated. This means that, in its fundamental structure, postliberal capitalism has become non-contradictory, a perspective which entails the impossibility of immanently establishing emancipation and an antagonistic subjectivity.

In this sense, Postone's critical theory can be considered an attempt to resituate contradiction at the very foundation of society, in a transformed capitalism, and to overcome the concept of one-dimensional society that emerged in Pollock's theory. Postone's theory is indispensable for the renovation of the critical theory of society, but it does not manage to go deep into the possibility of an antagonistic subjectivity; it rather focuses on refuting the idea of the proletariat as a subject of transformation. And this can serve as a starting point from which to advance beyond the classical theory of revolution.

That said, the conceptualization of postliberal capitalism as a one-dimensional society influenced the critical theory of Marcuse. From his text *The Struggle Against Liberalism in the Totalitarian View of the State,* written in the 1930s, he refers to Pollock's analysis and its foundations in order to understand the development of capitalist society in the twentieth century.[14] However, it is in the *One-Dimensional Man*, his most

[14] On Pollock's influence on the thinking of Marcuse, see Marramao (1975).

important work, that Marcuse extensively develops the idea of the one-dimensional society, whose origins can be traced back to the social theory of Pollock.

In this work, Marcuse argues that advanced industrial society has a one-dimensional character, post-war capitalism has been transformed. The one-dimensional society is a new phase of civilization, it is a technological society that creates a basic tendency, one which is characterized by the capacity to repress social contradictions and dominate or integrate the power of the negative, which has been historically concentrated in the proletariat.

According to the theory of the advanced industrial society, the bourgeoisie and the proletariat continue to be the fundamental classes of society. However, in this phase of social development, a type of technical and authoritarian rationality has emerged which has acquired a certain social autonomy and has become a political force that can repress the contradictions of society. The bourgeoisie has lost its control of the economy and the state in favour of this rationality, while the proletariat cannot bring about revolution for its class consciousness is blocked by the culture of the masses and the happy consciousness produced in the one-dimensional society (Cohen, 1984; Marcuse, 2007).

It must be stressed that Marcuse was very critical of the one-dimensional society and tried to understand the advanced industrial society from the viewpoint of its transformation, even if the understanding of this society as one-dimensional were to result in breaking with the very possibility of inherently theorizing emancipation and antagonistic subjectivity.[15] Beyond the decisive influence that the failure of the revolution in the West and the changes in postliberal capitalism had on his intellectual experience, Marcuse insisted throughout his work on substantiating the possibility of an antagonistic subjectivity; as we have seen, he did it anthropologically. This possibility was to be found in human instincts, in *Eros* as the revolutionary and creative "primitive counterforce".

[15] In a footnote in *Time, Labour, and Social Domination,* Moishe Postone (2003: 86) asserts that Marcuse continued to look for an inherent possibility of emancipation, even considering postliberal capitalism as a one dimensional totality. He did it in *Eros and Civilization* "he sought to locate that possibility by transposing the locus of contradiction to the level of psychic formation". I do not agree with Postone's affirmation, given that, for Marcuse, the psychic formation has an essentially ontological-anthropological character; therefore, this level is extrinsic to the very foundation of capitalist society and its historically specific character.

It is my opinion that the conceptualization of capitalism as a totality where the contradictions that are inherent in the basic forms of socialization are overcome influenced the theory of Marcuse; this, in turn, led to a shift of the foundations of antagonistic subjectivity from society and their reconstruction on the basis of a notion of human nature with instinctive nature at its core. What I have presented as the Marcusian model—in a somewhat heuristic sense—is characteristic of his theory of negative subjectivity and, as well shall see in the following and last section of this chapter, is also present in John Holloway's theory of praxis.

Antagonistic Subjectivity in the Theory of Holloway

Holloway's attempt to establish an antagonistic subjectivity can be found in his most important work, *Change the World Without Taking Power*; however, his most rounded theoretical elaboration unfolds in his book *Crack Capitalism*. The starting point in *Change the World Without Taking Power* is "the scream", which means opposition, negativity and the struggle of the subject that rebels against domination. After the scream comes "the doing", a concept that will be central in Holloway's theory of praxis. Doing has a broad sense; it is not only an action or a material condition for living, it goes beyond that. It is a negative practice of the subjects, a form of resistance and part of their struggle to change the world. Holloway establishes a link between doing and labour, one that is crucial in substantiating antagonistic subjectivity. In capitalist society, doing becomes labour.

Furthermore, according to Holloway, human doing is creative. He documents this characteristic on the basis of a well-known paragraph from *Capital*, where Marx speaks of a distinction between human beings and other species,[16] namely the awareness of a goal, the projection towards something that can be. This human characteristic that Marx points at is

[16] "A spider conducts operations that resemble those of a weaver, and a bee puts to shame many an architect in the construction of her cells. But what distinguishes the worst architecture from the best of bees is this, that the architect raises his structure in imagination before he erects it in reality. At the end of every labour-process, we get a result that already existed in the imagination of the labourer at its commencement. He not only effects a change of form in the material on which he works, but he also realises a purpose of his own that gives the law to his modus operandi, and to which he must subordinate his will" (Marx, 1965: 178).

not interpreted by Holloway as one characteristic among many others which distinguish us from animals; it is perceived as something essential, it is what makes us human: "The scream and the doing-which-is-a-going-beyond distinguish humans from animals. Humans, but not animals, are ecstatic: they exist not only in, but also against-and-beyond themselves" (Holloway, 2010a: 25).

Interestingly, one paragraph after stating the abovementioned, Holloway contradicts his own premise and, in a sense, tries to retract and distance himself from the idea of a human nature, as well as from the essentialist implications thereof:

> We scream and push-beyond not because that is human nature, but, on the contrary, because we are torn from what we consider to be humanity. Our negativity arises not from our humanity, but from the negation of our humanity, from the feeling that humanity is not-yet, that it is something to be fought for. It is not human nature, but the scream of our starting point that compels us to focus on doing. (Holloway, 2010a: 25)

However, he maintains the idea that it is possible to decipher what the human being is, for, according to Holloway, in capitalism we are separated from what humanity is. And we can only say that we are separated from something if we know what that something is. Holloway (2010a: 25) argues that he opts for doing and not being for "doing implies movement" and, therefore, doing is something historical.[17] This perspective involves an idea of the being as something static, but the notion of the being that we find in the most influential representative of ontology of the twentieth century, Martin Heidegger, is not precisely static, it moves. In *Being and Time*, being is understood as fundamentally historical; the category of historicity accounts for the movement that is inherent in being. However, Holloway's intention is not to follow Heidegger, it is to assume concrete human beings as his starting point and comprehend them as a moment of negation of that which is.

As in the theory of Marcuse, his goal is a concrete philosophy, a theory that is based on subjects as negation. And negation is founded on the idea of subjects as doers. Remarkably, Holloway (2010a: 26) claims that "the

[17] Holloway also mentions he does not opt for speaking or thinking; however, in *Crack Capitalism* he does not clarify why speaking or thinking do not imply movement and history and why they would be less relevant than doing.

doer is not" and that "any definition of the subject is therefore contradictory or indeed violent". However, to understand subjects as doers is already to define them and to identify them; arguably, the logic of identity is at work within the concept of doing, given that the idea of human beings as doers reduces the multiple to a common denominator, that is, doing.

Holloway's strategy to escape this problem is to establish an antagonism between movement and what it tends to rigidify. Given that he has established that doing is movement against-what-is, it is possible to define subjects as doers without apparently identifying them. Although to conceptualize human beings as doers is already to fix them within a concept.

Likewise, according to Holloway (2010a: 25) "there is no 'being', or rather [...] being can only be a frustrated becoming"; this approach entails a sort of negative ontology. Alex Callinicos (2005) also pointed this out: according to this author, the key to Holloway's negative ontology is a radical subjectivism. I concur in part with Callinicos in that one of the key aspects of Holloway's thinking is his radical subjectivism. However, to what extent this aspect allows us to understand his theory as a negative ontology is, I believe, not very clear in Callinicos's critique of Holloway.

From my perspective, Holloway's theory is a negative ontology, for the emphasis is not placed on the "being" but rather on its negation; or, as Holloway would say, in crisis, in the crisis of being. For that reason, in his interpretation, "being" can only exist in its frustrated becoming. Holloway rejects the philosophy of Martin Heidegger; however, this rejection does not allow his theory to escape an ontological content, as we have seen. On the contrary, his approach entails a negative ontology, given that it is founded on a concept that sets out to understand the very being of subjects in their frustrated historical becoming; this concept is the doing.

In *Crack Capitalism*, Holloway seeks to substantiate antagonistic subjectivity on the basis of Marx's theory of value, and in the centre of his theory of praxis one can find his anthropological reading of the dual character of labour that Marx developed in *Capital*. The purpose of this is to show that his concept of doing is central for an anti-capitalist praxis. Just like Marcuse, Holloway moves from ontology—which he unfolds in *Change the World Without Taking Power*—to anthropology—developed in *Crack Capitalism*—through the *Economic and Philosophic Manuscripts*.

Holloway's (2010b) argument is that the antagonistic relation between estranged labour and the conscious life-activity that the young Marx develops in *Manuscripts* is basically the same relation that the mature Marx deploys in *Capital* in terms of the categories of abstract labour and concrete labour, which express the twofold character of labour represented by the commodity. For Holloway (2010b: 93), "essentially, then, the abstraction of labour discussed in *Capital* is the alienation of labour discussed in the *1844 Manuscripts*"; the same would apply to concrete labour and conscious life-activity, they are both moments of expression of one same idea in Marx.

According to Holloway (2010b: 93), conscious life-activity and concrete labour can be understood as categories that account for the generic being of humanity, "that which makes him human". A generic being that is in a living antagonism with the capitalist social synthesis that Marx articulates through the categories of alienated labour and abstract labour. For Holloway (2010b: 93):

> The argument of *Capital* rests on the same distinction between humans and animals which is so central to the *1844 Manuscripts*. It is purposive doing that distinguishes us from animals…Capitalism robs us of the unity of project and performance, purpose and doing: it robs us, therefore, of our distinctive humanity.

Thus, the human power of doing encloses the potential to rebel against abstract labour, which is the historical form that the doing assumes in capitalist society. Human doing in capitalism is alienated or abstracted in labour, and in capitalism "the cracks are revolts of one type of doing against another type of doing" (Holloway, 2010b: 84).

In *Change the World Without Taking Power*, Holloway ontologically posits the category of doing through its difference with the category of being. Nevertheless, in *Crack Capitalism* his theory assumes an anthropological direction in that it derives the concept of doing from conscious life activity and from concrete labour, a concept that accounts for the generic being of humanity: human beings are, in essence, creative doers, and their doing struggles to free itself from abstract labour.

Conclusion

Holloway's theory of praxis is a version of the Marcusian model, in which the condition of possibility of antagonistic subjectivity is founded on an anthropological level. The potential to negate capitalism lies in doing, an activity that differentiates us, human beings, as a species. I have pointed out that the Marcusian model induces dualisms; doing against labour is the dualism that is implicit in *Crack Capitalism*. A dualism that Holloway seeks to overcome, albeit unsuccessfully, through the theory of form of Open Marxism.

The dualism reappears time and again in his theory, also in the very concept of the crack as a method for revolution and as the creation of a space where a distinct way of doing is asserted, different from abstract doing. Holloway (2010b: 115) refers to "the struggle of doing against labour"; in this approach, the relation between the two aspects of the twofold character of labour is interpreted as an antagonistic interaction between a capitalist aspect and another which is potentially non-capitalist. The latter exists in capitalism in the form of its negation and struggles to assert itself; upon the abolition of capitalism, creative doing will be realized.

This approach contains a very particular interpretation of dialectics. Schäbel (2018) has pointed out that it remits to an interpretation formulated by Proudhon. The latter considered categories to have a good and a bad side, the goal being to abolish the bad side and realize the good one; in Holloway's interpretation, the side to be abolished would be abstract labour, and the one to assert would be doing. From this viewpoint, Holloway's theory can be considered a practical normative theory, one that postulates anthropologically an essential principle which must be and which has been negated by history.

Marx's idea of dialectics is more complex and grounded on the contradictions that constitute social totality, social contradictions that produce an immanent social dynamic which points beyond itself.[18] It is not dualist, given that the contradictory coexistence in categories such as labour or commodity does not distinguish between a capitalist side and a side that is potentially non-capitalist, as value and use value or abstract labour and concrete labour arguably do. In this sense, the struggle of the proletariat against the capitalist class in the classical theory of revolution was not a

[18] On this, see Postone (2003).

struggle for the proletariat to realize itself as a class; it was a struggle to abolish itself as a class.

In his work, Holloway places special emphasis on the contradictory character of capitalist society. However, his interpretation of the social contradiction is basically that of the contradiction between the subject and society or, in other terms, the antagonism between human nature and the social–historical world. For Holloway, society is an environment that has been aligned by its creators, and what is theoretically relevant is to understand how subjects are the contradiction within the society that we have created and can stop creating. To that end, he metaphorically uses the image of a wall to refer to capitalist society; we, the human beings, bang our head against the wall and create cracks due to the misfitting of our doing within society. Thus, critical theory is understood as "the theory of our own misfitting" (Holloway, 2010b: 9).

This perspective implicitly contains the idea of the one-dimensional society, a weave of social cohesion that is closed within itself and can only be opened through the anthropological disposition of the subject towards emancipation. Thus, contradiction is understood only as the contradiction between society and the subjects that constitute it; this is one aspect of the dialectic between the subject and society, but it overlooks the contradiction that is inherent in the very fabric of society.

Drawing from the theory of Alfred Sohn-Rethel, Holloway (2010b: 52) posits that "to underline the close-knit character of the social cohesion of capitalist society, I refer to it as a social synthesis". Here, Holloway interrupts the negative dialectics that he aspires to attain in his theory, given that negative dialectics is a dialectics without synthesis. Adorno (2007) rejected the conceptualization of society in synthetic terms, for he thought of an open dialectics where contradiction lies in society itself. This does not mean that the subjects are the only contradiction in society simply because they constitute it. This perspective identifies society with the subjects that constitute it; society for Adorno has a dual and contradictory character. According to Adorno (2001: 38), society

> … is neither the mere sum or, agglomeration, or whatever you wish to call it, of individuals, not something absolutely autonomous with regard to individuals. It always contains both these moments at the same time; it is realized only through individuals but, as the relationship between them, it cannot be reduced to them. On the other hand, it should not be seen as a pure, over-arching concept existing for itself.

Insofar as it is a relation, society is also contradictory in its basic structure; hence Adorno's idea (2008: 2) of "the contradictory character of reality", largely the reason for which he refused to substantiate an antagonistic subjectivity anthropologically. To conclude, it is important to highlight that one of the most relevant aspects of Holloway's theory is that, like Marcuse, he does not give up on the effort to establish the possibility of an antagonistic subjectivity in contemporary capitalism. This is no minor matter; it is, perhaps, the decisive issue of the critical theory of society. However, a theory of praxis with an ontological and anthropological foundation is, ultimately, identitarian. It is a theory that reduces human diversity to an essential characteristic that distinguishes us as a species and has an alleged potential for emancipation. Holloway claims that critical theory does not seek to assert identities, but his theory falls into the trap of asserting an identity: that of human beings as doers.

Acknowledgements For their comments, observations, and suggestions on this text I am very grateful to Roberto Longoni, Panagiotis Doulos, Rogelio Regalado Mujica, Ignacio De Boni and Rodrigo Pascual.

References

Adorno, T. W. (1980). *Philosophische Terminologie 2*. Suhrkamp.

Adorno, T. W. (2001). *Introduction to Sociology* (1a ed.). Stanford University Press.

Adorno, T. W. (2006). *History and Freedom: Lectures 1964–1965*. Polity Press.

Adorno, T. W. (2007). *Negative Dialectic*. Continuum.

Adorno, T. W. (2008). *Lectures on Negative Dialectics: Fragments of a Lecture Course 1965/1966*. http://amazon.com.mx/

Bundschuh, S. (2004). The Theoretical Place of Utopia: Some Remarks on Marcuse's Dual Anthropology. In J. Abromeit & W. M. Cobb (Eds.), *Herbert Marcuse. A critical reader* (1a. ed., pp. 152–162). Routledge.

Callinicos, A. (2005). Sympathy for the Devil? John Holloway's Mephistophelian Marxism. *Capital & Class, 29*(1), 17–19. https://doi.org/10.1177/030981680508500104

Cohen, J. L. (1982). *Class and Civil Society: The Limits of Marxian Critical Theory*. University of Massachusetts Press.

Cohen, J. L. (1984). The Legacy of Herbert Marcuse. *Dissent*, (Fall), 90–93.

García Vela, A. (2020a). Objectivity and Critical Theory: Debating Open Marxism. In A. C. Dinerstein, A. García Vela, E. González, & J. Holloway

(Eds.), *Open Marxism 4. Against a Closing World* (1a. ed., Vol. 4, pp. 47–62). Pluto Press.
García Vela, A. (2020b). Reflexiones sobre las nuevas lecturas de Marx. La Teoría Crítica como un conocimiento no-identitario. *Constelaciones. Revista de Teoría Crítica, 11/12*, 311–330.
García Vela, A., & Longoni, R. (2020). El giro normativo de Jürgen Habermas como fundamentación ontológica de la Teoría Crítica. *Sociológica México, 35*(101), 9–33.
Grollios, V. (2017). *Negativity and Democracy. Marxism and the Critical Theory Tradition*. Routledge.
Habermas, J. (1981). *Gespriiche mit Herbert Marcuse*. Suhrkamp Verlag.
Habermas, J. (2015a). *The Theory of Communicative Action: Lifeworld and Systems, a Critique of Functionalist Reason, Volume 2*. Wiley.
Habermas, J. (2015b). *The Theory of Communicative Action: Reason and the Rationalization of Society, Volume 1*. Wiley.
Holloway, J. (2010a). *Change the World Without Taking Power*. Pluto Press.
Holloway, J. (2010b). *Crack Capitalism*. Pluto Press.
Honneth, A. (1993). *The Critique of Power: Reflective Stages in a Critical Social Theory*. MIT Press.
Jay, M. (1972). The Frankfurt School's Critique of Marxist Humanism. *Social Research, 39*(2), 285–305.
Johannssen, D. (2013). Toward a Negative Anthropology. *Anthropology & Materialism*. https://doi.org/10.4000/am.194
Johannssen, D. (2018). Humanism and Anthropology from Walter Benjamin to Ulrich Sonnemann. In B. Best, W. Bonefeld, & C. O'Kane (Eds.), *The SAGE Handbook of Frankfurt School Critical Theory* (Vol. 3, pp. 1252–1269). SAGE.
Kurz, R. (2007). Grau ist des Lebens goldner Baum und grün die Theorie. Das Praxis-Problem als Evergreen verkürzter Kapitalismuskritik und die Geschichte der Linken. *EXIT! Krise und Kritik der Warengesellschaft, 4*, 15–106.
Löwy, M. (2005). *The Theory of Revolution in the Young Marx*. Haymarket Books.
Maiso, J. (2018). Prefacio: la intempestiva actualidad de Herbert Marcuse. In J. Habermas, K. Popper, & R. Dahrendorf (Eds.), *Filosofía radical: Conversaciones con Marcuse* (2a. ed.). Gedisa. Kindle Edition.
Maiso, J. (2020). Ocaso: El hundimiento de Weimar y la génesis de la Teoría Crítica. In J. Maiso (Ed.), *Laboratorio Weimar: La crisis de la globalización en Euroamérica (1918–1933)* (1a ed., pp. 301–322). Tecnos.
Marcuse, H. (1969). *An Essay on Liberation*. Beacon Press.
Marcuse, H. (1973). The Foundation of Historical Materialism. In H. Marcuse (Ed.), *Studies in Critical Philosophy* (pp. 1–48). Beacon Press.

Marcuse, H. (1978). *The Aesthetic Dimension: Toward a Critique of Marxist Aesthetics*. Beacon Press.

Marcuse, H. (2015). *Eros and Civilization: A Philosophical Inquiry into Freud*: Beacon Press.

Marcuse, H. (2007). *One-Dimensional Man: Studies in the Ideology of Advanced Industrial Society*. Routledge.

Marquard, O. (2007). *Schwierigkeiten mit der Geschichtsphilosophie*. Suhrkamp Verlag.

Marramao, G. (1975). Political Economy and Critical Theory. *Telos, 1975*(24), 56–80. https://doi.org/10.3817/0675024056

Marx, K. (1965). *Capital* (Vol. 1). Progress.

Marx, K. (1998). *The German Ideology. Including Theses on Feuerbach and Introduction to the Critique of Political Economy*. Prometheus Books.

Pollock, F. (1989). State Capitalism: Its Possibilities and Limitations. In S. Bronner & D. Kellner (Eds.), *Critical Theory and Society: A Reader* (pp. 95–118). Routledge.

Postone, M. (2003). *Time, Labor and Social Domination. A Reinterpretation of Marx's Critial Theory* (1a ed.). Cambridge University Press.

Reitter, K. (2012). Flirting with Value Critique: Remarks on John Holloway's Crack Capitalism. *Journal of Classical Sociology, 2*(12), 248–255. https://doi.org/10.1177/1468795X12445605

Schäbel, M. (2018). *El Marxismo Abierto y la herencia de la Esuela de Frankfurt*. (Doctorado). Benemérita Universidad Autónoma de Puebla.

Schäbel, M. (2020). Is Open Marxism an Offspring of the Frankfurt School? Subversive Critique as Method. In A. C. Dinerstein, A. García Vela, E. González, & J. Holloway (Eds.), *Open Marxism 4. Against a Closing World* (Vol. 4, pp. 76–91). Pluto Press.

Schmidt, A. (2014). *The Concept of Nature in Marx*. Verso.

CHAPTER 9

The Crisis of Capital and the Conformist Rebellion: On the Need to Reflect on the False Solutions

José A. Zamora

The almost insoluble task is to let neither the power of others, nor our own powerlessness, stupefy us.

Th. W. Adorno

In capitalist social formations, social life and its reproduction are organized under two basic forms that both promise to safeguard it and submit it to its own reproduction: in general and abstract terms, these forms are Capital and the State. Both forms possess a pseudo- or almost natural character; that is, they appear as identified with the reproduction of the life itself of society and of its members, and in most cases they are

J. A. Zamora (✉)
Institute of Philosophy, Spanish National Research Council (CSIC), Madrid, Spain
e-mail: joseantonio.zamora@cchs.csic.es

A. García Vela and A. Bonnet (eds.), *The Political Thought of John Holloway*, Marx, Engels, and Marxisms,
https://doi.org/10.1007/978-3-031-34571-5_9

perceived as such. Most individuals cannot even imagine a reproduction of their life and of society other than the one provided by these two fundamental forms of organization, in spite of the fact that they are historical forms, and it is only by accepting that we are before the "end of history" that we can consider them as insurmountable. It is obvious that, along with the socio-economic and legal-political forms, the social ties and identities of the individuals are also mediated and organized under specific cultural and psychodynamic forms that evolve and transform with the contradictory and crisis-ridden dynamic of the system itself. In the constitution and consolidation stage of this social formation in the liberal capitalism of competitiveness, these forms become fundamentally crystallized around the objective illusions of the sphere of circulation and the theoretical constructions that accompany them in the bourgeois philosophical, aesthetic, and political thinking (autonomy, freedom, equality, contract, justice, citizenship…). However, as the promises fuelled by these illusions turn into a disappointment for the vast majority, other cultural and psychodynamic forms become more relevant in the constraint of individuals and in their identification with the capitalist organization of social reproduction, such as nationalism, racism, antisemitism, social Darwinism, authoritarianism, the entrepreneurialization of life, etc., forms that—at least since the beginning of the twentieth century, with the collapse or quasi-complete recruitment of precapitalist popular cultures and bourgeois culture—are subjected to the general framework of the cultural industry. All these forms constitute the structural and symbolic weave of capitalist societies in that they develop the processes of subjectivation subjectification. In any case, the very process of constituting individuals as social beings cannot be separated from the assumption of the need for their lives to be reproduced by means of and through the reproduction of these social forms; forms which have, in some ways, been autonomized from them and on which they depend, but with which they are mostly identified.

Certainly, none of the mentioned forms has been or is free of conflict, crisis, commotion, etc., neither of internal contradictions nor mutual antagonism. Likewise, the identification of individuals with these forms is never completely free of fissures, even more so when their coercive mediation has painful effects on them. However, to this day, they have been able to resist all their crises, even if none of these forms of subjectification and of the organization of social life have worked and work without demanding sacrifices. This becomes more obvious at times of crisis. Nonetheless, their "ordinary" operation also permanently causes suffering, alienation, exploitation, violence, exclusion, etc., which are unevenly distributed. The interplay between the forms of violence we could call structural—that is, those that emanate from the operation of the legal, institutional, and symbolic crystallizations of the systemic coercions—and the forms of explicit violence perpetrated by the military, the police, or criminal activities, has been uniquely successful in capitalism. Its history is not only one of democratic institutions and civil and political liberties, but also of authoritarian states and dictatorships, processes of colonization and the violence of war. Only with an immense dose of cynicism could we ignore the pyramids of sacrifice that have marked the global history of the Capital, State and Nation forms for centuries.

Focusing on the present, there is no doubt that the multiple crisis (economic, of reproduction/care, ecological, and political) that became visible during the 2008 crash has constituted one of the most forceful "stress tests" for the reproduction of these three forms of the organization of social life that are characteristic of capitalist social formations. The global reaction has obeyed one fundamental priority: to fortify these forms as a way of preventing the collapse. However, the tackling of this multiple crisis through the preservation of these forms has not only increased its coercive character and the sacrifices demanded; the reproduction of the Capital, State and Nation forms under the new conditions that resulted from the crisis has not been able to eliminate the threat of economic, state, or national collapse either. On the contrary, their capacity to ensure the reproduction of life in conditions of dignity, equality, and sustainability, which had never applied to the immense majority of individuals or to nature to begin with, is currently reduced in a radical and accelerated way. The destruction of the environment and the growth of the contingent of "excess" humanity are the most impactful effects of this combination of the depletion of the forms of Capital, State, and Nation and their reinforcement at all costs.

The structural dynamics, their contradictions, and their propensity to crisis currently pose immensely significant questions. Even if we cannot assert with utter certainty that there is an internal and impassable limit to the process of capitalist accumulation, as Wallerstein (2010) and Kurz (2012) point out, we must at least admit that there will be no lasting stabilization and that we will most probably face shorter or longer periods of recession—and perhaps of slight recoveries—without knowing for sure if these cycles are nothing more than a waiting period on our way to ecological collapse. In any case, the third industrial revolution does not seem capable of creating the "virtuous" economic cycles of Fordism. Maintaining the profit rates or avoiding their decrease leaves less and less margin for the financing of the reproduction of the life of those who are deemed "superfluous" by the valorization of capital. The expansive imperialism that incorporated territories and peoples to the process of capitalist valorization has given way to an imperialism of exclusion, whereby an increasing mass of individuals and territories have become useless or expendable for valorization, without this being translated into any type of liberation for them. Furthermore, the forms of "recognition" of *national* subjects of law—which accompanied the post-war capitalist expansion in the centres of the capitalist system as a model of abundance—are being progressively dismantled as the public debt that has sustained them for the past four decades becomes more and more unsustainable in the long term. The upkeeping of accumulation demands today forms of expropriation and plunder that unleash massive movements of flight and displacement. The unjustified rejections at the borders, as well as the fortification of the latter, follow an objective rationale in the same crisis of civilization that highlights the increasing impossibility of universalizing an alleged wellbeing that is mediated by the valorization of capital.

Systemic crises of such magnitude have always been associated by traditional Marxist movements of emancipation to the perspective of the collapse of capitalism and/or its overcoming through revolution. What is surprising in today's crisis is that, to most individuals who suffer personally from this crisis, the revolutionary overcoming of capitalism has become an unimaginable reality. There is certainly no lack of forms of protest and demand, of rage and rejection, be they local and temporary or more lasting through time. However, in most cases these forms do not point towards the overcoming of the Capital, State, or Nation forms. They either demand the impossible return of an allegedly more "human" capitalism which is generally identified with the "golden decades" of the Keynesian period, as the heirs to the integrated post-war forms of the left demand; or they call for the restriction of the protective state to a national "we" as a way of guaranteeing the undivided enjoyment of benefits that are becoming more and more exclusive; or try to ensure private enclaves of privilege and wellbeing through strategies of isolation and subtraction in the increasingly debilitated structures of redistribution and solidarity; or demand the authoritarian and despotic control of the chaos—such is the case of one part of the wageworkers who perceive themselves as the middle class—in the hope of shifting the most devastating effects of the crisis to those who have been rendered more vulnerable (the immigrants and the marginalized, the impoverished populations forced into precariousness in the metropolises or the so-called periphery countries of the world, etc.). It is difficult to find significant practices and movements that aim at abolishing wage labour and the state. I believe this is the framework that allows for the appreciation of the contribution made by John Holloway.

Crack Capitalism reflects the effort to think of revolution—and think of it in a radical way—in a setting such as the one described, where the need for revolution is more intense and more urgent, and where the feeling of its impossibility or improbability haunts the thoughts and actions of an infinity of individuals who feel this need (2010: 10). This is what Holloway called "the dilemma of the urgent impossibility of revolution" in *Change the World Without Taking Power* (2005: 74), a dilemma that can be escaped only through a conception of revolution which opposes the traditional conceptions that focus on taking state power under the leadership of vanguard political organizations. This new conception points towards a "radical reorganization of our daily activity" (2010: 86), considered at the same time the more obvious and simpler but more difficult task. The issue, therefore, is to ensure its possibility without negating or silencing its difficulty.

The former, its possibility, is founded on the thesis that, if man makes capitalism, man can also stop doing it. Behind this thesis hides the critique *ad hominem absconditum* of the fetishism of the commodity in Marx. "Capital" is presented as a desubjectified subject of the social process, but critique reveals the forms "value", "commodity", "money", and "capital" as reified and inverted social relations (Holloway, 1993: 76). The system is constituted by virtue of the actions of the individuals, it is their result, and therefore their "naturalness" is a "pseudo-naturalness" (*Naturwüchsigkeit*); however, as such, it appears to stand against them, following a dynamic that crushes them and turns them into mere executors and extensions of the objectivity they have produced. Autonomized social objectivity is therefore presented as something that is external and opposes them, whose genesis has become opaque, almost impenetrable for certain individuals who are not able to unravel the process of this autonomization, even if real abstraction is nothing more than the autonomized reification of their entire work: "Objectivity is nothing but objectified subjectivity" (Holloway, 1995: 172). Marx's theory of value allows for the unravelling of the dialectic between structure and action without dissolving one into the other or deducing one from the other. The concept of inversion (*Verkehrung*) in this dialectic prevents a simple derivation of the objectified forms from action, as if we were before a process of natural rationalization through differentiation and coordination—as functionalism claims—but also a complete subsumption of action under these forms practically without fissures or frictions—as structuralism asserts—no matter how much certain Marxian categories, such as the "automatic subject" or "personifications" (*Charaktermasken*), might seem to imply it.

It is well known that Holloway has taken the *ad hominem absconditum* critique of fetishism to an extreme that is not devoid of problematics.[1] His attempt to dissolve the reified rigidity of social objectivity leads him to interpret it as a contradictory process and as a process of struggle. Capital itself is not only a reified objectivity but also a struggle (of its producers with themselves or with the alienated product of their activity). Struggle does not oppose the system from the outside, it is inherent in the very constitution and development of the value, money, and capital forms. The cracks are part of the crust because the crust is created by those who incessantly rebel from the inside, who constantly look for alternatives and aim beyond it. Antifetishism constitutes fetishism. The revolution becomes or can become omnipresent and turn into an everyday affair that is crystallized in "the barely visible transformation of everyday activities" (2010: 12). Therefore, if fetishization is a process and its constitution is an everyday struggle, daily revolt is an unquestionable and ordinary fact and not an extraordinary event to be relegated to the future. What remains to be seen is whether and how this everyday revolt is supported, articulated,

[1] In focusing on the dissolution of the reifying rigidity of the capitalist forms, the contradictions that are inherent in the unfolding of these forms do not receive the attention that they probably deserve and that they do receive in Marx's analysis of form in *Capital*. The extreme "subjectivation" of reified objectivity emphasizes the contradiction between the capital form and the practices of resistance and rebellion; however, it might disregard the immanent contradictions of the very process of accumulation and of the "value" form, a point that is made by other interpretations, such as the "critique of value" (Kurz, 2005). To consider the contradictions that are inherent in the capital form and the self-destructive potential of the capitalist economy does not necessarily mean to reduce antagonism to a contradiction between capital and capital. However, the crises of capital are not only the result of the opposition to and rejection of its rule. Otherwise, there is a risk that the real struggles and goals of the actors be counterfactually assigned with a power of subversion that rests solely on itself (see Elbe, 2006).

and coordinated, and how it turns against the Capital and State forms. This approach culminates in the well-known formula of "we are the crisis of capital" which we already come across in *Change the World* and in subsequent formulations in all his works (2005: 202; 2010: 250; 2016) and which is the title of the last *reader* (2018). We could say that, at any given moment, in any given place and situation, the reproduction of the abstract social universality is at stake and it *is in our hands* to (begin to) prevent it by giving a chance to self-determination against and beyond capital: the decision and "the responsibility is ours" (2010: 169).

The latter, that is, the extreme difficulty of revolution, derives from the fact that creative potential and the capacity for action are not to be found outside the reified forms, but *in*, against and beyond these forms, what initially seems to indicate a distancing from a possible ontologizing of the subject—action, creativity, strength...—enclosed from the outside, one that autonomist currents tend to incur.[2] The category "fetishism" must not only be unravelled as a clotted social relation, as something that is constantly produced; it also accounts for "*the stability of bourgeois society.* It points at once to the dehumanisation of people, to our own complicity in the reproduction of power, and to the difficulty (or apparent impossibility) of revolution" (Holloway, 2005: 51). "Social synthesis" in

[2] J. Holloway wants to equally confront a structuralist and an autonomist reading of Marx (Bonefeld, 2009), but his wish to establish a starting point in "the particular" (2010: 11), to speak affirmatively of a "subject" (2016) or a "we" in the face of the fetishist reification of abstract social synthesis, to compare capital to a "procrustean bed" or a "corset", to refer to needs and use values that are distorted and disfigured by a form from which they must and can free themselves to be able deployed, ... all this runs the risk of betraying the (negative) dialectic to which Holloway claims to want to be faithful. Saying that that capitalism "takes" or "snatches" the wealth of our creative capacities can be understood, against Holloway's own interpretation of fetishism, as the assertion of an exterritoriality—albeit perhaps not as crude as the one that traditional Marxism assigned to the proletariat—now conferred to the common "doing", an exterritoriality that is plural, interstitial, and certainly problematic (see Starosta, 2017). Elsewhere, analysing the concept of "spectral materiality" in Marx and W. Benjamin, I have tried to show that to consider the commodity form as something that remains external to things would be an underdetermination of this form. Neither use-value nor concrete labour represent a external materiality to the capitalist form, which can be recovered outside of it in a simple way. On the contrary, this form shapes them in multiple ways and turns them into the concrete side of the abstraction (Zamora, 2020). This does not mean that this materiality and the living substance of the individual disappear and are left completely subsumed under the abstract form that mediates them. I will return to this point further on when referring to Th. W. Adorno.

capitalism possesses a "dense character" and exercises a powerful coercion (2010: 52). In fact, Holloway asserts, "abstraction is not external to the activity itself" (ibid.: 94). The fact that we might be the "creators" of the structures of abstract domination—which requires an explanation that is far from obvious—that they depend on us for their reproduction, does not make the opposite less true: our reproduction has also become dependent on the reproduction of these structures. This is what constituted the process of creating the "free" labour force in the shaping of the capitalist system; and the fact that the reproduction of the life of the individuals has never been a priority for this system does nothing to refute it.

If the categories and theories of bourgeois political economy reproduce the reversal we were talking about earlier and lose sight of the social relations that appear as relations between things, it is equally true that fetishism is the foundation of everyday "common sense" and its effects are universal. The extreme difficulty of even imagining revolution, but most of all of performing a radical reorganization of our activity, is also founded on the everyday thinking and practice of the individuals themselves. We cannot think of a "life world" that is not mediated by the capital form as a universe of permanent disposition to self-determination and solidarity. There is no critique of fetishism without a critique of our complicity in the reproduction of abstract social universality. The assertion that "we are the crisis of capital" cannot be understood but as a confrontation with ourselves. The reproduction of capital also takes place with our involvement, with our active participation. If objectivity is nothing more than an objectified subjectivity, to confront objectivity is to confront ourselves. Even more so if the way in which the value form is imposed is not always perceived as coercive, if it "may be very subtle and gradual" (2010: 68). Arguably, if there were no introjection of coercion, abstract social universality would not be reproduced. And this element must be considered as intensely and as seriously as the "constant drive towards self-determination" (2010: 39). For only from the consideration of the introjection of coercion does it make sense to demand of ourselves to go against ourselves in order to go against the "social synthesis". Thus, being aware of what makes us consider the domination we tolerate as inevitable, but also of why we would even want the "capital" form, becomes crucial. What makes us affirm that which destroys us? Neither "the mute compulsion of economic relations", nor do the great ideological constructions of bourgeois culture, the coercion of the legal-political structures, or the power of the disciplinary structures suffice to account for the integration of the majority.

The true reach of this issue becomes clear when the introjection of the coercion takes an irrational turn in the rise of the different forms of fascism and national socialism in Europe. We are confronted with the key question facing Critical Theory, forced to rethink the critique of political economy in the face of fascism, antisemitism, and the cultural industry. And this question once again acquires an urgent quality in the face of the shift towards authoritarianism that is taking place at the global level. This shift forces us not only to reflect on the difficulties of the revolution but also to think of the false solution of a conformist rebellion. I believe this is an aspect that open Marxism must attend to in more detail and grant it the importance it deserves in its relation to Critical Theory.

It is well known that authors such as Horkheimer and Adorno focus on the mediation between the structures of capitalist domination and the processes of subjectivation, where not only the constitution of the forms of consciousness is of importance but also the psychic-libidinal economy. Through the psychic-libidinal conflicts, this domination is inscribed within the individuals, it is part of their constitution as social individuals. This allows the recognition within these psychic-libidinal conflicts of the mediation of social antagonism, which in turn renders them an essential source of knowledge of antagonism itself and of its effects on the individuals (Adorno, 1967: 77). At the same time, the historical and social determination of the psychic-libidinal economy forces these authors to consider the new conditions of subjectivation, to which the thesis on the weakening of the individual responds. This thesis is crucial in the understanding of the perpetuation of a system that causes unjustifiable suffering. The self that is debilitated in the new social and historical constellation of monopoly and authoritarian capitalism is less and less able to perform its role as a mediating instance between social reality and its imperatives, on the one hand, and libidinal impulses, on the other—not even in the precarious and unstable forms that psychoanalysis set out to untangle and stabilize. The new social and historical conditions radically alter the access of the self to the satisfaction of its impulses, to a non-repressive sublimation, to a fortress without the shielding imposed by an absolutized self-conservation and, finally, to a solidary socialization without an excess of repression. It is in this sense that the situation of the individuals in monopoly capitalism, a situation that is responsible for a particular weakening of human beings and their subjectivity, processes new and more acute forms of experiential impoverishment and psychosocial regression.

In this regard, the concept of "administered world" tries to account for a condensation of the compact network of economic, bureaucratic-administrative, and political structures for which the relative autonomy of the self becomes a distorting factor that must be neutralized, even and above all where it is apparently glorified and celebrated. Contrary to what it might seem, this epochal diagnosis is not refuted in essence by the new emotional regime of the subjectivation of the post-Fordist phase of capitalism or by what others define as the passage from disciplinary societies to societies of control. In fact, the new corporate strategies do nothing but increase the instrumentalization of emotions for the creation of value and for capitalization. The incorporation of humanist psychology into the organization of labour increases the efficiency and amount of the results. Thus, the strategies of capitalization invade even the most intimate spheres of everyday life to subject them to a commodification that aspires to be all-encompassing. The priority is no longer the repression of desires and impulses, but their development and realization under a model of *indirect rule* that functionalizes and instrumentalizes autonomy in order to reinforce dependence. The demand to be oneself (!) amounts to perceiving oneself as an unlimited capitalization machine. It is an exacerbated individualism whose substance, however, is subjugation. Even so, power relations are no longer articulated through strategies of domination from the outside but through the activation of the potential of individuals for self-control.

In all these transformations, there is something that remains unchanged. Beyond the suffering caused by the situations of precariarization and exclusion that affect an increasing number of individuals, it is obvious that many others are finding it extremely difficult to "successfully" adapt to the new demands by leveraging the flexibility that is presented as an adaptive answer. For this flexibility does not emerge from a reinforced self but is rather a new figure of the weakened self. Many feel they have been left behind and are overwhelmed by the coercion that pushes towards a permanent self-optimization, and this seems to be the source of many mental disorders, addictions, or self-destructive behaviours. It is well-known that the demand to view oneself as a machine of limitless capitalization and to act accordingly is linked to increased rates of depression. In the so-called "control" societies, the emotional and expressive activation of the individuals does not reduce social suffering in the slightest.

In this sense, social suffering is the point of intersection between antagonistic objectivity and individual experience. This means that social mediation manifests itself and can be identified in what is mediated, in the singular individuals, in concrete situations. And, at the same time, in the suffering becomes identifiable the coercive character of this mediation. Adorno assumes the existence in individuals of the necessary freedom to experience and recognize real impotence in the face of abstract social universality. As we shall see, this is the paradoxical force of the subject with which we can "break through the fallacy of constitutive subjectivity" (Adorno, 1973: xx). Through the experience of this impotence, the subject conserves a power over itself that does not self-deceitfully appear as autonomy. This experience is not an ontological substratum but a potential. Therefore, it is not about imagining a free autonomy, where what really occurs is the subsumption of the individual under the relation of capital, but about becoming aware of social mediation by virtue of the indissoluble tie with nature which, in the subject and outside of it, is subjected to the coercion of abstract synthesis (Scheit, 2015: 25). The subject of the non-regulated experience is not the subject that believes to be autonomous, but the damaged subject who, in the damage it has suffered, is capable of remembering the broken nature within it and outside it. Therefore, openness to suffering is the fundamental cognitive function of the damaged individual: the experience both of the violence of mediation and of the fact that not everything in the subject and in the object is depleted and disappears within it.

However, this does not mean that Adorno conceives suffering as a safe port for critique, for the very society that produces the suffering also develops mechanisms to ensure its invisibility. "It is part of the mechanism of domination to forbid recognition of the suffering it produces" (Adorno, 2005: 63). That is why he is fully aware of the possibility that the awareness of oppression and suffering might even disappear. Therefore, the question that steers the research and theoretical reflection of Critical Theory in the 1930s is precisely why, in the face of the exponential increase of social suffering caused by an unprecedented systemic crisis, the rebellion of the oppressed acquires regressive and authoritarian characteristics. Empirical research has shown that conventionalism, submission, authoritarian regression, superstition and stereotypes, the exaltation of power, destructivity and cynicism, projection, and sexuality are necessary mechanisms for a self that is weakened by social processes that decisively affect the conflicts taking place within its psyche. Its capacity or incapacity to stand up to them was determined by the social processes and relations of domination. At the same time, this capacity or incapacity made them vulnerable before the political offers that reinforced domination. This analysis allowed them to establish a tie between the psychic-libidinal conflict, authoritarian dispositions in individuals that have been socialized in monopoly capitalism, and certain social phenomena such as authoritarian nationalism or antisemitism, which are once again coming to the forefront.

The conflict between the necessary libidinal occupation of the self so as to resist in the increasingly ferocious struggle for survival and the experience of helplessness in the face of structural changes that are incomprehensible and can barely be influenced is "resolved" in weakened individuals by virtue of an ambiguity between submission and the coagulated rebellion in the psyche of those who cling to the existing order. It is well-known that the authoritarian personality finds a way out from its internal conflict by identifying with the rule that is embodied in a personal figure and projecting aggressions against groups that are pointed out as weaker. The result is a paradoxical *conformist rebellion*: a sort of combination between the pleasure of obeying and aggression against the defenseless. Racism, nationalist chauvinism, or authoritarian populism act as a "false cure" (*Schiefheilung*) of sorts that sheds the individual symptom by participating in a "collective symptom". This false cure can only work if the nationalist or authoritarian images and myths allow for the integration in the collective; that is, if they become a movement of the masses, thus fulfilling the fantasies of omnipotence and fusion. This way the "collective narcissism" acts as a powerful means of integration. This clearly shows that there is no one-way street between suffering, feeling affronted, and anti-systemic political struggle. There are also false responses to the experience of suffering and victimization, as Th. W. Adorno himself points out: "Modern anti-Semitic ideology is the antidote against the sufferings entailed by rational civilization" (Adorno et al., 2019: xliii–xliv).

The same can be said of the tie between the experience of suffering and the capacity to unravel its structural causes. If the suffering that is rooted in the logic, temporality, and specific modality of systemic violence is perceived as an affront, it is highly likely that some will want to personify the responsibility for the suffering felt as a way to explain it. An example of this can be found in antisemitism and in its identification of capital with "the Jews". However, this type of identification does not occur exclusively within antisemitism. As the concept of "structural antisemitism" shows, there is a constitutive tie between antisemitism and the fetishism of the commodity and its transposition to forms of false consciousness that divide aspects of the capitalist system—the sphere of circulation, money, the capitalist class, financial capital, etc.—to personify the abstract forms of capitalist domination and turn these personifications into the object of a critique that is inevitably insufficient, on which forms of conformist rebellion are based and, in totalitarian contexts, policies of massive annihilation (Zamora & Maiso, 2012). Thus, all efforts to approach the political destinies of suffering must begin from an ascertainment of this caesura between experience and theory that does not sacrifice critique in the name of a false sublimation of common sense.

That said, suffering contains the possibility of a critique of the false identification of the universal and the singular, for "society becomes directly perceptible where it hurts" (Adorno, 2000: 36). The suffering that is socially produced is the sign of coercion, but it also opens up the gap from which the possibility to oppose social totality emerges, "convicting it of nonidentity with itself" (Adorno, 1973: 147). The coercion on the singular individual that reveals itself in the socially produced physical and mental suffering is the proof of the particularity of the dominant universality, which the theory of society must unravel. However, we must not forget, as V. Safatle points out, that the absence of a fair life amidst the falseness is experienced in our body and in our desires; this absence is inscribed in them (2017: 65). The cracks and ruptures of the mental life, which always include a physical dimension, are not only traces of the coercion of abstract social universality but also signs of the resistance of the individual in the face of this coercion, signs of a conflict that has neither been pacified nor utterly integrated. Suffering and malaise are not only symptoms of the violence inflicted by social mediation but the starting point for the possibilities of living a life that does not bow to the prevailing social order, possibilities that await their articulation and politicization. However, this life can only do justice to the experience of suffering if it does not forget its physical dimension and if it does not rest on a subjectivation that identifies with domination.

This physical overflowing certainly appears in pleasure, but it appears above all in suffering. The living body resists the instrumental reduction of the physical body to a mere substratum of domination and exploitation. That is why the living body "never completely coincides with the labour force, as its possessor painfully and pleasantly experiences, and it is only for this reason that the spirit is not subsumed under it" (Scheit, 2011: 51). The living body is not separate from the reified physical body, a natural stronghold that is safe from social mediation; it is, rather, the experience that the body does not disappear within this reification and thus allows it to recognize it (and resist it). The recollection of nature in the subject wants to do justice to what resists disappearing in the reifying mediation. It is true that the subject cannot make the process of repression disappear through which he has constituted himself renouncing themselves. However, through remembering the repressed, the subject can confront the domination on which he/she rests. The Enlightenment only distinguishes itself from this domination and opposes it in remembering the presence of nature in the subject. It is about "shedding light on the scars of the violence inflicted in the process of constructing the subject and showing them, at the same time, as fissures through which the possibility of another subjectivity might slip" (López Álvarez, 2011: 60).

A political subjectivation that assumes this premise as its starting point cannot be articulated around the struggles for the conditions of realization of a sovereign subject. The logic of identity or of self-realization is compromised by the abstract social universality and reproduces the violence that causes the suffering. The bourgeois subject, the proletariat and its countless substitutes—insofar as they are perceived from the logic of identity—will not be able to break the cycle of the violence that has tormented history and society since time immemorial. The critique of constituent subjectivity to which the experience of suffering leads would have to be transferred to the conception of the political subject. Similar to what V. Safatle (2015: 91) does in remembering that it is the force of the de-identity and the de-differentiation that defines the proletariat in Marx. Beyond impoverishment, the proletariat suffers a complete dispossession of itself, and this cannot be combatted by reaffirming oneself or by asserting for oneself the "properties" that define the bourgeois identity—family, nation, state, property—or other, different ones. This dispossession is, in fact, the condition for "transforming their helplessness into a political force for the radical transformation of life forms" (ibid.: 92). The total loss of humanity is the starting point for the overcoming of the identification of the human with the sovereign subject. That is why the practical determinations of a political subject that does not repeat the traps of identity must originate from a void, from a loss which prevents the identification of subject and self-possession, power, property, and authority. One of Adorno's more surprising contributions in the context of his critique of constitutive subjectivity and of his diagnosis of the weakening of the individual might, for that reason, possess a paradoxical character: it is precisely through the growing empirical and categorical cracks in the individual that certain perceptions can emerge, perceptions that remained concealed while the subject was interpreted as a firm dominant category. Through this process of its increasing fracture and erosion, the subject acquires certain critical potentials: possibilities of individual experience or even forces of resistance that point beyond what is given. The crisis of identity and of the agency of actors who are socialized under the "capital" form allows us to recognize certain new possibilities of political agency by radically questioning the principle of identity. This is what makes the experience of suffering politically relevant.

References

Adorno, T. W. (1951/2005). *Minima moralia. Reflections on a Damaged Life* (E. F. N. Jephcott, Trans.). Verso.

Adorno, T. W. (1966/1973). *Negative Dialectics.* Routledge.

Adorno, T. W. (1967–1968). Sociology and Psychology. *New Left Review, 46*, 67–80 and 47, 79–97.

Adorno, T. W. (2000). *Introduction in the Sociology* (Ch. Godde, Eds., E. Jephcott, Trans.). Stanford University Press.

Adorno, T. W., Frenkel-Brunswik, E., Levinson, D. J., Sanford, R. N. (2019). *The Authoritarian Personality*, in collaboration with Betty Aron, Maria Hertz Levinson and William Morrow with a new introduction by Peter E. Godon. Verso.

Bonefeld, W. (2009). The Principle of Hope in Human Emancipation: On Holloway, *Herramienta*, https://www.herramienta.com.ar/articulo.php?id=163. Accessed 28 Apr 2021.

Elbe, I. (2006). Holloways 'Open Marxism'. Bemerkungen zur Formanalyse als Handlungstheorie und Revolutionsromantik, *Z. Zeitschrift für marxistische Erneuerung*, *67*, http://www.zeitschrift-marxistische-erneuerung.de/article/727.holloways-open-marxism.html. Accessed 8 Apr 2021.

Holloway, J. (1993). Open Marxism, History and Class Struggle. *Common Sense, 13*, 76–83.

Holloway, J. (1995). From Scream of Refusal to Scream of Power: The Centrality of Work. In W. Bonefeld, R. Gunn, J. Holloway & K. Psychopedis (Eds.), *Open Marxism* (Vol. 3, pp. 155–181). Pluto Press.

Holloway, J. (2005). *Change the World Without Taking Power.* Pluto Press.

Holloway, J. (2010). *Crack Capitalism.* Pluto Press.

Holloway, J. (2016). *In, Against, and Beyond Capitalism: The San Francisco Lectures*. PM Press.
Holloway, J. (2018). *We Are the Crisis of Capital: A John Holloway Reader*. PM Press.
Kurz, R. (2005). *Das Weltkapital. Globalisierung und innere Schranken des modernen warenproduzierenden Systems*. Tiamat.
Kurz, R. (2012). *Geld ohne Wert*. Horlemann.
López Álvarez, P. (2011). Ocaso del individuo, recuerdo de lo vivo. Sujeto y naturaleza en Adorno. In J. Muñoz (Ed.), *Melancolía y verdad. Invitación a la lectura de Th. W. Adorno* (pp. 33–70). Biblioteca Nueva.
Safatle, V. P. (2015). Por um conceito 'antipredicativo' de reconhecimento. *Lua Nova: Revista De Cultura e Política, 94*, 79–116.
Saffatle, V. P. (2017). Freud em Frankfurt: A Função da Psicanálise no Pensamento de Theodor Adorno. In D. Kupermann (Ed.), *Por que Freud hoje?* (pp. 63–89). Zagodoni Editora.
Scheit, G. (2011). *Quälbarer Leib. Kritik der Gesellschaft nach Adorno*. Ça ira.
Scheit, G. (2015). Erfahrung und Jüngstes Gericht. Eine Anmerkung zum verborgenen Freiheitsbegriff der Kritischen Theorie. In D. Dumbadze & Ch. Hesse (Eds.), *Unreglementierte Erfahrung* (pp. 13–26). Ça ira.
Starosta, G. (2017). Fetichismo y revolución en la teoría marxista contemporánea: Una evaluación crítica de la *Neue Marx-Lektüre* y el *Marxismo Abierto* en clave metodológica. *Izquierdas, 37*, 162–190.
Wallerstein, I. (2010). Structural Crisis. *New Left Review, 62*, 133–142.
Zamora, J. A. (2020). Materialidad espectral, subjetivación y crítica inmanente del fetichismo. In J. M. Romero & J. A. Zamora (Eds.), *Crítica inmanente de la sociedad* (pp. 171–204). Anthropos/SigloXXI.
Zamora, J. A., & Maiso, J. (2012). TeoríaCrítica del Antisemitismo, Constelaciones. *Revista de Teoría Crítica, 4*, 133–177.

CHAPTER 10

John Holloway and the Dialectics of Revolution

Alberto Bonnet

Rings the bells that still can ring,
forget your perfect offering.
There is a crack, a crack in everything,
that's how light gets in.
Anthem, Leonard Cohen,
In memoriam

Introduction

One of the fundamental inputs of Holloway's political thought is the tradition of critical theory in a broad sense (Lukács, Bloch, Horkheimer, Marcuse) and, in particular, Adorno's negative dialectics. It is true that

A. Bonnet (✉)
Department of Economics and Administration, National University of Quilmes, Buenos Aires, Argentina
e-mail: abonnetprivado@gmail.com

A. García Vela and A. Bonnet (eds.), *The Political Thought of John Holloway*, Marx, Engels, and Marxisms,
https://doi.org/10.1007/978-3-031-34571-5_10

critical theory had already been present in *open Marxism* since its beginnings, certainly because of the influence it had had among intellectuals linked to the new European lefts of the 1960s and 1970s (see Bonefeld et al., 1991a, 1991b, 1995). But, in Holloway's recent writings, Adorno's negative dialectic wields a much more significant influence than elsewhere.[1] The negative dialectic, in Holloway's interpretation, is the dialectic of revolution. "This is the central theme in Adorno's thought: dialectics as the consistent sense of non-identity, of that which does not fit. It is both libertarian and revolutionary" (Holloway, 2009a: 13). Negative dialectics, in other words, becomes in Holloway's hands the way of thinking that allows to consistently push forward the attempt to open the categories that is characteristic to *open Marxism*. In this consists, ultimately, its revolutionary character. Furthermore, the recourse to dialectics distinguishes Holloway's way to rethink revolution from the non-dialectical way in which poststructuralist-inspired neo-autonomism does it (Holloway, 2010a: 160ff.; 2010b: 188ff.). Whereas, insofar as it is a negative dialectic, it also distinguishes it from other more traditional dialectical modes of thinking about it.[2]

This use of Adorno's negative dialectics may raise doubts. Indeed, in contrast to the young Lukács, to take one example, Adorno presents his most finished conception of dialectics, in the introduction and the first two parts of Negative Dialectics, in a philosophical register of a very high level of abstraction. And the "models" of the third also refer to traditional philosophical problems. What can such dialectics tell us about revolution? Holloway's answer, which we share, is that it can tell us a lot.

We cannot justify this answer in these few pages by a thorough examination of negative dialectics. We will limit ourselves to recalling an indication of Adorno himself: in the preface to *Negative Dialectics* and in his lessons inspired by it, Adorno stated that he aspired to "put his cards on the table" (2004: xix; 2008: 27). This does not mean that he was trying to expound some sort of method, of course, but to make explicit the way of thinking underlying his previous "material works". And among these material works are certainly his writings on the

[1] This can be seen, in parallel, in the writings devoted by Holloway to Adorno's own thought (see especially the volume Holloway et al., 2009).

[2] That difference led to interesting exchanges (see especially Holloway, 2009b; Negri & Cocco, 2006: 219ff.; Altamira, 2006 for a detailed reconstruction). The latter difference, on the other hand, did not give rise to much debate (but see Hudis, 2003).

critique of society. Negative dialectics is thus not a mere philosophical exercise. It is, in Adorno's thought, the dialectic underlying the consequent critique of capitalist society. This realization legitimizes—at least, in principle—the attempt to recover it within the terrain of revolutionary thought—although, of course, it does not immunize us from the dangers involved in this passage between such distant levels of abstraction.

In the following pages, then, we will assume the relevance of Holloway's attempt to recover negative dialectics for rethinking revolution and discuss exclusively the way he does it. Needless to say, this discussion does not respond to a scholarly eagerness to reestablish some presumed original meaning of Adorno's negative dialectic, but to the political concern that the way in which Holloway assimilates it erodes precisely its most radical edges.

Dialectics in *Change the World*

Holloway's starting point is always subjective and negative: the "we scream" (2010a: 1), the "we want to break" (2010b: 3), the "we" of a denied dignity (2016: 2). The adoption of this starting point implies a double rejection. A rejection, on the one hand, of traditional discourses about revolution that, although they contemplate a subject, conceal the subject of their own enunciation. This goes without saying. But, on the other hand, a rejection as well of the conversion of that subject into an affirmative point of departure, that is to say, ontological rather than dialectical, which is found in the aforementioned autonomist and especially neo-autonomist tradition of poststructuralist inspiration (see in this sense the interesting exchange between De Angelis, 2005 and Holloway, 2005).

The risk inherent in adopting such a subjective starting point, however, always lies in the fact that it can push the argumentation in a subjectivist direction. Of course, we are not repeating here the well-known accusation against the "subjectivist deviations" of a "leftist" who departs from the correct line of some party.[3] The issue is more relevant. It concerns a

[3] Callinicos (2003 and especially 2005), for example, simply invokes against Holloway the "papal bull of excommunication" (to use Otto Rühle's accurate expression) issued by Lenin against the Western "leftists" who in 1920 did not abide by the "21 conditions" of international discipline imposed by Bolshevism (and which would later be promulgated again by the bureaucrats of the Western communist parties against the leaders of the

relapse into subjectivism within the dialectic between subject and object, which is the matrix of all dialectics, underlying Holloway's argumentation. A relapse that Adorno's negative dialectic consequently strives to avoid, by the way, since it leads precisely to the identitarian and idealistic conception of dialectics with which it intends to break. Indeed, from that subjective and negative starting point, Holloway's argumentation works its way through a dialectic between the subjective "power-to" and the objectified "power-over", in *Change the World* (2002: 51ff.), and between "doing" and its conversion into "labour", in *Crack Capitalism* (2010: 93ff.). Both dialectics are naturally inspired by the Marxian critique of political economy: in the relation between labor and capital in the former, and in the dual character of labor itself in the latter (something that seems to be overlooked by Lebowitz, 2005). Let us examine these dialectics in this and the next section.

The problem, in the first case, lies in the fact that Holloway tends to interpret that critique of political economy in terms of an ad hominem critique and, consequently, of a critique oriented toward the reduction of the object to the subject. "In the young Marx there is the idea of the *ad hominem* critique. The idea of the true sun, the real sun, which he mentions in the *Introduction to A Contribution to the Critique of Hegel's Philosophy of Right*. The aim of the critique is to demystify those false gods such as money and the commodity, so that, theoretically and practically, the world revolves around its true sun, around human beings" (2017: 32).[4] Even if we reject with Holloway the peregrine Althusserian witticism of the existence of a *coupure épistémologique* in Marx's thought, we do not believe, however, that his mature critique of commodity and money as forms of social relations is simply assimilable to his youthful critique of religion. We do not believe, more precisely, that the subject-object dialectic that underlies this critique of commodity and money can be understood without remainder as a *reductio ad hominem*. The commodity form and the money form appear in the critique of political economy

student revolts of the late 1960s; see also Holloway and Callinicos 2005). These Vatican files, of course, do not concern us in these pages.

[4] "Theory is capable of seizing the masses once it demonstrates *ad hominem*, and it demonstrates *ad hominem* once it become radical. To be radical is to grasp matters at the root. But for man the root is man himself" (Marx, 1970: 123). These are the lines alluded to by Holloway and written by the still Feuerbachian Marx of 1844, that is to say, lines written about religion and not about forms such as commodity or money, whose status he was not able to unravel then.

as objective modes of existence of social relations in capitalist society. Fetishism is certainly an attribute of these forms. But the fetishized character of these forms does not simply explain their objective character. The critique of the socially necessary appearance—that relations between people appear as relations between things—does not dissolve the objectivity of these relations between people: reification and objectivity are not synonyms.

Holloway, however, tends to simply assimilate both concepts (as Löwy, 2004 and 2005 correctly objects). He thus states that "if, from the perspective of the social flow of doing, the objectification of the done is a fleeting objectification, immediately overcome through the incorporation of the done into the flow of doing, then capitalism depends on making that objectification a durable objectification, on converting the done onto an object, a thing apart, something that can be defined as property. Capitalism thus implies a new definition of 'subject' and 'object', in which the 'object' is durably and rigidly separated from the subject's doing" (2010a: 31). And he abounds in a footnote that "there is, then, not clear distinction to be made between alienation and objectification. Adorno and the late Lukács both insist on the distinction, almost, it would seem as a way of protecting themselves from the implications of their own theory (very explicitly so in the case of Lukács)" (idem: 248).[5] Holloway seems to recognize in that passage that social labor itself involves its objectification, albeit fleeting; he argues that capitalism brings

[5] In fact, both Adorno and Lukács were in this way trying to protect their dialectic against a relapse into idealism. We will return to Adorno's case in a moment. Regarding Lukács, Holloway refers to his self-criticism in the 1967 preface to *History and Class Conciousness* (Lukács, 1971, but see also Lukács, 2000). Löwy, during this polemic (2005), as well as in his earlier study of Lukács (1972), considers that the young Lukács did not engage in this (self-criticized) idealist assimilation between objectivity and reification. We are not sure about the latter (and see in this sense Adorno, 2004: 190). But, in any case, the arguments within that polemic are very clear. Löwy argues: "Wouldn't a good chair produced under socialism become 'an object with an enduring identity'? Your refusal to distinguish between alienation and objectification (see Footnote 25 in Chapter 3 [cited above])—a mistake the young Lukács did not make (despite his late self-criticism in 1967)—leads to a denial of the objective materiality of human products" (Löwy & Holloway, 2003: 108). And Holloway responds that "the distinction between objectification and alienation is a way of putting the brakes on revolutionary theory" (idem: 112) and, further on, that Marxism is "critique of all that appears to be independent of doing, to all objectivity" and that "critique attacks objectivity and shows it to be a projection of subjectivity" (idem: 113).

with it a more lasting objectification and consequently redefines the relation between subject and object; he equates that lasting objectification with property; and finally, in that footnote, he simply assimilates alienation and objectification. All very problematic statements. Let us see.

Labor always involves its objectification in a product—we use a more traditional terminology for now because Holloway's notion of "doing" includes activities which, like play, do not involve objectification in this sense.[6] And this objectification cannot be understood as "alienation" or "reification", except within a thoroughly idealistic conception of work, but we will return to this point later. The "fleetingness" attributed by Holloway to such objectification is, on the other hand, much more debatable. The objectivity of the products of social labor is not necessarily as fleeting as he suggests. An emancipated society, for example, would continue to grapple for decades with the concentration of housing in gigantic cities resulting from the secular process of capitalist urbanization. Even productive force itself, which, as Holloway (2010b: 245ff.) insists on pointing out, is an attribute of that social labor, is also necessarily objectified in the means of production. And any emancipated society, to consider another example, would be forced to continue employing for decades means of production inherited from capitalism. This represented, in fact, enormous challenges for the revolutions of the past. But if these considerations seem too distant for the reader, just remember that the objective efficiency of the means of production expropriated from the bosses is often a daily obstacle that is little less than insurmountable for the workers in the "recovered factories". To recognize in objectivities such as these, an objectification of social labor, that is, to de-fetishize them, does not reduce that objectivity one bit.

The conversion into private property and the capitalist character of these objectifications of social labor, consequently, do not depend on the greater durability or rigidity of their objectification. It can even be

[6] Marx states in *Capital* that "the commodity is, first of all, an external object, a thing which through its qualities satisfies human needs of whatever kind" (1982: 125). The objectivity of the commodity, in this first determination of it, lies simply in its being an object external to the subject. Holloway, however, hastens to assimilate this mere objectivity to reification—which, of course, is a different and ulterior determination: "The commodity is an object produced by us, but standing outside us. The commodity takes on a life of its own in which its social origin in human labour is extinguished. It is a product which denies its own character as product, a done which denies its own relation to doing" (2010a: 46).

conjectured that the products of social labor in the capitalist society, in many cases, have a much more ephemeral and gelatinous objectivity in this sense than that of their peers in pre-capitalist societies. The ancient temples, in any case, were more durable than our cell phones. The social form of the product does not derive from its objectivity. It is true that this objectivity, insofar as they are products of social labor, is conditioned by the form of their production. The planned obsolescence of these mobile telephones as commodities did not affect those temples of antiquity. But both the ephemeral character of the former and the quasi-eternal character of the latter rest on a material dimension of their objectivity that subsists behind their social form.

This material dimension ultimately refers to nature. And the objectivity of the products of social labor, in this material-natural dimension, cannot be reduced to their "alienated" or "reified" character either, except in the context of a completely idealistic conception of nature. This idealist conception of nature, which simply reduces it to a social form, is precisely what Alfred Schmidt, Adorno's disciple, objected to the young Lukács (Schmidt, 2014: 78ff.). And it is for this reason that Adorno conceptualizes the relation between society and nature in an emancipated society in the terms of a "reconciliation", a concept that involves an irreducible alterity, rather than in those of an "identity" (Horkheimer & Adorno, 2004: 358ff.). This identity, the *reductio* of nature to society, would only consummate for Adorno the process of domination over nature inherent to the dialectic of enlightenment (Horkheimer & Adorno, 2002). Meanwhile the concept of nature, symptomatically, plays no role within the subject-object dialectic inherent in Holloway's argumentation. The conception of this dialectic in terms of a *reductio ad hominem* is even more problematic at this point. For if that reduction of the objectivity of the products and means of production of social labor to the subject leads to a naive conception of the challenges facing the revolution, this reduction of the objectivity of nature to that subject involuntarily validates the destruction of nature.

Now, this tendency to assimilate the subject-object relation to a mere reduction of the object to the subject is certainly a tendency that has already been objected to in other critiques (see Reitter, 2003 and more recently, in the last volume of *Open Marxism*, Schäbel, 2020 and García Vela, 2020). And this is true not only regarding Holloway, but also regarding other representatives of *open Marxism*. Let us look at this problem from a broader perspective. While Adorno attributes to negative dialectics "to use the strength of the subject to break through the fallacy of constitutive subjectivity" (Adorno, 2004: xx), a *desideratum* recovered by Holloway himself (2009a: 16), the latter extols however that same "constitutive subjectivity" affirming that "dialectics seeks to bring to light the power of human creativity that lies in all that negates that power, to understand the world and not just the capital-labour relation (understood in traditional identitarian terms) from the perspective of human creativity" (ibidem). And this reinforces, precisely, that fallacy.

Bonefeld states that "the *reductio ad hominem* that for Adorno (1993: 143) characterizes the critical intent of Marx's work does not entail the replacement of the object by the subject. It means the comprehension of the object as a mode of existence of the subject. Just as objectivity without the subject is nonsense, subjectivity without the object is nothing" (2009a: 129).[7] These statements by Bonefeld condense, even better than those of Holloway, the misunderstanding in question. In the first place, Adorno does not attribute this *reductio ad hominem* to Marx, but to a tradition of "critical enlightenment" that goes all the way back to Xenophanes (even if, naturally, the young Marx's still Feuerbachian conception of critique as *reductio ad hominem* can also be inscribed in this tradition). "The *reductio ad hominem* which inspires all critical enlightenment is substantiated in the human being who would first have to be produced in a society which was master of itself. In contemporary society, however, its sole indicator is socially untrue" (Adorno, 1977: 122). The *reductio ad hominem* is problematized in this last statement by Adorno and in a very specific sense: critique cannot be equated to a *reductio ad hominem* insofar as the existing society continues to block the possibility of that *homo* (or *femina*) existing. And in the same sense Adorno affirms in *Negative Dialectics*: "Enlightenment thus transcends its traditional self-understanding: it is demythologization –no longer merely as a *reductio ad hominem*, but the other way round, as a *reductio hominis*, an insight into the delusion of the subject that will style itself an absolute. The subject is the late form of the myth, and yet the equal of its oldest form" 2004: 186). Criticism understood simply as a *reductio ad hominem* is, in these circumstances, nothing more than the perpetuation of the myth of constitutive subjectivity.

[7] Bonefeld refers here to the German edition of Adorno's "Einleitung" to *Der Positivismusstreit in der Deutschen Soziologie* but, in fact, it corresponds to "Die Logik der Sozialwissenschaften". We will return to this passage in a moment.

Secondly, it is interesting to note that Adorno states this precisely in the context of his argument in favor of the "object's preponderance" (*Vorrang des Objekts*) within the *Negative Dialectics*. This means that he not only rejects the reduction of the object to the subject, stating that "the duality of subject and object must be critically maintained against the thought's inherent claim to be total" (2004: 175). But it also gives priority to that object, since "carried through, the critique of identity is a groping for the preponderance of the object (*Präponderanz des Objekts*). Identitarian thinking is subjectivistic even when it denies being so" (idem: 183). It is precisely that critical maintaining of the duality of subject and object, that is, of the specific mutual mediation between both, which reveals the priority of the object. "Due to the inequality inherent in the concept of mediation (*der Ungleichheit im Begriff der Vermittlung*), the subject enters into the object altogether differently from the way the object enters into the subject. An object can be conceived only by a subject, whereas a subject by its very nature is from the outset an object as well. Not even as an idea can we conceive a subject that is not an object; but we can conceive an object that is not a subject. To be an object also is part of the meaning of subjectivity; but it is not equally part of the meaning of objectivity to be a subject" (ibidem).

It is evident, at this point, that for negative dialectics the object is not a mere mode of existence of the subject. The objectivity without the subject is not a nonsense: the object can *exist*, even if it cannot *be conceived*, independently of the subject. And, if the subjectivity without the object is nothing, it is for a very different reason: because the subject itself is an object, namely, first of all, a body.[8] In this object's preponderance lies precisely, for Adorno, the materialist character of the negative dialectic. And let us say it once and for all, to confirm the scandal: in this lies to a large extent, in our opinion, its revolutionary character. Negative dialectics does not therefore aim to any reduction of the object to the subject, but to a reconciliation between the two or, in other words, to a simultaneous emancipation of the subject and the object with respect to

[8] And we must not overlook this somatic dimension of the subject (Adorno, 2004: 192ff.) because it is, for Adorno, the ultimate substrate of suffering and, consequently, of resistance. See on this point the chapter by Zamora included in this volume.

the relation of domination (and self-domination) established precisely by that enlightened tradition.[9]

Let us now descend from this philosophical level of argumentation and turn to some of the consequences that this conception of dialectics entails for Holloway's argumentation. The concept of form plays, in principle, a fundamental role in such argumentation. However, in the same way that such dialectics deprives any object of its objectivity, social forms themselves are deprived of theirs and, consequently, the concept of form tends to become superfluous (see in this sense Elbe, 2006). Let us look at two important examples of this problem.

Holloway's indistinction between the concepts of "original accumulation" and "capitalist accumulation" properly speaking (2010a: 142ff.; 2010b: 165ff.),[10] justified precisely by virtue of the effort not to split the existence of those forms with respect to their genesis, that is, to understand them as process-forms, tends to convert the category of capital itself into an irrelevant notion. In effect, the (*sogenannte*, Marx clarified) "original accumulation" is not accumulation of capital in the strict sense, but violent expropriation of wealth, even when this wealth may subsequently take the form of capital; while "capitalist accumulation" properly speaking is the accumulation of surplus value, that is, of a wealth that takes the form of capital beforehand. And the social relations and antagonisms at play in both cases are very different. An indigenous community confronts the expropriation of its lands by a mining corporation (i.e., the "genesis" of capital) in a very different way from the way in which workers resist daily exploitation in the factories (the daily "existence" of capital). This difference, naturally, is very relevant when thinking about revolutionary processes.

Let us turn now to the state form. The derivation of the state allows us to rigorously conceptualize the state as a form, that is, as a

[9] We are aware that in these pages, for the sake of a more basic discussion of the subject-object dialectic, we are alternatively referring to different types of objectivity that in another context should be rigorously differentiated and considered separately, namely, to the objectivity of nature, of society in general and of capitalist society in its specific reification.

[10] This indistinction had already been introduced by Bonefeld (1988) and had given rise to an interesting discussion in the pages of *The Commoner* (later compiled in the first part of Bonefeld, 2009b).

differentiated mode of existence of capitalist social relations (2010a: 91ff.; 2010b: 130ff.).[11] And Holloway correctly criticizes, based on this conceptualization, the conceptions of revolution centered on the conquest of state power and the transformation of society from the state. However, here again the need to understand the state as a process-form leads Holloway to deprive this state-form of any objectivity. The state, then, "exists only as a node in a network of social relations" and its differentiation is merely the result of a fetishization that "abstracts it from the network of power relations in which it is immersed" (Holloway 2010a, 30 and 31). From the derivation of the state as a form of capitalist social relations perhaps it follows that revolution cannot be conceived as the conquest of state power and the transformation of society from the state. But it surely does not follow that its differentiation is a mere result of a process of fetishization. This difference may seem subtle, but it is also decisive when it comes to thinking revolution.

Finally, in the discussion of these issues we cannot even restrict ourselves to those general forms assumed by social relations in capitalism, such as capital and state, but must also attend to the specific characteristics they acquire in specific historical periods and social formations. The denial of the objectivity of these social forms becomes at this level an underestimation of the importance of the analysis of the latter and of the concepts necessary to analyze them. In his synthetic but excellent commentary to *Change the World* in *Das Argument*, Hirsch points out in this sense: "the call for negation, for a break with what exists, to not-participate-anymore is, undoubtedly, important, but it moves us forward politically only if it is combined theoretically with a precise analysis of the changing forms of capitalist reproduction and its concrete historical transformations; in short, of everything that Holloway denounces generically as a theory that legitimizes existing relations" (2006: 125). Holloway, in his response to Hirsch, rejects such analysis outright. He argues that underlying this critique is "a difference in our understanding of what Marxist or revolutionary theory should be trying to do" (2006: 71) and further asserts that "if we are consistent and insist on opening up the categories, then

[11] Recall—with regard of the problem we will address below—that Holloway relies for this argument (2010a: 93; 2010b: 65) on the German derivation debate (Holloway & Picciotto, 1978) and on Hirsch (1978) in particular.

no 'precise analysis of the changing forms of capitalist reproduction' is possible" (idem: 72).[12]

It is clear, however, that in his critique of political economy Marx did not limit himself to reducing commodity value to abstract labor or capital to surplus value, but advanced in the analysis of "changing forms of reproduction" of capital which he identified through specific concepts such as those of simple cooperation, manufacture, and big industry. It is also clear that, in their development of that critique of political economy, the participants of the German debate did not limit themselves to deriving the state form either, but also discussed some of the "changing forms of reproduction" of that state such as, *par excellence*, the post-war social state form. And what did Holloway himself do if not an "analysis of the changing forms of capitalist reproduction," for example, in his essay on the rise and fall of Keynesianism? (Holloway, 1996). Be that as it may, the analysis of the transformations of capital and the state in specific historical periods and social formations is an indispensable task for revolutionary thought. And the fact that such transformations are always contingent processes, traversed by class struggle, does not preclude such analysis.

Dialectics in *Crack Capitalism*

Now, the passage from that dialectic between the subjective "power-to" and the objectified "power-over" of *Change the World* to a dialectic between "doing" and its conversion into "labour" of *Crack Capitalism* tends to consummate this subjectivist tendency insofar as, in the second case, it is no longer a contradiction between subject and object. In this case, the latter is completely suppressed within the argumentation and the contradiction is consequently redirected to the interior of the activity of the subject himself. Let us now look at this passage between the two dialectics.

Holloway presents this passage as a descent to a more fundamental level of his argumentation. "The transformation of doing in abstract

[12] This problem was already present in the debate on post-fordism (Bonefeld & Holloway, 1991). In that debate, Holloway and Bonefeld rejected the deterministic consequences of the use of "intermediate categories" from Poulantzian and regulationist thought in Hirsch and Jessop's analyses of the transition to post-fordism. And this objection, at least in part, was justified. But, along with them, they ended up rejecting *any* analysis of the ongoing transformations of capitalism and *any* intermediate categories required to carry it out.

labour is a pre-condition of capitalist exploitation" (2010b: 148). "There are really two different levels of class struggle. Capitalist production is based both on the abstraction of doing into labour and on the exploitation of abstract labour. Without the abstraction of doing into labour, exploitation would not be possible. On the other hand, it is through the process of exploitation that the abstraction of labour is imposed and re-imposed (or not, as the case may be). The two forms of struggle are closely intertwined, and yet distinct. The distinction is important because in the one case we are talking of the struggle of doing *against* labour, and in the other case of the struggle *of* labour against capital" (idem: 155; author's underline). Holloway then intends to elaborate "a new revolutionary theory, a new Marxism: the theory not of the struggle *of labour against capital*, but the struggle *of doing against labour (and therefore against capital)*" (idem: 157; author's underlines). Here again, Holloway's assertions are problematic. In first place, the excerpt in question immediately raises a methodological problem. Holloway presents the passage from that dialectic between "power-to" and "power-over" to this dialectic between "doing" and "labour", as we pointed out, as a passage toward a more fundamental level of argumentation, because "the social synthesis is formed through the abstraction of doing into labour" (2010b: 95). Abstract labor thus appears as a sort of ultimate principle that structures capitalist society as a whole.[13] Holloway can (and does) invoke in his support Marx's claim that his discovery of the "twofold nature of the labor contained in commodities" is "crucial to an understanding of political economy" (Marx, 1982: 132).

But this does not prevent us from asking to what extent this notion of an ultimate structuring principle of society is compatible with a conception of society strictly based on a negative dialectic.[14] We cannot

[13] On this point Holloway agrees with Postone (even in the expression "social synthesis"), no matter that Postone understands abstract labor as a contradictory though not antagonistic category and Holloway conceives it as a permanent antagonism (Holloway, 2010b: 186ff.; we will return to this point later). Our objection, in this sense, concerns both.

[14] That is, a dialectic that unfolds its content in the form of "constellations" (Adorno, 2004: 162 et seq.). Let us clarify this point with an example. On the reduction of Freud's psychoanalysis to Jung's "collective unconscious", Adorno writes: "the truly important conceptions are almost always distinguished by the fact that they do not include any such magic words, that they do not have any specific category by which everything can be explained once and for all. Rather, they form contexts or constellations of categories

exhaustively develop this problem in these pages. Let us limit ourselves to pointing out, restricting ourselves to his argument, that the establishment of a hierarchy between the categories of abstract labor and wage labor is doubtful. The generalized existence of wage-labor separated from its character of value-producing abstract labor is as unthinkable as, vice versa, is the generalized existence of abstract labor separated from its character of wage-labor. For the monetary remuneration of the different kinds of concrete labor by means of a wage is already in itself an operation of abstraction of these labors. There is thus a mutual mediation, rather than a hierarchy, between the two categories.

Holloway, in any case, presents this conversion of "doing" into "labor" into an ultimate structuring principle of society as a whole. And this principle would explain not only capitalist exploitation and the formation of social classes, but also the dimorphization and genitalization of sexuality, the domination of nature, the particularization of the state, the homogenization of time, the conversion of society into a totality and so on (2010b: 14–20). Holloway's political intention is, of course, to redirect the diversity of conflicts that traverse capitalist society to a single primordial antagonism between those "doing" and "labour". "In this sense, the conflict between doing and labour is prior to other conflicts" (2010b: 223). But this expedient is also problematic. From a methodological point of view, because it threatens to reduce dialectics to a kind of deductive system and because it also requires turning this doing into a completely indeterminate principle, as we will see below. But also, from a more substantive point of view, because in fact it is very unconvincing: it implies reducing patriarchy in its multiple dimensions to the role of women in reproductive labor in capitalism, the domination of nature in all its complexity to capitalist production, and so on (see in this sense, for example, the objections of Cockburn, 2012).[15]

as a means of explanation, instead of calling on one of them to be a maid-of-all-work" (2000: 113). Does not the reduction of the critique of political economy—or worse, of the critical theory of society as a whole—to the supposed principle of the dual character of labor lead to a similar result?

[15] Our previous critique of *Change de World* (Bonnet, 2005) already pointed to this, although it was perhaps unsatisfactory, in the sense that the failure of Holloway's attempt to redirect all social struggles to a common matrix ended up validating, *malgré lui*, the postmodern proliferation of micro-politics. But it is decisive to note that here we are not simply assimilating Holloway with postmodernism as Bensaid (2003, 2005) and a chorus of less interesting commentators attempt to do, for it is oriented in a very different

In second place, Holloway's own presentation of this "conflict between doing and labour" is also problematic. The contradictions between concrete and abstract labor and between use-value and value—and we return to a more traditional terminology for now because the notion of "doing" includes activities that are not labor at all and therefore do not produce value—are, strictly speaking, contradictions between the forms that labor and the product of labor assume within capitalist society. This means that, as such, they are not only contradictory among themselves, but also in themselves. This implies that we are not dealing with a dualism between a "good" pole (namely, concrete labor, hypothesized as doing, and use-value) and a "bad" pole (abstract labor and value). Not even the most technical aspects of labor processes and their products can be understood, in capitalist society, disregarding their place within processes of capital valorization. And it can even be affirmed that the concrete labor done and the use values produced outside these valorization processes are also, to some extent, conditioned by their characteristics. Although it is still true that the housewife who cooks her children's meals on Sundays for the rest of the week can bring into play a commitment that belies the *Taylorization* of her activity, just as the worker who leads an insurrection can take pride in his *savoir faire* as a metalworker. Perhaps Holloway agrees with these assertions. But the point is that abstract labor and value are also contradictory social forms in themselves. They are certainly the way in which labor and products made by independent private producers are socially validated in capitalist society. But they are not only that, but also much more. I would dare to affirm that perhaps emancipation would be inconceivable without the historical presupposition established by the very development of capitalism which, in its perverse way, equated the priest's ceremony with the peasant's sowing. Substitutability in the exchange between different works and products of labor is, in this sense, both the perverse form and the presupposition of the equality to which we aspire (see Adorno, 2004: 146 et seq.).[16]

direction (see Holloway, 2010a: 27ff.). We are only asserting that the political challenge represented by this diversity of struggles is not resolved in this way.

[16] It is paradoxical at this point that the "anti-dialectic" Hardt puts forward a much more dialectical conception of this problem than the "dialectic" Holloway. Hardt states in his discussion with Holloway: "a political project that affirms use value over exchange value seems to me to be a nostalgic effort to recapture the pre-capitalist social order. As I see it, Marx's project, on the other hand, cuts through capitalist society to come

Now, we have been referring to "contradictions" (and not to "antagonisms") in and between these social forms. And this leads us to a third problem. Holloway (2010b: 87ff.), as we said, agrees with Postone in considering abstract labor as the ultimate principle of a kind of "social synthesis". However, while Postone limits himself to considering abstract labor as a contradictory form in a merely objective sense and turns capital into an authentic "automatic subject" (Postone, 1993: chaps. 8–9), Holloway avoids this mystifying conclusion (2010b: 186ff.). But he avoids it at the price of simply suppressing any distinction between contradiction and antagonism. Holloway states that "Postone make a clear distinction between contradiction and antagonism [...] whereas the starting point of this argument makes such a distinction impossible" (2010b: 188). Negative dialectic, in this controversy, succumbs in both cases. For it is true that there can be no contradiction (much less antagonism, of course) in any object that lacks subjective mediation. It is precisely in this sense that there is no dialectic in nature, except insofar as it is socially mediated. But this does not enable us to simply dissolve the distinction between contradiction and antagonism because this subjective mediation of the object, which can give rise to a contradiction, is not equivalent to the subjectivation of this contradiction, which can give rise to an antagonism. To return to the previous example, the relation between capitalist accumulation and nature is manifestly contradictory but is not antagonistic, for nature itself cannot become the subject of an antagonism.[17]

But let us leave this extreme example aside. The fact that this capitalist accumulation unfolds through competition carries in itself contradictory consequences such as, for example, simultaneous tendencies to the concentration of capital and the incorporation of new individual capitals into this competition. This and many other contradictions inherent to the forms that capitalist social relations assume do not give rise to any antagonism, at least in the anti-capitalist sense involved in Holloway's

out the other side" [...]. "I don't think abstract labor is the rival. It is a simplification (although I think it is an important simplification) to say that without abstract labor there would be no proletariat. If the labor of the bricklayer, the cabinetmaker, the weaver, the agricultural laborer, and the self-employed remained concrete and incommensurable labor there would be no concept of labor in general (labor without regard to the manner in which it is expended, as Marx puts it), labor potentially linking them to each other as a class" (Holloway & Hardt, 2012: 134–135).

[17] See in this regard the article by Piva included in this compilation.

arguments. Holloway's intention here is to recognize, in opposition to so-called "orthodox Marxism", the various individual and collective ways in which the antagonistic character of capitalist society manifests itself every day, and the importance they have when it comes to thinking about revolution (Dinerstein, 2018). However, just as these diverse antagonisms cannot be traced back to a single primordial antagonism, neither can the contradictions of capitalist society be reduced to those that are effectively subjectivized as antagonisms.

This difference between contraction and antagonism leads us in turn to a fourth and final problem. When we distinguish between "subjective mediation" and "subjectivation" we are trying to acknowledge the fact that the forms assumed by social relations have an objectivity before individuals whose contradictory character may or may not give rise to an antagonism per se, on the one hand, and that the fact that this happens or not depends on a process of subjectivation of the individuals involved in them, on the other. We have already referred, in the previous section, to the question of the objectivity of social forms; let us now look at this question of subjectivation. This question of the subject represents a real problem in Holloway's arguments. The invocation of "the antagonism between human creativity and its negation" (2010a: 146), of "the revolt of doing against labour" (2010b: 83) or other similar metaphors does not solve the problem because neither creativity nor doing are subjects at all but, at best, presuppose a subject. Holloway refuses to identify that subject because, certainly, such an identification could give rise to the narrow definitions of the revolutionary subject proper to that so-called orthodox Marxism. But his abstract denial of identity does not solve the problem because, in the meantime, there is no antagonism without a subject, and no subject without an identity.[18]

[18] Here we are interested in subjectivation on a collective scale, but it is worth remembering that this is also (and above all) true on an individual scale. The abstract negation of the identity of the individual (of the self-consciousness) and collective (of class consciousness and other antagonistic identities) subject has no place within the negative dialectic: identity itself is rather a moment of it. This explains the somber tone of Adorno and Horkheimer when they write that "the elimination of qualities, their conversion into functions, is transferred by rationalized modes of work to the human capacity for experience, which tends to revert to that of amphibians" (2002: 28), or of Adorno when he writes that "the oppressed who today, as predicted by the theory, constitute the overwhelming majority of the mankind are unable to experience themselves as a class" (2003: 97).

Indeed, the subject in question can only be thought of as the result of a process of antagonistic subjectivation and this process again involves a subject-object dialectic. This dialectic implies in turn a double objectification on the part of the subject: that of the other and that of himself. Let us look at the case of capital itself. Capital is a contradictory social relation sustained by the exploitation of labor power. But the conversion of this contradiction into antagonism is not given beforehand but requires a process of subjectivation of that labor force as a class.[19] And this subjectivation requires in turn the objectification of both poles of the social relation: that of capital, as capitalist class, and that of labor, as working class. The constitution of the subject is always a process of recognition that requires a self-objectification on the part of the subject. Holloway is right when he warns against the fetishization of labor in the history of the labor movement (2010b: 151 et seq.). But neither can this problem be solved by simply suppressing the subject-object dialectic involved but, once again, by "critically sustaining" this dialectic.

Holloway carries this problem over from *Change de World*. "The struggle against capital is the struggle against identification. It is not the struggle for an alternative identity" (2010a: 100). "We do not struggle as working class, we struggle against being working class, against being classified" (idem: 144). It is difficult to understand the precise meaning of statements such as these. If they mean that the existence of the working class is the result of the development of capitalist society, they are evidently correct—and for this reason Marx considered it to be potentially revolutionary, as its immanent negation. If they mean that this class, insofar as it becomes that revolutionary subject, struggles for its own abolition as a class, they are a reasonable bet—Marx did not bet on anything else. But if they mean that the identity that turns that class into a collective subject or, in other words, its class consciousness, is the result of some classification mechanism of capitalist society, they are neither self-evident nor reasonable.[20] And they are a *requiem* for dialectics. Capitalist society can in its own way recognize the working class as a distinct social

[19] See in this sense the debate around "The Revolt of Dignity" (Holloway, 1997) between Wildcat (1997) and Holloway (1998). Also, the Aufheben collective (2003) is right on this matter when it recovers the autonomist emphasis on the processes of class composition and recomposition.

[20] This question of the concept of class had already been motive of controversy in Dinerstein and Neary (2002; see Bonnet, 2021).

group. The capitalist state, for example, differentiated the labor contract from the other contracts of commercial law to subsume it within a new jurisdiction of specific labor law. But, even in cases like this, this class classification was a result of the struggle of that class. The struggle against capital, then, is not the struggle against identification. It is, above all, the struggle of the working class to articulate its own identity, against the mechanisms of disarticulation of that identity proper to capitalist society.

Conclusions

We cannot retrieve in these conclusions the entirety of our arguments. We will simply point out that, in our opinion, Holloway is right in his objections to the traditional conception of revolution, in the need to rethink it and even, to a certain extent, in the path he chooses to follow to do so. However, negative dialectics, which is one of his fundamental inputs, gets lost along the way.

The subjectivist tendency toward the reduction of the object to the subject, which we examined in the second section, tends to the suppression of the subject itself, as we have just pointed out in the third section. This result may seem paradoxical, but it is worth remembering that such a paradox has always accompanied idealism like a shadow—especially on its way from Fichte to Schelling. The sacrifice of the object at the altar of the subject drags with it, inexorably, the subject itself. And in this double sacrifice the matrix of dialectics—of any dialectics—is lost.

Once this subject-object matrix is lost, Holloway has only a residue in his baggage: the *power-to*, the *doing*. It is a residue because now we are no longer referring neither to labor nor to concrete labor, concepts that can only be determined within that sacrificed dialectic, but to a completely undetermined activity. An undifferentiated flow is devoid of proper subjects and objects. Power-to and doing then become authentic ontological principles.[21] And reality as a whole appears as a

[21] This is where the tension between Adorno and Bloch within Holloway's argumentation becomes relevant (see Dinerstein, 2005, 2012). *Power-to* and *doing* resemble the Blochian *not-yet*. The problem is that this *not-yet* has, within Bloch's thought, the status of an ontological principle (see especially his assimilation of Aristotelian *dynamis* in Bloch, 1995: 223ff.). Whereas, for negative dialectics, there is no place for such principles: "hope is not a principle", Adorno replied to Bloch (1980: 60; see also Habermas, 1969).

sort of repressive scenario in which these principles struggle to express themselves.

The problem is that, in this indeterminacy, such principles become sterile for rethinking revolution (see Stoetzler, 2005 and especially 2012). The *power-to* or the *doing* can be virtually any activity. Individual or collective activities. Activities that challenge the capitalist order more or less openly, but also activities that do not challenge it in any sense, or even unintentionally contribute to its perpetuation. Disruptive activities that prefigure an emancipated society or that herald a society even worse than the capitalist society in which we live. To discriminate between these diverse expressions of human activity is something unavoidable for revolutionary thought and requires more determined concepts. And, naturally, it requires the preservation of dialectics.

References

Adorno, T. W. (1977). On the Logic of the Social Sciences. In T. W. Adorno et al. (Eds.), *The Positivist Dispute in German Sociology*. Heinemann.

Adorno, T. W. (1980). Bloch 'Traces': The Philosophy of Kitsch. *New Left Review, I*(121), 49–62.

Adorno, T. W. (2000). *Introduction to Sociology*. Stanford University Press.

Adorno, T. W. (2003). Reflections on Class Theory. In R. Tiedemann (Ed.), *Can One Live After Auschwitz?* Stanford University Press.

Adorno, T. W. (2004). *Negative Dialectics*. Routledge.

Adorno, T. W. (2008). *Lectures on Negative Dialectics: Fragments of a Lecture Course 1965/1966*. Polity Press.

Altamira, C. (2006). *Los marxismos del nuevo siglo*. Biblos.

Aufheben. (2003). Review of Change the World Without Taking Power. *Aufheben* 11. Disponible en. https://libcom.org/library/review-change-world-aufheben-11

Bensaid, D. (2003). La Révolution sans le pouvoir? A propos d'un récent livre de John Holloway. *Contre Temps* 6.

Bensaïd, D. (2005). On a Recent Book by John Holloway. *Historical Materialism, 13*(4), 169–192.

Bloch, E. (1995). *The Principle of Hope* (Vol. I). MIT Press.

Bonefeld, W. (1988). Class Struggle and the Permanence of Primitive Accumulation. In *Common Sense* (Vol. 6, pp. 54–65). London.

Bonefeld, W. (2009a). Emancipatory Praxis and Conceptuality in Adorno. In Holloway, Matamoros and Tischler (2009).

Bonefeld, W. (Ed.). (2009b). *Subverting the Present, Imagining the Future. Class, Struggle, Commons*. Autonomedia.

Bonefeld, W., Gunn, R., & Psychopedis, K. (Eds.). (1991a). *Open Marxism I. Dialectics and History*. Pluto Press.

Bonefeld, W., Gunn, R., & Psychopedis, K. (Eds.). (1991b). *Open Marxism II. Theory and Practice*. Pluto Press.

Bonefeld, W., Gunn, R., Holloway, J., & Psychopedis, K. (Eds.). (1995). *Open Marxism III. Emancipating Marx*. Pluto Press.

Bonefeld, W., & Holloway, J. (1991). *Post-Fordism and Social Form: A Marxist Debate on the Post-Fordist State*. Palgrave Macmillan.

Bonnet, A. (2005). Hopeful Voyage: Unexpected Port? In *Capital and Class* 25 (1). Conference of Socialist Economist.

Bonnet, A. (2021). Clase y estado. Notas sobre la constitución de la clase y su relación con el estado en Marx. In *Antagónica. Revista de investigación y crítica social* 2. IESAC-UNQ.

Callinicos, A. (2003). How Do We Deal with the State? *Socialist Review, 272*, 11–13.

Callinicos, A. (2005). Sympathy for de Devil? John Holloway's Mephistophelian Marxism. *Capital and Class, 29*(1), 17–19.

Cockburn, C. (2012). Who Are 'We'?, Asks One of Us. *Journal of Classical Sociology, 12*(2), 205–219.

De Angelis, M. (2005). How?!?! An Essay on John Holloway's *Change the World Without Taking Power. Historical Materialism, 13*(4), 233–249.

Dinerstein, A. C. (2005). A Call for Emancipatory Reflection: Introduction to the Forum. *Capital & Class, 29*(1), 13–17.

Dinerstein, A. C. (2012). Intersticial Revolution: On the Explosive Fusion of Negativity and Hope. *Capital and Class, 36*(3), 521–540.

Dinerstein, A. C. (2018). John Holloway: The Theory of Intersticial Revolution. In B. Best, W. Bonefeld, & C. O'Kane (Eds.), *The SAGE Handbook of Frankfurt School Critical Theory*. SAGE.

Dinerstein, A. C., García Vela, A., González, E., & Holloway, J. (Eds.). (2020). *Open Marxism 4. Against a Closing World*. Pluto Press.

Dinerstein, A. C., & Neary, M. (2002). *The Labour Debate: An Investigation into the Theory and Reality of Capitalist Work*. Ashgate.

Elbe, I. (2006). Holloways 'Open Marxism'. BemerkungenzurFormanalysealsHandlungstheorie und Revolutionsromantik. In *ZeitschriftfürmarxistischeErneuerung*, 67.

García Vela, A. (2020). Objectivity and Critical Theory: Debating Open Marxism. In A. C. Dinerstein et al. (2020).

Habermas, J. (1969). Ernst Bloch—A Marxist Romantic. In *Salmagundi* 10/11. Skidmore College.

Hirsch, J. (1978). The State Apparatus and Social Reproduction: Elements of a Theory of the Bourgeois State. In Holloway and Picciotto (1978b).

Hirsch, J. (2006). Poder y antipoder. In J. Holloway (Ed.), *Contra y más allá del capital*. Herramienta.
Holloway, J. (1996). The Abyss Opens: The Rose and Fall of Keynesianism. In J. Holloway & W. Bonefeld (Eds.), *Global Capital, National State, and the Politics of Money*. Palgrave Macmillan.
Holloway, J. (1997). *La revuelta de la dignidad*. In Chiapas 5.
Holloway, J. (1998). Open Reply to an Open Letter. *Wildcat-Zirkular* 45. Disponible en. https://www.wildcat-www.de/en/zirkular/45/z45e_hol.htm
Holloway, J. (2005). No. *Historical Materialism, 13*(4), 265–284.
Holloway, J. (2006). La imprenta del infierno. In J. Holloway (Ed.), *Contra y más allá del capital*. Herramienta.
Holloway, J. (2009a). Why Adorno? In J. Holloway, F. Matamoros, & S. Tischler (Eds.), *Negativity and Revolution. Adorno and Political Activism*. Pluto Press.
Holloway, J. (2009b). Negative and Positive Autonomism: Or Why Adorno? Part 2. In J. Holloway, F. Matamoros, & S. Tischler (Eds.), *Negativity and Revolution. Adorno and Political Activism*. Pluto Press.
Holloway, J. (2010a). *Change the World without Taking Power: The Meaning of Revolution Today* (New). Pluto Press.
Holloway, J. (2010b). *Crack Capitalism*. Pluto Press.
Holloway, J. (2016). *In, Against, and Beyond Capitalism: The San Francisco Lectures*. PM Press.
Holloway, J. (2017). *Una lectura antiidentitaria de El Capital*. Buenos Aires: Herramienta / ICSyH-UAP.
Holloway, J., & Callinicos, A. (2005). Can We Change the World Without Taking Power? A Debate Between John Holloway and Alex Callinicos (World Social Forum, 27 January 2005). In International Socialism 2 (106).
Holloway, J., & Hardt, M. (2012). Commonwealth y Agrietarelcapitalismo. Una lectura mutua. In Bajo el Volcán 11 (18). ICSyH – UAP.
Holloway, J., Matamoros, F., & Tischler, S. (2009). *Negativity and Revolution. Adorno and Political Activism*. Pluto Press.
Holloway, J., & Piciotto, S. (1978). *State and Capital: A Marxist Debate*. Edward Arnold.
Horkheimer, M., & Adorno, T. W. (2002). *Dialectic of Enlightenment. Philosophical Fragments*. Stanford University Press.
Hudis, P. (2003). Rethinking the Idea of Revolution. In *News & Letters* 48 (1). News and Letters Committees.
Lebowitz, M. (2005). Holloway's Scream: Full of Sound and Fury. *Historical Materialism, 13*(4), 217–231.
Löwy, M. (2004). John Holloway, Change the World without Taking Power. In *New Politics* 35. New York.
Löwy, M. (2005). To Change the World We Need Revolutionnary Democracy. *Capital and Class, 29*(1), 22–24.

Löwy, M., & Holloway, J. (2003). Intercambio entre Michel Löwy y John Holloway. In *Bajo elVolcán* 6. ICSyH – UAP.

Lukács, G. (1972). Preface to the New Edition (1967). In *History and Class Conciousness. Studies in Marxist Dialectics*. The MIT Press.

Lukács, G. (2000). *A Defense of History and Class Conciousness. Tailism and the Dialectic*. Verso.

Marx, K. (1970). *Critique of Hegel's 'Philosophy of Right.'* Cambridge University Press.

Marx, K. (1982). *Capital: A Critique of Political Economy* (Vol. I). Penguin Books.

Negri, A., & Cocco, G. (2006). *Global. Biopoder y luchas en una América Latina globalizada*. Paidós.

Postone, M. (1993). *Time, Labour, and Social Domination: A Reinterpretation of Marx's Critical Theory*. Cambridge University Press.

Reitter, K. (2003). Wo iststehen. In *Grundrisse* 6.

Schäbel, M. (2020). In Open Marxism an Offspring of the Frankfurt School? Subversive Critique as Method. In A. C. Dinerstein, A. García Vela, E. González, & J. Holloway (Eds.), *Open Marxism 4. Against a Closing World*. Pluto Press.

Schmidt, A. (2014). *The Concept of Nature in Marx*. Verso.

Stoetzler, M. (2005). On How to Make Adorno Scream: Some Notes on John Holloway's *Change the World Without Taking Power. Historical Materialism, 13*(4), 193–215.

Stoetzler, M. (2012). On the Possibility That the Revolution That Will End Capitalism Might Fail to Usher in Communism. *Journal of Classical Sociology, 12*(2), 191–204.

Wildcat. (1997). Open Letter to John Holloway. *WilcatZirkular* 39. Disponible en. https://www.wildcat-www.de/en/zirkular/39/z39e_hol.htm

CHAPTER 11

Doing the Locomotive: On Running Towards Disaster, Being the Disaster and Some Bad Screams in John Holloway's Contribution to Open Marxism 4

Marcel Stoetzler

John Holloway's 'The Train', the concluding chapter of *Open Marxism 4* (2020a), contains Holloway's rejoinders to challenges thrown at him in the same book by some of those who co-edited the book with him. 'The Train', like most of the first part of *Open Marxism 4* and some of the remainder, deals with one of the fundamental questions of critical theory, and indeed most forms of modern social theory: to what extent is our social world an oppressive, object-like 'thing', and to what extent is it merely the ephemeral effect, however reified, of the actions and relationships of the human beings who constitute society? Mainstream sociology knows this as the old 'structure and agency' problem, Marxists

M. Stoetzler (✉)
Bangor University, Bangor, UK
e-mail: m.stoetzler@bangor.ac.uk

A. García Vela and A. Bonnet (eds.), *The Political Thought of John Holloway*, Marx, Engels, and Marxisms,
https://doi.org/10.1007/978-3-031-34571-5_11

more elegantly refer to the dialectic of subject and object, usually putting the subjective-agentic part first as befits a theory that itches for practice. Holloway has always been a master juggler of these two dimensions of the dialectic, while evolving the high art of experimental theory bricolage as the Anansi spider among Marxist crisis theorists. Keeping these balls in the air, white hair flowing, vibrato cracking, no one performs the prophet like Holloway, channelling trusty old eighteenth-century vocabulary like 'dignity' and 'recognition' via Marx, Bloch and the Frankfurt School into what most contemporaries mistake for a post-Marxist era. Not least for these things, of all members of our small tribe of Adornoite autonomists (or whatever else it is that we are, or that in the state of being we are not-being) he is the one who is most successful in getting a hearing in social movement contexts. Success in academic publishing, as in political pamphleteering, presupposes a healthy dose of ambiguity, polyvalence and honest straightforward sloppiness which allow combined and uneven audiences to hear what they came to hear. The same thing that brings exoteric success brings therefore esoteric quarrelling: you cannot have the one without the other, and anyway we concept-sticklers would be out of a job if no one established a paradigm first by writing a bestseller for us to split hairs about. In 'The Train', Holloway has an easy time refuting-embracing his critics, but then again, not entirely. Like in *Change the world without taking power* and *Crack capitalism*, there is an undercurrent that undermines his own argument.[1] On this occasion, it is manifest in the guiding metaphor itself, *the train*.

Allegory and metaphor only work when the relationships between the elements that make up the image are identical to the relationships between the elements of the reality which the image is meant to illuminate. If 'the train is capital', or the totality of society that 'we live inside', then the relationship between the train and the passengers should represent the relationship between individuals in capitalist society and the society that they constitute. The train metaphor does not transport this concept, though: it rather obscures and confuses Holloway's argument. As many critics chiefly accuse him (and the Open Marxism 'school' in general) of 'voluntarism' and 'subjectivism', he may have chosen the train metaphor in an attempt to over-compensate for this crime and ends

[1] Stoetzler (2005, 2012).

up reproducing, against himself, the rather rigid conceptual distinction between things and doings, structures and agency of which Open Marxists tend to accuse the structuralists: if Open Marxism stands for anything at all, it is the refusal, attempted and reaffirmed ever anew, to accept this dichotomy. Like raccoons do with sugar cubes, we obsessively wash these concepts in the waters of the dialectic, and even if we end up with nothing, we have no regrets and do it again. This defines our love for the infinite, the in-through-and-beyond of refusing finite-making, static-making and state-making. (It is also beyond the dichotomy of materialism and idealism.)

A train is a thing. It would be very perilous to assume otherwise. A train is of course a product of society (in the technical language used by Hegel and Marx, a *Gegenstand*) but when it rushes at you it is very much an *Objekt*, not to say a projectile. It is well out of your hands, even if you happen to have designed or built the train: when it hits you, the difference between *Gegenstand* and *Objekt* does not matter anymore. It is *aufgehoben* (and so are you). It is more complicated with social things, or less immediately tactile objects: they may, or may not be like the train that runs you over no matter what. Here Holloway's signature catchphrase comes in: *Stop making capitalism*. We cannot 'stop making' the train in whose headlights we are caught, because we *have* made it—past perfect tense!—and now it exists. We cannot 'stop making' the train we sit in, either. But we can 'stop making capitalism': if all value-producers on the planet go on a general strike, capitalism objectively ends after a day or two. It is as simple as that. (A different and much more difficult question is, what would have to happen next in order to make the post-capitalist world a *better* place, rather than just the next instantiation of a recurring nightmare. The capitalist mode of production is not the temporary corruption of a benign natural order that we can simply revert to: quite the contrary, it is the apex of several thousand years of increasing domination of human and non-human nature whose enormity and absurd brutality, we hope, may still produce a revolutionary reaction so strong that it allows us to overcome the patriarchal civilization that produced capitalism as its latest, most systematically exploitative and oppressive form.)

At the same time, 'stop making capitalism' is as utopian an idea as they come, as there is no mechanism conceivable now, in the reality of this current moment, through which this could be organized.[2] But this is beside the point: 'stop making capitalism' is a theoretical postulate, and it is irrelevant whether philosophers and activists can anticipate, let alone agree on, how exactly it might play out. (The point of a revolution—i.e., a radical opening—would be that the likes of us will play no special role in it at all. When it comes along, we must make sure that we do not ruin it by projecting any of our ready-made blueprints on it, and we can help preventing others from doing so—as, after all, it takes a thief to catch a thief.)[3]

Holloway's chapter 'The Train' is built around the image of 'us' sitting in a train that 'rushes forward into the night' (Holloway, 2020a: 168). Once one sits inside a train, one is not anymore producing this train, though, as its production has been completed. The train *is* a thing, a separate entity that exists as such, while society is *not*. The only way to think of 'doing the locomotive' that would illustrate Holloway's argument would be to imagine it as an effect of the combined performative acts of people sitting down on seats *as if* they were in a train: something children do as a game, or actors on a (non-naturalistic) stage set. They really *are* the train (because the budget was not big enough for an actual train). Or else, one could think of a party dance like the one evoked in the classic song 'Do the Loco-Motion'.[4] Holloway's argument

[2] It is not even clear what kind of transformation would have to take place to create enough of an overlapping of interests among all humans at the planetary level to bring that about, considering that a very large number of people find capitalism serves them just fine. Some people, like Bookchin, have suggested that the climate crisis may be about to provide this point. This could perhaps be true, considering that it forces people to look at capitalism as a global issue (not even the most nationalistic tankie would suggest 'stopping global warming in one country'), and it does not allow one to distract from what capitalism *is* (a dynamic-destructive totality with an inbuilt runaway logic) by focusing on one or several of its manifestations (the unequal distribution of wealth and related forms of injustice).

[3] 'Open Marxism' is revolutionary in asserting revolution as an opening. It is negative in fighting the closing-down of the opening.

[4] 'Now that you can do it, let's make a chain now/(Come on baby do the loco-motion)/ A Chugga-chugga motion like a railway train now/ (Come on baby do the loco-motion)/ Do it nice and easy now don't lose control/ A little bit of rhythm and a lot of soul/ So come on, come on, do the loco-motion with me.' The song (by Carole King and Gerry Goffin) states that the everyday performance of the dynamic totality (the train) needs to be well-rehearsed, with control but nice and easy—with 'soul'. It may be a fetish, but as a dynamic fetish it is not *literally* ossified (which would result in flat-footed and unpersuasive dancing).

that is awkwardly loaded onto the train metaphor is that the totality of society that humans produce every single day anew may *seem* like but *is* not in fact an 'automatic subject', whereas a train is. Marx's formulation that capital is an 'automatic subject' is best understood as rhetorical, a deliberate exaggeration that rams home the point that reification and alienation have become extreme in capitalist society. Reification, ossification or petrification never mean that any social things *actually* turn into things, bones or rocks.

The chapter begins with a statement of the horror of the accelerating development of capitalism: 'The train rushes forward into the night, faster, faster. Where is it going? To the concentration camps? Or to nuclear war? Or to annihilation by global warming and ecological disaster? To extinction?' (168) The energy that drives the train comes from human sacrifice—Holloway writes that passengers 'are actually being thrown, one after another, into the engine of the train and burned up'. This element of the allegory is rather ill-chosen, too: a train that 'actually' runs on burning up its passengers will not go far, unless the passengers are given an opportunity to reproduce, as is the case in capitalism. Capitalism does look after its own sustainability, the reproduction of its conditions of existence such as a sufficient supply of labour power, albeit not necessarily that of anything else.[5]

Holloway's text does not reference but evokes a famous fragment by Walter Benjamin: 'Marx says revolutions are the locomotive of world history. But … perhaps revolutions are how humanity, traveling on this train, reaches for the emergency brake'.[6] The travellers in Holloway's train look for but cannot find the emergency brakes, though. Circumspect engineers must have removed them from the train of history since

[5] In the allegorical 2013 film *Snowpiercer*, that I cannot help thinking of when reading Holloway's 'The Train', passengers are not actually burned but, more plausibly, children are used to do some kind of dangerous maintenance job inside the engine (clearly echoing Marx's descriptions of child labour). Another beautiful but unsettling image is provided by Pixar's films *Monsters Inc.* (2001) and *Monsters University* (2013), where monsters—obviously representing capital—derive their energy supplies from the screams of children, which is why they need to learn at university how to be scary. Different from the Open Marxism approach, the *Monster* films take a pessimistic, system-theoretical approach suggesting that capital deliberately and systematically provokes our screams which it recuperates and uses for its own reproduction.

[6] This is found in one of the 'paralipomena' to 'On the concept of history', which are notes that were produced in the latter's preparation or in the same context (Benjamin, 1977: 1232).

Benjamin's days. Instead, they 'seize control of the engine room, but it makes no difference, the engine is more powerful than any driver'. (We seem to be dealing with an automatic train-subject-object that is not actually controlled by a human driver.)

> We grow more and more desperate. ... We organise protests, rebellions, even revolutions. We walk in the opposite direction, hoping that this might affect the forward rush of the train. We organise spaces within the carriages where we try to take control over our lives on a harmonious, non-hierarchical basis. We even rush from one side of the carriage to the other, thinking this might derail the train. (168–9)

This sequence sounds like Holloway wants to make fun of forms of blind activism (especially the one about walking inside the train in the opposite direction...). Then he leaps out of the image plane and lists some of the measures that previously have failed to make the train stop: 'The Russian Revolution, the Chinese, Vietnamese, Cuban revolutions, the uprisings and revolutions in Africa and Latin America in the seventies, the Zapatistas, the alter-globalization movements, the Occupy movement' (169)—a rather disjointed list, especially as most of these were revolutions that explicitly aimed to bring the train (the capitalist mode of production) up to speed, or get it started in the first place. (Certainly, most of these were attempts to change the world by taking, and massively expanding, modern state power.) Next, back on the image plane, 'we examine the train', which means reading works by 'people like Backhaus, Reichelt, Postone, Heinrich, Kurz, Krisis and so on' who 'help us to understand the movement of the engine and where the train tracks are heading'. Holloway writes that they are useful for explaining why we need to get out of the train but are not able to tell us anything about how to do so, which seems slightly uncharitable, as at least some of these writers do have their own ideas on what's to be done, and what not.

In the second compartment of 'The Train', Holloway asserts that the subject and its suffering—'the scream'—are the *point of departure* of theorizing, which does not mean that it is and remains at its centre. Holloway goes out of his way to assert how much of the object has migrated into the subject: 'the object penetrates the subject' which sits inside the object (the train; society). This is true: when you spend too much time on a train, you become train-trained. Furthermore, you cannot look at the train very well when you are inside it: your vision becomes train-shaped. You become part of the train's furniture. 'The object cripples the subject' (170), yet 'never totally'. A degree of non-identity remains. 'The relation … between damaged subject and terrifying object' is unstable (171). Things are getting worse:

> [T]he train penetrates more and more deeply into our minds, bodies, imaginations, damaging us ever more profoundly; and also it forces from us a scream that grows louder and louder, a scream of desperation. A scream of desperation that throws us back to the subject, however damaged. The caravans of Central American migrants camp just around the corner from where I live, on their way north towards the US border, where, subjectively-desperately-absurdly they hurl themselves often quite literally against the objective frontier, sometimes climbing 5-meter high fences with their children and then throwing themselves down to the other side. (171)

At this point Holloway grants that one of his interlocutors has a point:

> Alfonso García [Vela] is right then when, referring to Adorno, he says "the more anonymous and alien the relations of domination are, the more unbearable it is for the subject to experience its own impotence. Therefore, thinking will tend towards a higher subjectivity. At the same time, the desperate self-exaltation of the subject stands in the way of its self-reflection. Generally speaking, the rise of subjectivity in theorising and the reification of the world are correlated." (171; quoted from García Vela, 2020: 57)

The more overwhelming capitalism becomes, Holloway continues, the more we become like those migrants. He suggests that this confirms, rather than questions the notion that the 'screams' of the subject need to be the starting point of theory, though. What else could be? The point is, though, that the starting point does not determine where the journey goes. The starting point is in fact what we leave behind. By beginning and going on, we negate the beginning because we move elsewhere.

Holloway then discusses—still in the second compartment—an important phrase by Adorno, the 'primacy of the object', that is used by two of his critics, Mario Schäbel and Alfonso García Vela. Holloway suggests an important distinction crucial to understanding Adorno's phrase:

> The first sense of the object is nature, the natural object. In this sense, to recognise the primacy of the object is to respect the natural limits on human action, to accept that humans are just part of a totality of natural conditions in which they constantly intervene, but which they do not control. The non-conceptual is then that which goes beyond human control and indeed human understanding. (171–2)

This is Adorno's rejection of idealist subjectivism, especially its extreme, Fichtean form: because we create the world in our minds, for ourselves, as a set of perceptions that we actively produce out of meaningless raw sense data, we are tempted to think that we create the world *in itself*, which we do not. We can hardly control our mind, but certainly not the world, and we need to control our urge to control.

The second sense of 'the object' is the objectivity of 'the totality of social relations', a 'socially constituted reality' (172). Also this objectivity has for Adorno (and, I would suggest, for Open Marxism and Critical Theory in general) a preponderance ('primacy' sounds too strong here), but it is itself socially constituted and, most importantly, fragile and changeable. This preponderance is what we are struggling against and which we are out to overcome. It differs from the 'primacy' of 'natural' objects. Holloway then equates this distinction to that between *Objekt* and *Gegenstand* in Hegel and Marx, which seems mistaken to me: if a carpenter makes a table, this table is a 'Gegenstand' for her but it is also (for everybody else) an 'Objekt'. This is not the same as the distinction between social and natural objects. This misconstrual may play a role in the confusing use of the train metaphor: a train is a 'Gegenstand' inasmuch as it is a product of society, but it is clearly an 'Objekt', too. Capital is a 'Gegenstand', perhaps (although we do not produce it intentionally, which makes it again different from the carpenter's table) but most importantly it is a *social thing* whose ontological status is that of a 'real abstraction'—terribly real.

When the second compartment is the clearing the throat section of 'The Train', Holloway brings it all home in the third and last compartment. The train seems very happy to note our acceptance of its 'primacy'. But: the train 'is the totality of social relations' (174) that 'we humans' continuously produce which is 'the key to the fragility of the train'. Holloway quotes again Alfonso García Vela paraphrasing Adorno:

> Adorno ... acknowledges that, in capitalism, human practice has produced a social objectivity that is independent from particular subjects to a certain extent and rules over them universally, preventing their becoming subjects. (174; quoting from García Vela, 2020: 58)

Holloway points to the phrase 'to a certain extent' which indicates that Adorno does not actually suggest independence. He could also have pointed to the word 'particular': the social objectivity is quasi-independent from *particular* subjects, not from subjects as such or collectively. Theoretical emphasis on the fragility of the capitalist mode of production has always been central to Open Marxism (and to autonomist Marxism where it is the signature feature), whereas in the Critical Theory of the Frankfurt School it has tended to be hidden away and covered up to avoid the impression of cheap and cheerful optimism. Both stand in stark contrast to positivistic, structuralist and functionalist Marxisms where it plays no part at all. Holloway argues that the importance of Marx's labour theory of value lies precisely here:

> Capital depends on human action not just for its original creation but for its continued existence. That is surely the significance of Marx's labour theory of value: capital depends for its existence on labour, that is, on the constantly repeated conversion of human activity into abstract labour. It is the channelling of human activity into labour that constantly re-constitutes capital, that constantly re-constitutes the apparently autonomous existence of the train. It is perhaps not accurate to say that there is no separation between constitution and existence, but rather that that separation is always a fragile, momentary separating of existence from its constituting. Capital exists as an autonomous force to the extent that we constantly re-constitute it as an autonomous force. (174)

It is due to the imperfection of the object's domination of the subject that Holloway is writing this chapter and some people read it. Both he and they are

> part of a great world of resistance and refusal and rebellion, part of a world of confused No's saying "take control of the engine", "pull the emergency brake", "jump out through the door", "climb out through the windows" and our own preferred "stop making the train, stop them from throwing us into the engine-furnace". (175)

This sequence again is somewhat muddled: if 'we' continuously make the train, who are 'they' who throw 'us' into the furnace? Would that not terminate the train? No such 'they' was mentioned before. 'Stop making the train' is not consistent with 'stop them from throwing us into the engine-furnace'. A small detail, of course, but it indicates a crack in the argument where the traditional world of theorizing subject and object as strictly separate invades the critical argument of 'Stop Making Capital'.

In the last paragraph, Holloway explicitly reasserts the autonomist starting point of his argument:

> It is easy to see how the object penetrates the subject, more difficult to see how the subject penetrates the object and constitutes its crisis. That capital is in crisis is clear, but often we see our struggles as being the consequence of the crisis rather than the other way around. We have to make explicit how our struggles are the crisis of capital, the crisis of its capacity to channel our activity into the labour that creates and re-creates it.
>
> The relation between subject and object, far from being an identity, is a dissonance that is present within both subject and object. The presence of the object within the subject has been much emphasised, but what interests us more is the destructive force of the subject within the object, the presence of the subject in-against-and-beyond the object as its crisis. (176)

The fact that Holloway ends the chapter on this note surely suggests that the autonomist version of Marxist crisis theory as developed in *Change the World* and elsewhere remains at the core of his theorizing. The autonomist reversal of the 'Marxism from above'—assumption that capital *does* things while labour *reacts* to the effect that *capital* is now understood to be reacting to something that *labour* does, or rather refuses to do, can on its own easily become voluntarist. This is where the notion of the 'preponderance' of social objectivity over the individuals, articulated for example by Adorno, needs to be asserted. The latter does not mean, though, that critical theory reverted to a Marxist form of structural-functionalism or system theory.

In capitalist society there is no conflict between 'us' and 'the totality' but, in the dialectical perspective that was so powerfully set out in the first two volumes of *Open Marxism* and in parts of the third volume, 'we' are the-totality-which-is-not-one.[7] 'We' are everything, the totality as well as its opposite. In society, anyway, there is nothing else (except all the other things that there are, but they are literal, not social things which is what we are talking about here). In capitalist modernity, society constitutes a totality in the sense that everything is linked up with everything else through the universal mediation by abstract labour. 'We' are the ones who do this, that is, the 'we' of people who do social things in the capitalist way: activities that take the twofold form of concrete and abstract labour.[8]

Its contradictions and sloppy phrases notwithstanding, 'The Train' is still the most enthusiastically dialectical text in a volume that seems strangely addicted to dichotomies and separations. The problems begin with the title. While the first two *Open Marxism* volumes of 1992 had dry scholarly titles, *Dialectics and History* and *Theory and Practice*, respectively, and the third volume of 1995 the somewhat more playful *Emancipating Marx*, OM4 (Dinerstein et al., 2020) declares itself to take a stance *Against a closing world*. Call me old-fashioned, but why the indeterminate article? Marxists don't normally believe in the existence of several parallel worlds, which is why they cannot oppose 'a closing world' from the perspective of some other one. Proponents of Open Marxism normally posit themselves 'in-against-and-beyond the closing world', or perhaps, 'against the closing of the world that we constitute'. It is not possible to be 'against a world', closing or otherwise: humans can only be opposed to something that happens *to* and *in* the one world that we inhabit. In the self-reflective mode of Critical Theory we must in the process acknowledge our own role in constituting whatever it is we oppose. The unique selling point of Open Marxism is that we understand

[7] There is, though, a conflict between we/totality and *the individual* as in capitalist society, one cannot be different without fear, as Adorno writes.

[8] This obviously means the wage-form of labour based on labour power as a commodity, but there is an argument that also increasingly many of the remaining activities not actually performed as wage labour are coloured by the wage-form: the fact that you are not paid for what you do does not mean that you are entirely outside the wage/commodity form of social relations—which is even more depressing.

that *we constitute the world we oppose*. That's why we think we can *change* it, not just *be against* it. We are the closing world, and we look for ways not to be closing.

Two of the chapters in OM4, those by García Vela (2020) and Schäbel (2020) already mentioned, accuse Open Marxism, and Holloway in particular, of 'subjective idealism' as 'it dissolves the object within the subject dialectically' (García Vela, 48). I think it is possible to read Holloway's writings and others this way only by reading selectively as there are many passages that say the opposite. It seems fair to say that the (quite large) text corpus of Open Marxism is uneven and contradictory. When dealing with a contradictory body of texts, the interpreter needs to look to the rhetorical dimension of theoretical writing. When I say, for example, 'We are the closing world', this may grammatically look like a statement of identity but in fact it is a rhetorically stated challenge to the presupposed existence of the separate identities of 'we' and 'the world'. An analytical philosopher will probably take the grammatical meaning at face value and leave it at that, whereas a dialectical philosopher will look for an explanation in terms of what the rhetorical meaning of an obviously paradoxical statement is (and then either find, or not find one).

In Open Marxism/Critical Theory, the key lies in always thinking the concept of 'form' even when it is not explicitly printed on the page: this gives you 'we exist *in the form of* being the closing totality as well as *in the form of* being the anti-totality, the non-identity, the bad infinity of still somewhat hapless attempts at pushing back and reversing it'. No subject/object-identity there, certainly no 'subjective idealism'. Many serious readers are probably frustrated by the style of many of Holloway's texts and their sometimes wooly and flowery passages; well-meaning teachers may recommend to leave rhetoric to the priests and politicians and just speak the truth *clare et distincte*, the Cartesian way, *more geometrico*; but the practice of switching between a more analytical and a more rhetorical style (of which Marx was a grand master) can be defended by pointing to one of our eighteenth-century ancestors, Giambattista Vico, who thought that language bereft of its rhetorical, fantastical, literary, imaginary, non-mathematical, playful (and plain silly) dimensions cannot deliver truth, certainly not truth that will metamorphose the world (that is, us).[9] Besides, without some flowery language we will sell even fewer books.[10]

García Vela's actual position does not seem to differ from what I understand is basically Holloway's, or generally Open Marxism's position. The same is true of Schäbel, who is equally emphatic, though, about the 'subjective idealism' of Open Marxism, while at the same time offering plenty of evidence to the contrary (which he explicitly admits undermines his argument [77]). The strange tendency to exaggerate differences and build ideal-types linked to 'idealism' and 'materialism'—words that have only limited validity in the Marxist context—might have to do here with the fetishization of the brand names of supposed 'schools' of critical theory that are anything but schools: 'Frankfurt School' versus 'Open Marxism' versus 'New Reading of Marx'.[11] These are names of overlapping tendencies, or perhaps 'discursive fields', that contain *within* themselves nearly as many differences as there are *between* them. The article 'Open Marxism'

[9] I made the surprising experience, though, that many of my students disliked Holloway's 'The scream' when I used it in class. Some very serious students found it not serious enough, some others seemed to resent the rhetorical style as if they were being sold something.

[10] In a complementary manner, García Vela argues Moishe Postone turned 'the object' into 'the subject', despite reporting correctly that Postone presents the 'structures of social relations' as 'constituted by a type of objectifying practice' (García Vela, 2020: 58).

[11] Frederick Harry Pitts constructs the supposed contrast between OM and NRM in a different manner: 'Value-form approaches to the Marxian theory of value have their roots in the mature economic works of Marx, but differ in important ways from orthodox, traditionalist approaches to his output, redressing the disproportionate emphasis placed upon the value-producing properties of labour in favour of a perspective which foregrounds the abstract process of *social validation* which renders labour productive of value, and, in turn, the concrete antagonistic social relations that undergird this. The New Reading of Marx focuses primarily on the first, Open Marxism primarily on the second. Together, their Frankfurt-School inflected reading of Marx's *Capital* emphasizes the status of Marx's theory as a critical theory of society rather than a positivistic economic account...' (Pitts, 2020: 64–65). This seems overall very well put: my labour only reveals itself as having been abstract value-producing labour once the social process has validated it as such (in circulation, through the medium of money). I would be reluctant, though, to make too much of the different emphasis on 'the abstract process of *social validation*' versus 'the concrete antagonistic social relations that undergird this'. Pitts might have a point here, though, given that Open Marxists tend to use the concept of class more regularly. I have always seen this as merely a difference in emphasis in presentation, but maybe there is more to it.

by Werner Bonefeld in the first issue of Common Sense (1987) as well as the original three volumes of the *Open Marxism* series (1992, 1992 and 1995) sound pretty 'Frankfurt School' to me, OM1 and OM3 containing long canonical texts by *bona fide* Frankfurters Backhaus and Reichelt, who have only subsequently been rebranded the 'New Reading of Marx'. Adorno seems, after Hegel and Marx, the most often referenced author, especially in OM1. While these basic facts of the publication history roughly delineate the shared core between FS™, OM™ and NRM™, they also make clear the differences: in OM there have always been influences from Italian autonomism, world system analysis and socialist feminism, whereas both OM and NRM tend to ignore psychoanalysis, whose integration into a 'new reading' of Marx was the Frankfurt School's most momentous theoretical innovation with huge implications for the large-scale empirical social research projects that were the Frankfurt School's third defining field of work. (In all four volumes of OM, according to the indexes, the only reference to Freud is in OM3.) Autonomists have always had a soft spot for 'workers enquiries', but apart from that, Open Marxism does not generally seem to take much note of the empirical work done by the Frankfurt School, or empirical research in general, except for those OM authors most strongly influenced by autonomism. (The openness of autonomist Marxism to empirical sociological research might have to do with the Weberian influence at its origins.) Reading the four volumes of Open Marxism or indeed anything from the NRM canon, one would not learn that the Frankfurt School pioneered in the 1940s interlinked empirical and theoretical research on race and antisemitism. These are significant differences. If we consider the three-volume *Sage Handbook of Frankfurt School Critical Theory* edited by Best et al. (2018) as another product of the Open Marxism tradition, its much more inclusive openness is in this respect a major breakthrough: reading Marx differently is not the only thing that matters in the modern world. It is one of several important things.[12]

Also Ana Cecilia Dinerstein's chapter in OM4 (Dinerstein, 2020) erects a false dichotomy: arguing for turning back from Adorno's supposed negativity to Bloch's 'philosophy of hope', she exaggerates the differences she perceives between them. Adorno consistently defended

[12] Very illuminating on the relations between Critical Theory, Open Marxism and autonomism are Chanson and Monferrand (2018) and Memos (2018).

the utopian dimension in thinking, asserted 'identity against its identifications'[13] (which is not entirely different from the 'critical affirmations' Dinerstein argues for) and agreed with Walter Benjamin that '[i]t is only for the sake of those without hope that hope is given to us'.[14] If there was disagreement between Adorno and Bloch, it was on other things.[15]

The fact that such a large part of OM4 is dedicated to constructing rather unhelpful separations is frustrating specifically because it masks the absence of critiques that *would* be necessary. The 'idealism' that is problematic in Holloway's writings and those of some others who operate more closely at the coalface of political activism is not so much the philosophical, 'subjective' variety but the more practical one that idealizes some rather dubious associations. While I am inclined to argue that the philosophical conception of the classic Open Marxism texts is more dialectical than that of the critics who demand more dialectical dialectics, I have serious misgivings about how the philosophically sophisticated dialectical position translates into assessments of the more down-on-earth, grubby world of political practice and the coalitions that it is always inevitably based on. The theory's in-built drive towards being practical, inclusive, non-judgemental and accommodating becomes its own undoing when it remains blind to the fact that not every crack or scream is necessarily progressive and emancipatory.

Dinerstein, for example, writes that crises, such as financial crises, produce moments of 'de-mediation' (a term she borrows from Bonefeld), which are 'instances of de-fetishization when capitalist mediations cannot hide their true fetishising character. In those moments, the space for autonomous organizing opens wide because the possibility of appropriation of resistance seems difficult' (Dinerstein, 2020: 41). This is politically naïve and dangerous. The problem is not only that resistance could be

[13] 'What is, is more than it is. This "more" is not imposed upon it but remains immanent to it, as that which has been pushed out of it. In that sense, the nonidentical would be the thing's own identity against its identifications' (Adorno, 2004: 164).

[14] This is the last sentence of Benjamin's essay on Goethe's *Wahlverwandschaften* (Elective Affinities). In English it is best known as a quotation in Marcuse's *One-Dimensional Man* (Beacon Press, 1964), p. 257.

[15] Blumenfeld (2021) provides a pertinent discussion of the role of utopia and representations of utopia with reference to Bloch and the Frankfurt School. He suggests that '[c]linging to an image of utopia like an idol would ... be anti-utopian, while criticizing the utopian image in the name of what the image represents would confirm one's utopian consciousness'. Spot on.

'appropriated' but more importantly the resistance itself could be reactionary. The breakdown of capitalist, bourgeois mediations, such as the rule of law, opens the space also to any number of *additional* fetishizations that might result in a fascist's smashing my head in rather than 'a great moment for autonomous organising'. At the same time, the chaos of 'de-mediation' might make many people (at least temporarily) find the stability of bourgeois mediations look rather attractive—as was the case in the USA after Trump, a master practitioner of his own brand of 'de-mediation'. An emancipatory outcome remains possible, of course, but there is no guarantee that the open space created by the disintegration of bourgeois social forms will be filled by emancipatory movements. The underlying view of social mediations is undialectical: the latter are best understood as the institutionalized results of previous struggles, reflecting as compromises the existing power relations in the class struggle. Furthermore, not only progressives fight struggles against the existing social world, and social mediation is much more than just the recuperation of our emancipatory struggles by the capitalist state.

Already Holloway's books *Change the World* and *Crack Capitalism* suffered from the problem that the dance of the dialectic occasionally freezes up, takes a breather and reaches for the firm ground of a positive that seems deserving of affirmation. Only a real philosopher, a Stoic perhaps, could totally resist the urge to forego the austere grift of *la critique de la critique critique* for the warm-as-blood temptation of the embrace of this or that really existing negative positivity. Like in 'musical chairs', though, the music has a nasty habit of stopping at the worst moments.[16] My reservations concerning the vagueness resulting from expanded use of the concepts of 'the scream' and 'cracks' would similarly apply to confusing passages in more recent contributions by Holloway, such as the passage quoted above listing a hodgepodge of events from the Russian Revolution to the 'Occupy' movement as if they were all somehow of the same essence. Perhaps the most troubling recent example is Holloway's approving foreword to Abdullah Öcalan's treatise *The Sociology of Freedom* (Holloway, 2020b), an attempt to articulate a civic and democratic form of Kurdish (supposedly non-state) nationalism as

[16] See Stoetzler (2005, 2012). My work on antisemitism is grounded in exactly this issue; see Stoetzler (2019, 2021) as well as my forthcoming edited volume *Critical theory and the critique of antisemitism* (Stoetzler 2023).

a critique of civilization in the name of all of humanity. Öcalan's 'manifesto', which seems to me even more reactionary than the regular Stalinist nationalism of the PKK it emerged from, rests on antisemitic *Kulturkritik* that links not only capitalism (as usual) but also the state as such, and the nation-state in particular, to something called 'the Jewish ideology'.[17] Using a well-established philo/antisemitic trope, Öcalan points out that 'the Jews' *had to* develop civilizational techniques like the nation-state and capitalism to defend themselves from supposedly eternal hatred. He also grants that there have always been democratic, albeit much weaker, counter-currents within 'Judaism', but nevertheless writes of 'the Jews' as one transhistorical force or identity. Many of the numerous passages concerning 'the Jews' or 'the Hebrews' establish a dichotomy that opposes a democratic, republican, confederalist and market-based, to a 'capitalist' and statist concept of the nation, the former rooted in ancient and universal, quasi-natural 'moral and political society' (Habermas's 'life world' writ large), the latter on power, hierarchy, monopolies, the deification of rulers, exploitation and 'the Jewish ideology'. Kurdish liberation, expanded now to a notion of general human emancipation as opposed to ordinary nation-state building, means getting rid of all those aspects of 'capitalist civilization'. Another element of Öcalan's discourse is a naturalized, ahistorical celebration of women who are supposed to be central to the effort of saving humanity from 'capitalist civilization'.[18]

Holloway puts forward several criticisms but fails to address the antisemitism and the sexism of the book. His chief objection is that the critique of capitalism should not be interlinked so closely with that of

[17] 'Jewish Ideology, Capitalism, and Modernity' is the title of a section of chapter eight of *The Sociology of Freedom* (Öcalan, 2020: 221–238), which contains most of the book's antisemitic material.

[18] Öcalan suggests feminism be replaced by a 'science of woman' (Öcalan, 2020: 294–300) that would radically break with liberalism and explore 'the nature' of woman. 'Taking the economy out of women's hands and putting it into the hands of usurers, merchants, capitalists, power, the state and its agents … was the greatest blow to economic life' (ibid.: 299). Like the 'admiring' form of ('philo'-)antisemitism, the idealization of women as civilization's last hope is also a trope common in the late nineteenth century, not least among male supporters of (some aspects of) the women's movement of the time (Georg Simmel would be an example). Given that the expropriation of 'woman' would have begun thousands of years ago, the fact that Öcalan puts 'usurers' (a word traditionally connoted as Jewish) first in the list of the oppressors and usurpers of 'natural woman' suggests that (subconsciously, perhaps) the word is not used here in its literal sense.

civilization (Holloway, 2020b: xv).[19] Furthermore, Holloway correctly argues that 'it is better to think of the struggles for another world as being necessarily not only anti-state but also anti-national' (xviii) as well as critical of 'the market'. He warns against romanticizing indigenousness and unequivocally opposing it to modernity, and asserts that 'moral and political society … does not exist positively: it exists negatively, in the mode of being denied and, therefore, as struggle against its own negation' (xvi). These vintage 'Open Marxist' criticisms, if taken seriously, should pull the rug from under Öcalan's constructions but they are drowned out by Holloway's puzzling assertion that still, '*The Sociology of Freedom* is an important contribution to current debates about capitalism, patriarchy, ecology, and the state' (xiv). Not least given that central passages read like a more radical version of Werner Sombart's 1911 *The Jews and Modern Capitalism*, the classic example of a (nationalist-) 'socialist' argument that is antisemitic while seeming to celebrate the supposed 'achievements' of 'the Jews', it definitely is not such a contribution. It seems that the desire and hope to find positive connection points with a variety of political movements has here eclipsed the critical and emancipatory perspective, even though Holloway undermines the rationale for recommending Öcalan's text in several important respects. It is depressingly unsurprising that the antisemitism and the sexism are not among them.[20]

Those who endorse the false kinds of screams and cracks sometimes defend themselves by tarring their critics with the brush of metapolitical, ivory quietism. This is another false dichotomy. The point is not never to be positive about anything at all: the point is to control the urge. At the core of Open Marxism, if defined politically, sits an anti-authoritarian reading of Marx that is anti-Bolshevik as much as anti-Social-Democratic and opposed to all state-centric forms of Marxism: an anarchist kind of

[19] Holloway rejects therewith the one similarity between Öcalan's grand narrative and the critical theory of the 'Frankfurt School', in particular *Dialectic of Enlightenment* which does a lot of what Öcalan aims to do, but from a Marxist perspective (and without the antisemitism, albeit arguably with traces of a kind of 'positive' sexism not entirely unlike Öcalan's).

[20] Öcalan references Sombart repeatedly despite stating his arguments were 'exaggerated'. On Sombart, see Bodemann (2014) and Stoetzler (2014). The antisemitic mythology around Jewish 'money lending' etc. has been debunked repeatedly, most recently by Mell (2017, 2018).

Marxism, as it were.[21] Such a definition seems best to provide some coherence to all the different philosophical and meta-theoretical positions that can be found within Open Marxism. Open Marxists have often shown that they look for contemporary engagements beyond concept maintenance, though. A currently obvious and germane field are the movements around the climate crisis. In this context, the *specific* task of Open Marxism would be not to say and write things that are as inclusive and network-happy as possible but, to the contrary, to be *specifically* useful by being *critical*, i.e. to push for non-authoritarian solutions, when state-centric traditions of Marxism will be happy to feed into the increased authoritarianism that inevitably results from the attempt by our rulers and their proxies to manage the ecological disaster within the framework of the capitalist mode of production and the world-system of nation-states that is its political form. (For a compelling image of this, see *Snowpiercer*.) Connecting to a larger cause or movement means trying to make a useful contribution by way of insisting on, and remaining true to, the *specific difference* of what one is. One should better not be part of a movement that would not allow that.

References

Adorno, T. W. (2004). *Negative Dialectics*. Routledge.

Benjamin, W. (1977). *Gesammelte Schriften Vol. I, 3*. Suhrkamp.

Best, B., Bonefeld, W., & O'Kane, C. (Eds.). (2018). *Sage Handbook of Frankfurt School Critical Theory*. Sage.

Blumenfeld, J. (2021, July/August). Lifting the Ban. *Brooklyn Rail*. https://brooklynrail.org/2021/07/field-notes/Lifting-the-Ban. Last accessed November 2021.

Bodemann, Y. M. (2014). Coldly Admiring the Jews: Werner Sombart and Classical German Sociology on Nationalism and Race. In M. Stoetzler (Ed.), *Antisemitism and the Constitution of Sociology* (pp. 110–134). Nebraska University Press.

Chanson, V., & Monferrand, F. (2018). Workerism and Critical Theory. In B. Best, W. Bonefeld, & O. Chris (Eds.), *Sage Handbook of Frankfurt School Critical Theory* (pp. 1302–1313). Sage.

[21] Beyond that, the concept becomes the more complex the more other aspects of 'Frankfurt School' critical theory assert themselves, such as the psychoanalytically informed critique of fascism and antisemitism, and the critique of civilization based on the critique of labour as developed in *Dialectic of Enlightenment*.

Dinerstein, A. C. (2020). A Critical Theory of Hope: Critical Affirmations Beyond Fear. *OM4*, pp. 33–46.

Dinerstein, A. C., Vela, A. G., González, E., & Holloway, J. (Eds.). (2020). *Open Marxism Vol. 4. Against a Closing World*. Pluto Press.

García Vela, A. G. (2020). Objectivity and Critical Theory: Debating Open Marxism. *OM4*, pp. 47–62.

Holloway, J. (2020a). 'The Train'. *OM4*, pp. 168–176.

Holloway, J. (2020b). Foreword. In A. Öcalan (Ed.), *The Sociology of Freedom. Manifesto of the Democratic Civilization, Volume III* (pp. ix–xix) . PM Press.

Mell, J. (2017 and 2018). *The Myth of the Medieval Jewish Moneylender (2 Volumes)*. Palgrave Macmillan.

Memos, C. (2018). Open Marxism and Critical Theory: Negative Critique and Class as Critical Concept. In B. Best, W. Bonefeld, & O. Chris (Eds.), *Sage Handbook of Frankfurt School Critical Theory* (pp. 1314–1331). Sage.

Öcalan, A. (2020). *The Sociology of Freedom: Manifesto of the Democratic Civilization* (Vol. III). PM Press.

Pitts, F. H. (2020). Value-Form Theory, Open Marxism and the New Reading of Marx. *OM4*, pp. 63–75.

Schäbel, M. (2020). Is Open Marxism an Offspring of the Frankfurt School? Subversive Critique as Method. *OM4*, pp. 76–91.

Stoetzler, M. (2005). On How to Make Adorno Scream, Some Notes on John Holloway's *Change the World Without Taking Power*. *Historical Materialism, 13*(4), 193–215.

Stoetzler, M. (2012). On the Possibility that the Revolution that will end Capitalism might fail to usher in Communism. *Journal of Classical Sociology, 12*(2), 191–204.

Stoetzler, M. (2014). Sociology's Case for a Well-Tempered Modernity: Individualism, Capitalism and the Antisemitic Challenge. In M. Stoetzler (Ed.), *Antisemitism and the Constitution of Sociology* (pp. 66–89). Nebraska University Press.

Stoetzler, M. (2019). Capitalism, the Nation and Societal Corrosion: Notes on "Left-Wing Antisemitism." *Journal of Social Justice, 9*, 1–45.

Stoetzler, M. (2021). Capitalismo, nación y corrosión social: notas sobre el "antisemitismo de izquierda". In *Bajo el volcán, revista del posgrado de sociologia de la Benemérita Universidad Autónoma de Puebla*. Año 2, número 4 digital, 327–359.

Stoetzler, M. ed., (2023). *Critical Theory and the Critique of Antisemitism*. Bloomsbury

Afterword

I have been in-against-and-beyond-ed, and fabulously so! There is no higher compliment.

In: because the authors in this collection display a knowledge and understanding of what I have written that I find overwhelming, wonderful. *Against* because the various chapters criticize me in different ways, running from my subjectivism to my negative ontology to my undialectic emphasis on antagonism rather than contradiction to my concept of human nature to my opening-up of categories better left closed. And *beyond* because the criticisms open up debates that can take us forward in critical theory and even action. I am profoundly grateful.

And in this Afterword, what? Is there some way in which I can *in-against-and-beyond* the authors? It would be impossible for me to do them justice, to respond adequately to all the points made in criticism. Something much simpler, then. I have decided not to respond to particular criticisms and not to mention names. Most of the criticisms point in the same direction, so it is unnecessary for me to mention names and anyway the particular references should be clear.

We are attacked, we react. Start from there.

We are the starting point. There is no alternative. To put pen to paper, or finger to keyboard, is already to start from the subject. To start from the third person is a suppression, a lie.

A. García Vela and A. Bonnet (eds.), *The Political Thought of John Holloway*, Marx, Engels, and Marxisms,
https://doi.org/10.1007/978-3-031-34571-5

As in Marx's *Capital*. Richness (which I prefer to "wealth") is the starting point, not the commodity. "The richness of those societies in which the capitalist mode of production prevails, presents itself as 'an immense accumulation of commodities'...". Elsewhere, Marx characterizes richness as the absolute movement of becoming. We.

We or *richness* is the starting point. But within a few words, we see that *we* are attacked, that *richness* exists in the form of the commodity. We are attacked, but not completely defeated. Richness exists as an accumulation of commodities, but it is not completely contained within the commodity form. How do we know that? Simply because I am writing this and you are reading it. If I were entirely enclosed within the commodity form, it would not be possible for me to write in protest. The moment Marx wrote the first line of *Capital*, he proclaimed its untruth. It is only possible to say that richness exists in the commodity form if it is simultaneously true that it overflows from that form, if it is-and-is-not contained in that form, if it exists in-against-and-beyond the commodity.

We start from *we*, from the subject, a subject that is contained within the commodity form, but not entirely so, a subject that overflows, a subject that is-and-is-not contained, a subject that is-and-is-not objectified. A self-divided, schizophrenic subject. The overflowing is inseparable from the containment. The containment, the sucking of our every thought and action into the logic of the commodity, of money, is totalizing, but it is not a totality. It is not total, simply because I write and you read, and we are not so special. To speak of "abstract labour as only form of social validation" would imply that containment was complete, but that is true only if we see the world through the eyes of the commodity. Abstract labour is the centre of the sucking of our thoughts and actions into the logic of money, but it is a totalizing, not a totality. It is the dominant, but not the only form of social validation: friendship has not yet been obliterated. It is a process, not complete, a struggle, an antagonism.

We are attacked-and-react. We are contained and we overflow. The world is a battle between attack and reaction, between containment and overflow, between the commodity and richness. And yes, that is my view of human nature. It is not a trans-historical view, because the commodity-attack does not exist trans-historically: in its developed form, it is peculiar to capitalism. It is a human nature that does not exist positively: it exists negatively, as negation of its own denial. But yes: I confess that I do have this view of human nature. If we are slapped on the face, it is impossible not to react. If we are dominated, it is impossible for us not to say No. If we are channelled into a form of thinking that is determined by the logic of money, the pursuit of profit, then it is impossible for us not to overflow. Our overflowing may not be the communizing resistance-and-rebellion that could open up other worlds, it can be an overflowing easily re-channelled, the overflowing of drugs or madness or fascist violence. Or indeed it can be an overflowing that challenges the channelling/containment that is pushing us towards extinction. That is my human nature, my optimism, my subjective idealism, my anthropological Marcuseanism (what an honour!): I cannot imagine a containment without overflowing. Perhaps we are headed in that direction: towards a world in which there is no longer any dissent, any critical thought, any protest. But we are not there yet. The idea that *we rebel, the masses accept, we must save the masses* is an elitist concept that has shown its murderous content over the last century. Domination cannot be separated from refusal. Power-over cannot exist without the revolt of power-to, abstract labour cannot exist without a doing that pushes in-against-and-beyond it, the commodity cannot exist without a richness that overflows.

Class struggle, then, comes from above. It is the unceasing attack of capital, of the commodity, of money, driving us into a certain dynamic of behaviour. And therefore we overflow, react against this channelling of our thoughts and actions, we fight to de-classify ourselves, from our first tantrums and even before. We are born into class struggle. Commodity, money, capital, state: these are the great fetishized categories of this attack, categories that conceal the murderous violence of what is taking place. These are categories of antagonism. Money is an antagonism: it shapes what we do today, every day. We may or may not see it as such. We may not see our resistance in the thousand ways in which we sidestep its determination of our lives. Whether we do or not, the antagonism is there all the time: we are attacked, pushed each day into a social dynamic that has an intensity that did not exist yesterday. This is antagonism, not just contradiction. The alarm rings in the morning: the antagonism is there, even if we do not throw the clock against the wall, even if we just turn over and go back to sleep, even if we jump out of bed.

The attack, the antagonism, is a channelling. It is already expressed in the first sentence of *Capital*, the existence of richness in (and necessarily against-and-beyond, as overflowing) the totalizing-but-not-total form of the commodity. The violence of the antagonism is already there. It acquires a more direct, intense form when we come to exploitation, but it is already present in the commodity form.

The attack has a dynamic, a logical coherence that pushes us deeper into catastrophe. It is the train taking us who knows where. Capital is indeed an automatic subject, the creation of the way in which we relate to one another. The fact that we relate to one another through exchange, and therefore through commodity and money and capital, creates this Monster-Subject that is destroying us. Kill Money, stop the money-train, the capital-train, the train that bears on its side the dread words "Accumulate! Accumulate! That is Moses and the Prophets!"

One Monster? Or Many Monsters? It has become common in recent years to emphasize "and" in analyses of the oppressive nature of current society. We struggle against capitalism *and* sexism *and* racism *and* speciesism, for example. The connection between these struggles is seen as an intersectoral connection, an alliance between different struggles. It is suggested that to focus just on one Monster is to be blind to the other forms of domination.

One Monster? Or Many Monsters? My bet is on One Monster. A many-headed monster, a Hydra, as the Zapatistas put it. But it is only a bet, perhaps we shall have to wait for the owl of Minerva to take flight before we can know the answer. Certainly, we experience the attack as a series of distinct attacks. We are attacked on the basis of our identities, as women, as black, as indigenous, as old, as young, as disabled, as homosexual, as poor. Each attack is a monster-head and our response is and must be to fight back against that monster-head: for the rights of women, blacks and so on. The question is whether these are distinct, separate heads or whether there is some heart that connects them and generates them: a heartless heart lost in the mists, a heart that does not present itself, a force that generates and re-generates the identifying heads that attack us directly. My bet, my reasoned bet, is that there is such a connecting heart and that it is the fact that we relate to one another through the exchange of commodities, a heart that we can call Money. Money, by separating us, by breaking community, creates identities that are the substance of the multiple heads. It is a bet, a reasoned bet. When we succeed in killing Money, then we shall see if it at least becomes easier to chop off the different heads. This does not mean a hierarchy of struggle, that the *real* struggle is against capital/money and the rest are secondary. Quite the contrary: perhaps the only way of reaching the heart is through the struggles against the heads: or rather, through overflowings from the struggles against the different heads.

We are attacked, we react. We are channelled, we overflow. The problem is that *we* are a damaged subject. Domination penetrates us, weakens our ego, reproduces within us the hierarchical, authoritarian characteristics against which we rebel. *We* overflow, *we* resist-and-rebel, but *we* are not a pure subject. The rebellion may turn out to be a conformist rebellion, a rebellion that strengthens the system, the monstrous automatic subject against which we rebel. Capital attacks, we react by defending a nostalgic view of an imagined past in which there were no immigrants, no homosexuals and certainly no trans, and in which women, blacks and the indigenous knew their place. This is at the core of the rise of fascism in the 1930s and of the rise of the extreme right at the moment.

A common response to the rise of the right is the identifying separation: they are reactionaries, we are progressives; or they are fascists, we are rebels. Perhaps it would be more helpful, or at least more honest, to suggest that we are all angry conservatives. We are attacked and our first response is to defend. Coming out of the pandemic, we in the universities want to defend the type of classes we had before against the attempt to digitalize education more and more. A mining company wants to open a mine that will destroy the basis of our community: we defend. The Brazilian government promotes the deforestation of the Amazon: we defend. Tesla wants to intensify its work practices: we defend. The notion common on the left that *they* are the conservatives, *we* are the supporters of progressive change, is complete nonsense. Most social conflict is born from our conservative response to the aggression of capital. They attack, we react. That is something we share with the angry right.

What is important is what comes next, the shape that our reaction takes. What we are defending is a becoming, but at our own pace, as we would determine it. The attack is the attack of a being, an enclosure within the logic of identity, of money. The "we are attacked, we react" is common to left and right (I use the obnoxious terms for convenience). There is a shared scream. What is different is that one reaction overflows, breaks barriers, the other turns back to seek refuge within existing barriers. In one case the resistance overflows into rebellion, a more profound questioning. In the other case, the resistance re-encloses itself. In other words, one reaction is anti-identitarian, the other retracts into imagined identities. The distinction between "left" and "right" does not help us at all: on the contrary, it leads us into an identitarian way of thinking and doing. If we start from the idea of "we are attacked, we react", then, rather than distinguishing between "left" and "right" reactions, it is more helpful to think of identitarian and anti-identitarian reactions but not in an identitarian way, but in way that recognizes the interpenetration of identity and non-identity, the subversive potential of non-(or anti-)identity within identitarian responses and the corresponding danger of identitarian enclosure even within anti-identitarian movements. Contained rivers of anger can burst their banks, but it is also true that free flows of anger can be re-enclosed within walls. The identification and dis-identification of anger is surely the central issue of revolutionary and perhaps all social theory.

P.S. When I was very little, just starting my PhD, I went through a phase of reading German legal theory. Sometimes the articles I read would be gathered in *Festschriften,* weighty tomes dedicated to a worthy professor on his 60th or 65th birthday. "Perhaps one day ...", I would dream, much as, some years earlier, I had dreamt of playing rugby for Ireland. I never played rugby for Ireland and it seems unlikely now that I shall do. On the other hand, here I am, approaching my 75th birthday, a very suitable moment for a Festschrift, and I am jumping up and down with happiness, as perhaps those other worthy professors did too. My deepest, most heartfelt thanks to Alberto and Alfonso and to all the contributors to this wonderful book.

John Holloway
Cholula, 6 May 2022

John Holloway is a professor in the graduate school in sociology of the Instituto de Ciencias Sociales y Humanidades "Alfonso Vélez Pliego" in the Benemérita Universidad Autónoma de Puebla. His books, *Change the World Without Taking Power* (first published by Pluto Press, London, in 2002) and *Crack Capitalism* (first published by Pluto Press, London, in 2010) have each been translated into a dozen languages and have stirred international controversy. The third book of the trilogy, *Hope in Hopeless Times*, published by Pluto Press in 2022, follows the same disreputable path.

Index

A. García Vela and A. Bonnet (eds.), *The Political Thought of John Holloway*, Marx, Engels, and Marxisms,
https://doi.org/10.1007/978-3-031-34571-5

M

N

O

The manufacturer's authorised representative in the EU is Springer Nature Customer Service Centre GmbH, Europaplatz 3, 69115 Heidelberg, Germany. If you have any concerns regarding our products, please contact ProductSafety@springernature.com

Printed and bound by CPI Group (UK) Ltd, Croydon, CR0 4YY
01/10/2026
02225854-0005